The Deer Hunter's Encyclopedia

Steve,

Thanks for the delicious deer sausage. I hope you Drew & Reagan enjoy the book.

Ray

Books by Leonard Lee Rue III

The Deer of North America

How I Photograph Wildlife and Nature

How to Photograph Animals in the Wild

The World of the White-Tailed Deer

Leonard Lee Rue III's WHITETAILS

Leonard Lee Rue III's Way of the Whitetail

Furbearing Animals of North America

Meet the Beaver

The World of the Raccoon

Cottontail Rabbit

Pictorial Guide to the Mammals of North America

New Jersey Out-of-Doors

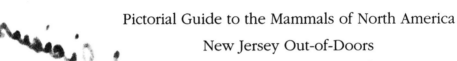

The Deer Hunter's Encyclopedia

Dr. Leonard Lee Rue III

All photographs by the
author unless otherwise indicated.

THE LYONS PRESS
Guilford, Connecticut
An imprint of The Globe Pequot Press

The Lyons Press is an imprint of The Globe Pequot Press.

Printed in the United States of America

10 9 8 7 6 5 4 3 2

ISBN 1-59228-064-1

The Library of Congress Cataloging-in-Publication Data is available on file.

Contents

Introduction

A number of years ago, I was hired by a Vermont hunting club to conduct three evening seminars on white-tailed deer. The club hoped that my presentation would help hunters, and the general public, understand that hunting does was needed for better deer herd management. Prior to the seminar, a belligerent old-time hunter, whom I judged to be in his late 60s, came up to me and said, "I've been hunting deer all my life. What do you think you can teach me about deer?" My answer was, "Not a damn thing with a closed mind like yours."

Thankfully, that attitude is rare among deer hunters. Most hunters—and I've talked to thousands—are like sponges: They just can't get enough information on deer. Neither can I.

As I say at the start of every seminar, "Although I have been studying the white-tailed deer since 1939, I don't want anyone to think that I think I know everything about deer, because I don't. I'm just trying to give you the benefit of the knowledge I have acquired about deer in the intervening years." I'm sure I'll learn something brand new about deer today or tomorrow, because the quest for answers is unending.

My thanks to the biologists who are constantly adding to our knowledge about deer; to all my friends, who continually relate their latest experiences with deer to me; to all my readers, who continually send me their questions; to Debbie Knauer, Publisher, and Pat Durkin, Editor, of *Deer and Deer Hunting* magazine, where these questions and answers were first published; to Jay Cassell, my editor, for helping me arrange all the material in this book; to Marilyn Maring, my secretary, for deciphering my handwriting and typing the manuscript; and, especially, to my lovely wife, Uschi, who shares my love of deer, for putting up with me and not being jealous of all the time I spend with "other deer."

God be with you all.

Leonard Lee Rue III
March 2000

This book is dedicated to some friends of a lifetime:

Dan Bacon
Manny Barone
Jim Gaucher
Charlie Heidecker
Earl Lawton
Fred Space
Lou Stout

CHAPTER
1

Hunting

As more Americans move from rural to suburban areas, they lose contact with the land, their roots, and basic knowledge of wildlife. Most folks don't even have to move, either, as suburbia is expanding outward and gobbling up rural areas. With less hunting land available, the number of licensed hunters is consequently declining in many of these developing areas. In all too many situations, hunting is no longer a family tradition, with knowledge being handed down from grandfather to father to son.

The bright side is that with the recent advent of bowhunting, many hunters are becoming better hunters. To be an efficient bowhunter, you have to know your quarry intimately, you have to spend more time in the field, and you have to get closer to the game in order to take a shot.

Many gun hunters are also becoming better hunters because they are restricting themselves to the taking of trophy, mature animals. This takes a lot more time and calls for a lot more experience.

All these factors, plus liberalized seasons, mean that many hunters are having more enjoyable outdoor experiences, and I honestly believe that this is why most of us hunt in the first place. We all would like to get a trophy deer, but that's really secondary to being able to spend quality time in the out-of-doors.

The following questions and corresponding answers are designed to not only make you a better hunter but also help you better understand deer and their environment.

Q: My first question concerns the distance that a stand could, or should, be from a deer's bedding area. I originally hunted feeding areas, but I found myself moving farther from the food and closer to the beds to become more successful and to find more and bigger bucks. The question is, exactly how close is too close? One hundred yards? Fifty yards? Three hundred yards?

My second question may also seem elementary. What makes a doe "blow"? It seems that if a doe sees or hears you, she just goes away, but when she smells you without visual or audio contact, she seems to blow. Is this true? Do does also blow if approached by a coyote or other predator? I have never heard a deer blow except when it has smelled my presence.

R. R., Randolph, Massachusetts

A: I have found that when deer are not being hunted, they go no farther than they have to to reach good cover to bed down.

If they have been feeding in a field, deer seldom go more than 300 to 400 yards into the woods to bed. In hilly country, deer usually go up on a sidehill so that thermals will bring scent up to them, and also so they can watch down the slope for potential danger.

I have long advocated that to be more successful, bowhunters should move their stands from the edges of feed fields and place them about halfway between the fields and the deer's bedding areas—which in most cases would be 150 to 200 yards.

If you approach your stand quietly, you should not alarm the deer at this distance, but you will have to be quiet. Because most areas have a prevailing wind, the deer should not be able to smell you; if the prevailing wind is blowing from you to the deer, your stand is in the wrong place.

You should be more successful, because deer move much more freely in the woods than they do in the open. They often hang up or hold back when they come to the edge of the woods. If you are deeper in the woods, you should have a shot at a deer much earlier in the afternoon than if you waited for the animal to step into the field. By getting an earlier shot, you have a better chance of recovering a deer, because you will still have some light by which to see its trail.

White-tailed deer bed no farther from their feeding areas than they have to.

To answer your second question, deer snort or "blow" to warn other deer of potential danger. Both bucks and does snort, but does do it much more frequently. The reaction of the deer hearing the snort depends upon which of two types of snorts the deer is giving.

The first snort is given with the mouth held open. Air is forcibly expelled from the lungs through both the mouth and nose. This snort alerts every deer that hears it, but that's all it seems to do. Listening deer will try to locate the potential danger that the first deer warned about.

The second snort is given with the deer's mouth closed, so that expelled air is forced out through the nostrils. This produces a higher-pitched whistling snort that causes all the deer within hearing range to explode into action. While the regular snort alerts the other deer, the whistling snort literally blows them away. There is no hesitance; they are gone!

I have found that deer give the alarm snort when they have either seen or heard me, but haven't identified me. In either case, they know that something is amiss but, because they haven't smelled me, they aren't sure what it is. It's when they have circled to get my scent, or I'm betrayed by a shifting breeze, and they have confirmed that I am a human and close at hand that they give the whistling snort, which I call the snort wheeze.

Q: Last month I had an interesting experience involving deer and turkeys.

Just before quitting time on November 2, I arrowed a fine doe on the edge of a pine woods. She dashed into the pines. I left my tree stand and walked about 50 yards into the woods. Suddenly a turkey flew up in the area where I suspected the doe had run. I could see another turkey on the ground and thought there might be several, since I seldom see them in groups of less than five in the fall.

My immediate concern was that I might flush the turkeys, thereby creating such a disturbance that the doe might run if she had bedded. Because of this, I snuck out of the woods and returned to my hunting shack.

The following morning I was able to walk right to the doe. She lay exactly where I had seen the turkeys and probably was already dead when I saw them the previous evening.

The doe was shot through the neck but had spun in a semicircle before dying. Behind her, and within a yard, there were deer hairs strewn about. Had I gathered them, I'm sure it would have been a large handful. However, examination of the hide revealed no patches of hair missing. It was as if they had been pulled out one or two at a time. I suspect the turkeys did this.

Do you think turkeys will peck at a dead deer? If so, what would they be seeking? If not, what might have done it? Thank you for information you can give me concerning this incident.   G. B., DePere, Wisconsin

A: I have never heard, nor have I seen, any evidence that turkeys would peck at a dead deer. I don't say they wouldn't do it, because many creatures do odd things out of curiosity. There would just be absolutely no reason for the turkeys to pull the hair out of your deer other than curiosity.

Q: My brother and I are planning a trip to Saskatchewan to hunt whitetails. Could you let us know where we can find a book or books on Saskatchewan whitetails? Also, could you help us find a good place to hunt—one where there would be heavy-necked and large whitetails? We are interested in your opinion. I have written to the Saskatchewan Department of Wildlife for their rules and information.   G. L., Cumberland, Maryland

A: Although I am not all that familiar with the hunting locations in Saskatchewan, I have found that Raymore, Langham, and Esterhazy Counties are producing the biggest bucks and generally conceded to be the best whitetail hunting areas.

You have already done what was probably the most important thing by contacting the Saskatchewan Department of Wildlife. I suggest you also get in touch with the province's Department of Tourism.

Q: How long will scent stay in an area?   J. B., St. Louis, Missouri

A: On a dry, warm day, the scent you leave when walking through the woods to your stand will probably dissipate within two hours—or at least after that time, deer will pay little attention to the slight odor that is left. Deer are not as frightened by the faint odor that your shoes leave on the ground as they are by whatever body odor you leave in the air. The reason is that odor detected in the air is *fresh,* and dissipates rapidly. The scent from your feet may last for two to four days. Bloodhounds have keener noses than deer, and they can follow a trail that is two to four days old. Deer are not really frightened by the faint odor of man, because they are constantly being subjected to it.

On days with lots of humidity, your scent will stay near the ground for a long time. On a cold, overcast day, your scent will roll along the ground,

Smell is the keenest of all a deer's senses and the one it counts on the most.
Credit: Len Rue Jr.

because cold air seeks the lowest level. A cold, dry day will see your scent dissipate rather rapidly: Such days normally have bright sunshine, and any amount of sun will start thermals rising. They, in turn, will carry your scent upward and away.

A hard rain will carry all of your scent downward but also dilute it so that it will dissipate very rapidly, often in less than half an hour.

When you use scent in hunting, apply no more than two or three drops at one time. It should not be splashed about like aftershave lotion. I usually place a few drops on a tree 5 to 6 feet off the ground, about 50 feet from my stand or blind. I may also lay a scent trail to the tree by placing the scent on a drag. I never put the scent on my shoes or clothing; I don't want deer to follow me. I don't want them coming to my stand or blind, either. What I do want them to do is follow the trail to the tree I put the scent on, and then stop.

Actual drops of scent placed on a tree or the ground will give off scent for at least five days unless washed off by rain. The concentrated scent that trappers use has a working life of about five days; deer scents are about the same.

Q: My question concerns scents. Can you tell me exactly what "human scent" smells like? If I work a shift at my factory job, I don't think I have the same odor I would if I had just taken a bath using any of the many scented deodorant soaps.

When I hunt, I do everything I know of to control my scent; I do believe it is a key element in deer hunting. But these questions have crossed my mind. If you can shed any light on this subject, it will be appreciated.

J. T., Lewisburg, Tennessee

A: Human odor is as diverse and as distinctive as the individual. It is affected by who you are, where you live, what you eat, what type of work you engage in, and so on. There is absolutely no way that human odor can be eliminated, although there are many things you can do to minimize it.

The term *human odor* usually refers to body odor. The human body has about three million sweat glands. Most are eccrine glands which, through the moisture of sweat, secrete salt as well as uric and lactic acids from the body. These glands also carry out the odors of the foods you have eaten, such as spiced foods and garlic. Apocrine sweat glands are much larger and emit a heavier sweat. They are located in the armpits and pubic regions. Bacteria work upon the sweat and sebum produced by these glands and cause them to give off body odor. Also, millions of dead skin cells collect between your toes and become odorous. The main defense against these odors is, of course, frequent washing with soap and water.

If your hunting clothing is washed in a scentless detergent or baking soda, air-dried, and kept outdoors, it should be as nearly odor-free as possible. I always keep my bowhunting outfit in a plastic bag with some evergreen branches. The Indians stood in a smoky sweet-grass fire before hunting.

The fact is that as long as you breathe, you are giving off your individual body odor with each breath. Your body not only absorbs many chemical odors to which you are exposed, but also gives off the same odors constantly.

The best advice I can give you is to keep yourself and your gear as clean as possible and refrain from eating garlic and spicy foods during hunting season.

Q: When I am hunting, I walk from my house to my tree stand. Once I saw a tree in a cornfield that had two buck scrapes near it. There is a tree nearby that has fallen down. The distance from my stand to the scrapes is too far for my bow to reach. Would it be okay to hunt from under the fallen tree? J. L., Belleville, Illinois

A: By all means hide yourself under the fallen tree. Just be sure that the prevailing wind is not blowing from the fallen tree to the tree with the scrapes or it will not work for you. If you use the fallen tree, be sure as well that you have room to get your bow into position to shoot. Get some camouflage material or use natural material—brush, cornstalks, and so on—to build a shield around the area where you plan to stand.

More deer have been taken by hunters on the ground than will ever be taken from tree stands. Tree stands have been extremely popular with bowhunters for the past 20 to 25 years. Prior to that, most bowhunters stood on the ground. Some gun hunters also use tree stands, but the majority of them still take their deer from ground stands.

Q: I have a question about injured deer. Someone told me that a deer that's been gut shot will fill the wound with leaves to stop the bleeding. I have never heard of this anywhere else and was wondering if deer are capable of it. If so, is it mainly on a gut shot, or is it on any wound that a deer may survive? J. H., Williamsburg, Virginia

A: I have never heard of deer using leaves to stop up a wound. I believe that the person telling you this has misinterpreted what he saw.

Browse and leaves make up a large part of a deer's diet, particularly in September and October when jillions of leaves are falling from the trees. Deer walk through the woods and pick up the freshly fallen leaves by the hundreds and eat them. An arrow wound in the paunch would leave at

Deer prefer browse over all other foods except acorns.

least a 1-inch-wide cut. The gases in the paunch would cause some of its contents, in this case leaves, to bubble out through the hole. I feel sure that the leaves your friend saw in such a hole came from inside the deer.

Q: I know the most important thing in archery deer hunting is scent. I've been bowhunting for 20 years and every year I wash my clothes in baking soda, hang them out to dry for two weeks before the season, and bag different clothes with different scents—pine, oak leaves, dirt, and so on—for different stand locations.

My question is, how do I know if I need the UV blocker that I see advertised on all these different scent-killing washes? Is there any way I can check my clothes to see if they're reflecting UV rays? Am I doing the right thing by washing with baking soda? If not, which UV wash do you recommend? M. C., Mountain Top, Pennsylvania

A: The only way you can test for the UV brightness that is put in most clothing is to use a black light at night. If the material has been treated with brighteners, the black light will cause them to glow.

For the past two to three years, most camouflage manufacturers have used material without brighteners. But you can't be sure unless the label says so or you test it yourself.

Prior to the discovery of the fact that deer can see color on the cold, or blue, end of the spectrum, brighteners were put in all clothing. Any camouflage clothing you have that is five or more years old will almost surely contain brighteners.

If your clothing is old, then washing it in a UV killer can help. Most detergents have brighteners in them so they get your clothes "whiter than white." If you wash your new camo clothing in household detergents, you are putting UV brighteners in that the manufacturer did not, nullifying the entire procedure.

You seem to be doing everything right, and washing your clothing in baking soda is a good idea. However, I have found that washing my clothing in Sportwash, made by the Atsko Company, makes them cleaner and odorless as well as UV negative.

Q: Last September my father and I were bowhunting when he arrowed a big doe. He was 15 feet up in a tree and the doe was 12 yards away broadside. His bow was set on 65 pounds, and his broadheads had three blades with a 1¼-inch cutting diameter. He was using a Game Tracker; after the shot, the line peeled away but the arrow stuck in the ground. The line broke from the arrow but stayed with the deer. My dad felt the shot was behind the shoulder but high. But when we examined the arrow, only one fletching was creased with blood. We could find no blood on the broadhead or shaft, so it was obviously not a pass-through. We figured the line had wrapped around the deer somehow, to explain why it was still with the deer.

Thinking it was only a superficial hit, we (probably unwisely) followed right away just to be sure. Over the course of about 300 yards, we found maybe 10 small drops of normal-colored blood (made possible only because of the Game Tracker); there was nothing in the blood to indicate what kind of hit it was. We also found one piece of flesh-colored tendon (or something) about 3 inches long that we could not identify, nor could we tell where it was from. It was not bloody and had no hair on it. It resembled a thinly sliced piece of raw chicken breast.

The deer stayed on a main runway and never circled or veered from the trail. What blood we did find was on both sides of the trail but, again, in extremely small amounts. We figured the blood could have splattered around while the deer was running. The deer had been shot from the right side. Blood on the brush was approximately 2 feet high. As we followed, the deer jumped up 40 yards away, moving with long bounds and tail up. This was about 20 minutes after the hit and thoroughly confirmed our thoughts of a superficial wound. We followed the line for another 100 yards and lost the trail at a stream, where the line pulled out.

The problem with this scenario is that, while scouting the area the following February, we discovered a large doe carcass not 20 yards from the spot where we had lost the trail. Although this might not be the same deer, due to its size, body position, and location, we think it is. We are both experienced bowhunters and have taken and trailed many deer. We are confused. What could have happened?   S. K., West Bend, Wisconsin

A: I am as confused as you are.

With no blood on the shaft or fletching, the arrow could not have gone through the doe. If the arrow did not go through the doe, how could blood get on both sides of the trail? You said that the drops were small, and small drops would not splatter enough to be on both sides of the trail.

The wound may have been a superficial one, just passing through the skin. How else could the line have been fastened to anything strong enough that it could be pulled from the container?

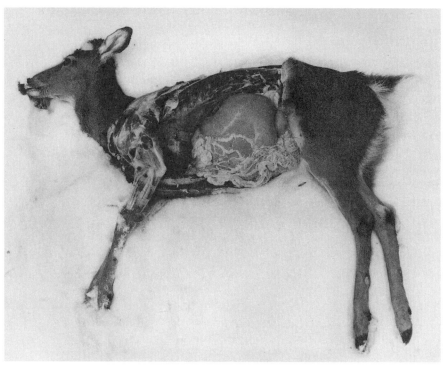

You can plainly see the location of the heart just behind and below the deer's shoulder.

You say that the blood was on the brush approximately 24 inches above the ground. On a good-sized doe, the brisket, on the bottom of the chest, is 20 to 21 inches above the ground. If the brush along the trail actually brushed against the deer, the arrow hit just 3 inches above the bottom of the rib cage. If the brush was a foot or more from where the doe passed, the shot was probably high, as the splattered blood would drop rapidly.

I can't imagine what the arrow could have hit hard enough to knock out a 3-inch piece. I could see a piece the same 1¼ inches as the broadhead being cut out, but anything else would be severed on just one end; the other end would still be attached to the deer, not knocked out. Yes, tendon does look a little like a piece of raw chicken breast.

When the doe jumped up, she made long bounds; that is not indicative of a severe wound. When the doe ran, she held her tail up, which is not indicative of a severe wound either.

While it is possible that the carcass you found is the doe your dad shot, there is nothing to indicate that the wound was severe enough to be fatal.

Q: At the outset, I must tell you that my sighting of a "handstand" cannot be verified, because I was in the woods alone.

When I sighted the buck, which I estimate was very old, with 10 to 12 points, I was carrying an over-and-under 20-gauge .22, Savage 24 D. The gun was loaded for small game.

As soon as I saw the whitetail, I broke the gun's action, withdrew the bird shot, and sought a rifled slug. He had his head down to clear his antlers of the alders and other brush.

We met at the bottom of a shallow creek bed. Apparently the buck did not see me.

By the time I finally got the rifled slug into the chamber and had the gun up ready to shoot, he was no more than 15 yards away. I aimed and fired.

The barrel selector on the hammer was in the upper, .22 position, and the gun misfired. My cursing alerted the buck to my presence. His eye (right—he was broadside, with his head to my right and tail to my left) must have caught me, and he must have realized that the day was one of salvation for, as I broke the action of the gun to withdraw what I thought was a dud rifled slug, he stood on his forelegs and lifted his hind legs up into the handstand position. The angle of his handstand was better than 45 degrees, but not quite 90 degrees to the ground.

When his hind feet touched the ground again, he seemed to coil and then bounded off to my right around some alders.

I chased him and saw him twice after that, but never clearly enough to try another shot. He escaped by staying ahead of me. That is, he'd get ahead into the brush and, when I came up, he'd quickly move off. I made a large circle downwind and lost his sign completely.

B. J. S., Yarmouth, Nova Scotia, Canada

A: A number of years ago, I reported that people had seen a deer apparently doing a "handstand"—actually walking a short distance on its front feet with its hind feet held up in the air.

I said then, and I say now, "No, I have never seen anything like that." I also said that just because I hadn't seen it doesn't mean it didn't happen. Over the years I know I have seen wildlife do things that perhaps no one else has ever seen—or, if they did, I don't know about it.

After I wrote that report, two other people contacted me and said that they had also seen deer do handstands. Evidently three people have seen this phenomenon.

Q: I want to ask you a question on rattling and calling that you mostly answered in your book *Whitetails*.

I've hunted in northern Maine the last two years and I am returning this year, Lord willing. It's outside of Ashland, so it's well north.

They claim up there that you really have to hunt on or around November 10 through the end of the month, which is the peak of the rut. Bad weather at that time (snowstorms) really sets the rut off. Only stand hunting is successful, because most of the bucks are traveling nonstop.

You mention that rattling and calling will work anytime during the rut. I read somewhere that grunt calling works throughout the rut, but especially so during the peak.

I've also heard that rattling is not effective during the peak of the rut, because bucks are not interested in fighting, just breeding—and that this is especially true in Maine, where there are not as many does. Do you agree?

Also, should I use larger antlers for rattling if I hunt in northern Maine, where the bucks tend to be bigger? C. W., Boonton, New Jersey

A: The peak of the rut in Maine, as in New Jersey, is around November 9–12, with it extending up to November 20–21. This is definitely the period of peak activity for bucks.

Rattling and grunting will work for deer at any time during the rutting season, but they are most effective at the peak. Don't believe whoever wrote that the bucks won't pay attention to rattling and grunting at the peak of the rut; that's not true. It is true that the bucks are mostly interested in breeding, but they are also intensely interested in all other deer activity. Fights usually occur over the breeding rights to a doe; every buck knows

Most buck fights are over in five to 10 seconds.

this, and wants a piece of the action if at all possible. Bucks following estrus does grunt frequently, so any other bucks that hear grunting will assume it's being made by a buck tending a doe. They want in on that, too.

Rattling and grunting work in all parts of the country, but they work better in the South than in New Jersey because, in the South, the doe:buck ratio is about 50:50, while here in New Jersey it is more like 80:20 or 90:10—eight to nine does to one adult buck. With this many does available, the bucks do not make as many rubs or scrapes. They don't have to advertise their presence when they have just about all the does they can handle.

You mention that they don't have as many deer in Maine as we do in New Jersey. Most states don't. The bucks are bigger, however, which is to be expected where the hunting pressure is light: Bucks live longer and so have time to grow bigger. Yes, I would use larger antlers for rattling.

When he's rattling and grunting, a hunter ordinarily tries it for a minute or so, then waits 10 minutes, then tries again. I suggest that you just "tick" the antlers together and grunt softly at first. Don't startle deer that may be close by starting with a loud crashing of the antlers. If there is no response, try louder. If there's still no response, really crash the antlers together on your third series. Most hunters then move, if they haven't gotten a response. However, in the peak of the rut you don't have to move, because the deer are traveling constantly. If there are any bucks in your area, they should pass nearby if your stand is on a major deer trail. So do a little moderate rattling and grunting every 10 minutes or so, and stay put.

Be extra cautious about not moving about at your stand between rattling sessions. A buck that is responding to your rattling and grunting may not come running; he may tiptoe in instead. A disadvantage to rattling and grunting is that the buck will be able to pinpoint your exact location by the sounds you are making. If he comes in behind you, he may spot you without your even knowing he was in the area. Keep all motion to a minimum. Using a tree stand will also help, because you can see farther and the deer may not look up.

Q: I was not raised on hunting; I just kind of drifted into it and, over time, learned to respect hunting and the ways of nature. I have read your book *Whitetails* and noticed and took particular interest in your scent chapter. You say that skunk scent is basically a no-no, and your reasoning makes sense. If I recall correctly, you say that fox urine is better because foxes naturally go around urinating here and there. Well, while recently reading an old copy of *Field & Stream,* I found a segment on just those two scents— fox and skunk. The writer said that *both* of the scents are warning signs, and that deer usually shy away from them. He told of an experiment he'd done with both of them, and both were negative. The skunk I can understand, but the fox has me confused. I am inclined to believe his experiment may have been under different circumstances, because you say fox is okay and I believe it. So until I'm told differently, I'm sticking with your theory.

G. F., Morrow, Georgia

A: I don't know who wrote the article you read, or what kind of experiments he ran. I do question the validity of his conclusions.

As everyone knows, skunks do not use their scent except in self-defense. They don't use it in their fights with one another, and they don't use it on the various kinds of small animals. They use it chiefly against dogs, coyotes, and man. They will also discharge their scent if attacked by a great horned owl. The great horned owl is no threat to a deer, but the dogs, coyotes, and man certainly are.

Creatures are extremely alert to the danger calls, signs, and scents of all other creatures. They also know that the skunk discharges its scent only when its life is threatened. Skunk scent means danger.

You may have noticed that your dog, or your neighbor's dog, will urinate on your car tires every time he passes the car. The dog does this to in-

The red fox is not an enemy of the deer.

Credit: Len Rue Jr.

corporate the car into his territory—your yard. Foxes are also territorial and urinate constantly on twigs, grass clumps, rocks, stumps, and the like on the perimeter of their territory, to claim ownership. Foxes are no danger to deer. I have witnessed deer playing with foxes on several occasions. Because deer are constantly encountering fox scent, it does not mean danger to them. It is for this reason that I say that fox scent is one of the best cover scents you can use for hunting.

Q: Would you please give me your views on smoking and smoke in relation to deer hunting?

Our hunting shack has 18 regular hunters and has kept an accurate log since 1986. The two most successful hunters are chronic pipe smokers (the only smokers in the group) and smoke almost continuously in the woods. They each have shot more than 50 deer—far, far above the camp average. (Minnesota is a one-deer-per-license state, but it is legal to party hunt.)

I also personally know of three bucks that have walked up to fires that hunters had built to warm themselves.

Does the smoke mask human odor and/or attract deer, or is this all happenstance? Thank you. J. C., St. Michael, Minnesota

A: I have heard hundreds of stories just like yours, and most of them have merit. As you say, your records are documented. These two men smoke and still have chalked up the best record for the number of deer taken.

I will be the first to admit that deer do many things out of curiosity, and I know they have been attracted to campfires. They may have been attracted to the pipe smoke, and perhaps it did cover the human scent.

I am also willing to bet that these two men are among the oldest in the group, that they have been hunting the camp longer than anyone else, and that they hunt from the same spot every year.

My brother-in-law, Dave Markle, took me on my first deer-camp hunting expedition when I was 17. Dave got his deer every year because he hunted the same spot every year and his experience had proven that when the deer were pushed, they invariably used the same intersecting trails he watched. The rest of us learned that it was a great spot, but we also knew that it was Dave's spot. The fact that he smoked did not make any difference: When the deer were pushed, they used those trails consistently in their travels.

A number of the real old-timers had a custom in the early 1940s that made great sense then and still should today. The war was on, and flashlights and batteries scarce. In order to find their way into the woods, these men carried a kerosene lantern. But they also carried a large wooden milk crate and a blanket. After getting to their stand, they put the lantern in the up-ended milk crate and then used it as a stool. Wrapping the blanket around the crate and their legs funneled all the warmth from the lantern to the lower half of their bodies. Their feet and rear ends stayed cozy and warm all day, and this kept their entire bodies warm. They could sit in comfort from before dawn until they left in the late afternoon. And the winters were a lot colder than they generally are now.

Some of these men smoked, and it's a sure fact that the burning kerosene lanterns gave off odors.

There are two schools of thought today about odor. The first is that all wildlife is becoming more used to human odor because there are so many more of us. Animals are coming into contact with human odor more often and, as a result, don't fear it the way they used to. A good example of this is the fact that, several years ago, I caught two adult gray foxes in metal box traps. When I was trapping big time, 50 years ago, I would have said that it was impossible to catch foxes in a box trap. Have the foxes gotten so used to human odor and the smell of metal that they are less cautious? Can it be that the lack of any trapping pressure has made the foxes less cautious?

The second idea is that the deer become even more wary of human scent as they contact it in places that they don't usually encounter it.

A deer knows if a dog is chained, penned, or allowed to run loose, and it reacts accordingly.

*Deer are highly adaptable but
never lose their inherent wariness.*
Credit: Irene Vandermolen

Deer expect to encounter lots of human odor around what used to be a rural area and is now being developed. It's when they encounter human odor in the woodlands that they react differently. Perhaps the kerosene lantern would be more detrimental today than it used to be.

I know one thing for sure: White-tailed deer become more wary as hunting pressure increases. And hunting pressure has increased tremendously in my area. It may not have increased in your camp area, though, or it may even have lessened. Although the number of deer hunters has dropped in New Jersey over the past few years, the total acreage open to hunting has decreased at an even more rapid pace. This results in increased hunting pressure on the available land.

I can't tell you for sure which idea is absolutely true. I do believe that smoking is a detriment not only to your health, but also to your success in hunting. I firmly believe that everyone should do everything possible to decrease any human or foreign odor while in the deer woods.

Q: If most animals are born at a sex ratio of 50:50, why do I see far more does than bucks at all age levels in the area where I live (Hunterdon County, New Jersey)? I realize that, with adult deer, hunters often shoot more bucks than does. But even with the yearling deer, before the annual gun season, I see more does.   P. D., Clinton, New Jersey

A: I am familiar with your area and am aware of your large deer population. It's estimated you have about 40 deer per square mile. For years, I did a lot of my best deer photography in Hunterdon County. Once I saw 53 deer in a field, of which 11 were bucks with antlers large enough to meet the 3-inch minimum to be legal. This was before gun season, and the herd included yearling and adult bucks. Eleven bucks out of 53 gives you an antlerless:buck ratio of 4:1. However, some of the deer were buck fawns, which don't yet have antlers, so it's hard to pinpoint the exact doe:buck ratio. Still, it's safe to say that before hunting season, there are up to seven antlerless deer for each antlered buck.

After gun season, the ratio is skewed much further—perhaps in the range of 15:1 antlerless deer to antlered bucks.

Yes, it is true that most animals are born at about a 50:50 sex ratio. With deer on adequate range, the sex ratio is about 52 males to 48 females at

The cryptic spotted coat helps the fawn to stay hidden in the woodlands.

birth. If the deer population has not peaked, the percentage of females might be even higher. On an overpopulated range, however, more bucks will be born.

For up to two weeks after birth, fawns are secluded and stay hidden to escape predators. The mother stays away from her fawns to prevent attracting danger to them, and to keep her body odor out of the area. She goes back to nurse the fawns four to six times a day, with most of the activity occurring during daylight, especially at dawn and dusk. While nursing her fawns, the doe licks their anal regions to stimulate their bowels. The doe then consumes any feces or urine they have voided. After nursing, fawns usually seek the densest cover they can find. They instinctively avoid lying in open areas.

After two weeks, fawns spend more time with the doe at each nursing, and they start sampling a wide variety of vegetation. At four weeks, fawns follow their mothers most of the time, because they are now capable of outrunning most predators. After this stage, mortality for the little bucks increases over that of their sisters. The buck fawn is more curious and adventurous, and he travels greater distances. This last trait stays with the buck his entire life. And, unfortunately for him, the more he travels, the more danger he encounters.

A deer's home range typically covers 1 to 2 square miles in spring and summer, and might expand or shrink in winter according to the severity of the weather and the availability of food. In the rutting season, a buck's range can increase to 10 or 12 square miles. That means he will be in unfamiliar territory, will cross more roads, and will be exposed to more hunters. Plus, during the rut, a buck is less cautious.

All these factors contribute to the much higher buck mortality rate.

Q: I have now grunted mature bucks to me in each of the past two deer seasons by using a small buck grunt call. The first buck ran along the edge of a thick swamp but stepped out to investigate, offering me a successful shot. The next buck, this past deer season, ran along the edge of the swamp but stayed in just enough cover so that no shot presented itself. The buck became nervous and went back into the swamp. Luckily, five days later—after I had abandoned my grunting—the buck came out on his own just before dark, giving me another successful hunt.

I am now considering the use of a decoy to help lure these mature bucks out of the thick cover. I am requesting your opinion on which decoy—a buck, a doe, or both—might work best. Along with the use of a decoy, what type of grunt should I use with this to increase my odds of getting a shot at these big bucks?

J. S., Wayside, Wisconsin

A: The use of a decoy deer should definitely improve your success in hunting, although you have done well in the past.

What I'll tell you now is pure conjecture on my part, but it's based on my lifetime observance of deer. It may make absolutely no difference, but I believe that you would probably have the best luck using a buck decoy before, and up to, about November 5—or in does' pre-estrus period. At that time, bucks are most interested in proving their dominance over all the other bucks and, if possible, driving any potential rival out of the area. They are busy checking out the does, but does will have nothing to do with a buck until they are in estrus.

Conversely, once the breeding season is in full swing, the doe decoy may work better. At that time, the bucks are primarily interested in which does are in estrus; other bucks are only an annoyance.

Mind you, either decoy may work equally well at either time. All I've got to go on is the deer's probable reaction at each period.

I would also use doe urine with the doe decoy and buck urine with the buck decoy. Still, this again may not make one iota of difference.

You seem to be doing well with the grunt call you have been using, so I would not change. To paraphrase Lucille Ball, "Don't mess with success."

This buck is urinating on his tarsal, or hock, glands while he is rubbing them together. Try using buck urine with a buck decoy to lure deer into range.

Many grunt calls have an adjustable O-ring. The farther down the reed the ring is pushed, the deeper the sound of the grunt. Big bucks make deeper grunting sounds than do small younger bucks, perhaps because their diaphragms are so much larger.

Should you use a higher-pitched grunt call? Should you use smaller deer antlers for rattling? Actually, both questions have the same answer. You will probably get more deer to come in using medium-sized antlers and the small buck grunt, but you will get bigger deer if you use larger antlers and push the O-ring down to get the lowest tone.

Q: I've recently received a grunt tube. I've been wondering how many seconds I should grunt at a time and how many seconds I should pause in between grunts?   M. H., Rosebud, Missouri

A: If your grunt tube has an O-ring controlling its tone, I suggest you move it down the reed toward the base to get the deepest tone possible.

I have heard bucks, following a pre-estrus doe, grunt every three or four steps. Each grunt was about 1 second long, spaced about 15 to 30 seconds

When tracking a doe, the buck keeps his nose down to her trail and has his tail raised. He also grunts every three to five steps.

apart. I have also heard bucks grunt before and during a fight. These grunts were longer—about two seconds—and spaced at least a minute apart.

If you are using the grunt call while rattling antlers, do what the deer do: make grunts one minute apart. If you are using just the grunt call, one short grunt every 30 seconds repeated 8 to 10 times would be about right.

Q: The following clipping appeared in the February 1993 issue of *Good Housekeeping* magazine:

> WHAT IF . . . WE STOPPED SPORT HUNTING? Our 34 million American sport hunters tend to defend their recreation with the claim that it keeps wild-animal populations "in balance" with their habitat. This happens to be true for the overpopulated white-tailed deer. But 95 percent of the animals they hunt—from grouse to grizzly bears—do not exceed their habitats; their populations are stable or declining; and they do not all need sport hunting to keep them "in balance." What the hunters' claim overlooks is that wildlife did rather well on its own—even before the first boatload of sport hunters arrived in the New World.

Are they right? And, if they are, should we give up sport hunting for the other species?

A: Well, they are half right. At least they got the part about the deer right, but they are way off base on the rest. They either don't know, or choose to ignore, four basic, fundamental points.

1. Ninety-four percent of all of the various forms of life that have ever lived on this earth were extinct before man appeared; man had nothing to do with their extinction.

2. No species of wildlife has ever been pushed to extinction by regulated sport hunting. Regulated sport hunting is the best game management tool that we have. Money from license fees and the self-imposed excise tax, has purchased huge tracts of land and refuges that have been saved for all time, for everyone to use. The money from excise taxes has provided for the Pittman-Robertson Fund which has paid for most of the basic wildlife research that has taken place over the past 50 years. Although the lands were purchased to provide space for game species, they have also benefited all the nongame species.

   It was through the efforts of the sport hunter that the deer, the elk, the moose, the pronghorn, the wild turkey, the Canada goose, and more were brought back from abysmally low numbers to their present-day highs. The preservationist groups shout louder and get more press but have only well-paid organizers and staffs to show for the millions of dollars they collect.

The white-tailed deer is a prime example of what good management and good, enforced laws can do for a species. For example, in the 1890s there were fewer than 200 deer in my own state of New Jersey. Today we have a whitetail population of between 150,000 and 155,000. Yes, the folks at *Good Housekeeping* were right: We do have to hunt the whitetail constantly to keep the population under control.

Deer are not cyclic in a predetermined pattern. With deer, it's boom or bust. When we had a low deer population, we had a bucks-only law—and it was needed. When a species population is below the carrying capacity of the land, it pays to protect the females in order to increase the birthrate and maximize the population.

When a species has reached a density such that it is in balance with its habitat—for deer this is about 20 animals to the square mile—then the females must also be hunted, because they will soon outproduce the vegetative growth. Nature itself tries to reduce the deer population, as they destroy their range by overbrowsing, by altering the sex ratio of the fawns. Does on poor range have fewer young, and there will be a preponderance of bucks born to does. This cuts down on the herd's breeding potential, but it is usually a case of too little, too late. Nature is superefficient; anytime the population of any species, including man, exceeds the carrying capacity of the land, it is cut back by disease, starvation, or stress.

A prime example of this was the mule deer boom and bust on the Kaibab Plateau in northern Arizona. This occurred before game management was thoroughly understood and is an outstanding example of game mismanagement.

In 1906, President Theodore Roosevelt was so impressed with the great size and massive antlers of the mule deer bucks on the Kaibab that he set aside the Grand Canyon National Game Preserve to protect them. Through lack of knowledge, the deer were coddled and protected—overprotected. Hunting was banned, predators were exterminated, and the deer herd grew and grew. As the deer population increased, so did their food requirements, and the forage plants began to suffer. In 1922–23, it was estimated that the herd of over 100,000 mule deer was creating a desert out of what once had been a plateau lush with vegetation. Conservationists of that time became alarmed, and some corrective steps were taken. Commercial grazing of ranch

An exceptionally fine mule deer buck. Credit: Len Rue Jr.

livestock was prohibited, and some hunting was allowed. It was too late. The deer began to starve, with more than 40,000 dying in one winter. Even with this evidence, political pressure by the state of Arizona prevented the proper management steps from being taken. From 1929 on, hunting on a large scale relieved some of the pressures, and the range began to come back. Again the deer herd multiplied, and the state went back to a bucks-only law. Drought and an excessive deer population combined in 1935 to bring the herd crashing down to about 12,000 animals, an all-time low. Proper game management has since allowed both the deer herd and the vegetation to increase.

3. It is a proven biological fact that 80 to 85 percent of all small birds and animals die, or are killed, each year, whether they are hunted or not.

Good Housekeeping is right to say that grouse do not exceed their habitat. But grouse follow a 10-year cycle, and their population fluctuates widely whether they are hunted or not. The Gardiner Bump, et al., study conducted in New York State in 1947 proved that even when the ruffed grouse population was at its lowest point, the birds could not be hunted out of existence. Even if no hunting were allowed, the grouse population would still crash and nothing could be done to save it. You cannot stockpile wildlife; you cannot save a cyclic species by not hunting it. Sport hunters are merely taking a part of the surplus of a renewable resource that would be lost even if that species was not hunted.

The cottontail rabbit and snowshoe hare are cyclic species, with the cottontail on an 8-to-9-year cycle and the hare on a 10-year. Sport hunters take millions upon millions of both species each year, but it is not this hunting that determines each species' population.

Studies done by the Pennsylvania Game Commission show that that state alone loses an estimated five million cottontails to predation, highway kills, accidents, and poaching between September 1 and November 1, when the cottontail season opens. That's five million rabbits that sport hunters did not shoot, but that are gone anyway. And this is happening throughout the cottontail's entire range. By the time the legal hunting season opens, about November 1, 60 percent of the year's total cottontail population is already gone.

Still, hunters do well. In 1958 Missouri—which has the largest cottontail population of any state—tallied 6,018,914 rabbits killed by hunters. Yet the state figured that more than 10 million cottontails were still left for breeding stock. Ohio came in second with more than 3,500,000 rabbits killed. The total hunting harvest for cottontails in the United States that year was estimated to be more than 25 million.

The varying, or snowshoe, hare is on a nine- to 10-year cycle.

Cottontail populations have decreased in many areas, notably Ohio, but not because of sport hunting. This brings up point 4.

4. As Pogo said, "I have seen the enemy and it is us." The most basic, incontrovertible fact is that all wildlife of all kinds either is declining or will decline as our human population continues to explode. Every time we stand upon, build upon, or pave over 1 square foot of ground, that's 1 square foot that cannot ever support another species of wildlife. It is our constant destruction of habitat, our invasion of wilderness that is threatening the future of not only the grizzly bear but all species. If we cannot control our human population, we cannot halt the decline of other species. Sport hunting will not have anything to do with it.

Q: I've read so many articles about the correct caliber to use for deer hunting. Most will tell you that the minimum caliber to ever use is the .243 Winchester. Now, I am not a professional by any means, but I am definitely not a novice. I have some deer hunting friends who have been renowned guides in the past in Alabama, Montana, and a few other places. We all agree that one of the best calibers to use is the .22-250 Remington. There are several reasons for this. It is an extremely flat-shooting bullet that, of course, offers long-range shots. Although it has less energy than most calibers at long ranges, we opt for the neck area whenever possible. One thing people argue with us is that, even at short distances, the .22-250 has low energy. But the bullet doesn't pass right through the deer like a 7mm Magnum. It stays in the deer, which means that every foot-pound of energy is contained within the animal—unlike what happens with the shoulder-knocking calibers. Also, with the little kick it has to offer, you are able to shoot it without flinching, which offers extreme accuracy. You are also able to shoot it more at the practice range and still come home without a bruised shoulder, which means you know how your gun handles better than you would otherwise. Note: It's legal to use this caliber in the states I hunt in, which include Alabama, Georgia, and Florida.

I'd like to know exactly what you think of this caliber for deer. I'd like to add that together we've all taken many, many deer that didn't need to be tracked more than 30 to 40 yards.

M. N., Fort Walton Beach, Florida

A: I have a .243 with a bull barrel and a 10X Unertal scope. It's not a deer rifle by any means: It weighs 12 pounds. However, it is an unbelievable varmint gun, and 300-yard shots at varmints are easy.

I have shot .22-250s and have also found them to be extremely accurate at long range.

I endorse your thinking completely about using a lighter, faster cartridge. You can place it exactly where you want it, while heavier cartridge will not reach out. They talk about heavier cartridges being "brush loads," but almost every bullet will blow up or deflect on hitting any brush. You need the heaviest load possible for big dangerous game but, for deer, the .22-250 is fine if your state allows it and the deer are standing still.

I do not claim to be a ballistics expert or even a gun nut.

Q: Is it possible for a state like Pennsylvania to develop a trophy deer hunting program? I hunt in several of the state's northern counties, and it seems the deer and their antlers are getting smaller. I have a mounted deer head shot by my grandfather in the 1920s, and it came from the same area I hunt. It scores 157 points. Believe me, we never see deer like that up here these days. I would love to shoot one good buck.

N. J., Eric, Pennsylvania

A: You are not alone. I would also love to shoot a good buck. Today, Pennsylvania has more deer hunters than any other state.

In contrast, there just weren't many deer hunters during your grandfather's time. A buck might live two to five years before being shot, which gave it the chance to grow up and produce big antlers.

In my home state, New Jersey, 85 percent of our bucks are killed when they are 1½ years old. Pennsylvania probably has about the same percentage. At 1½ years, a buck hasn't lived long enough to grow big antlers.

In the 1920s, Pennsylvania and New Jersey deer herds were just starting to rebound from the all-time lows reached in the 1890s. Because the herds were far below the land's carrying capacity, deer had an unlimited food supply. The forests in New Jersey and particularly Pennsylvania were heavily logged during World War I for timber, firewood, railroad ties, and other products. In the 1920s, the forests' regeneration cycle was just starting, producing endless miles of good deer browse. That produced more food than deer could eat, which maximized body weight and antler size. The grandfather of a nearby neighbor shot a deer on the mountain behind my home in the 1920s that I'm sure would have scored enough to be in the Boone & Crockett record books.

Could Pennsylvania have a trophy buck program? Yes and no. It has the potential to produce huge bucks, and it could set aside areas to manage for trophy deer, with a lottery system deciding which hunters could shoot bucks. But I doubt you could do this on a statewide level, nor could my state. A deer herd must be strictly managed to produce trophy animals, and in my opinion the hunting public in our two states would not be willing to make the sacrifices necessary for such a program to work on a widespread basis.

A fine 10-point white-tailed buck.

Trophy deer hunting can be achieved on club lands and private property, however, because you can impose a program that regulates access and harvests.

To produce trophy deer, you must be willing to pass up yearling bucks and maintain heavy pressure on the does to keep the herd below the land's social or biological carrying capacity. In heavily forested areas, the land's carrying capacity is based on the amount of forage the forest can produce. In agricultural areas, the carrying capacity is usually determined by how much crop damage farmers can tolerate.

In either case, you want bucks to have access to unlimited food, which allows them to grow larger bodies and antlers at every age level. An unlimited food supply also allows does to optimize their reproductive potential and increases the survival rate of fawns. The herd will grow substantially each year, meaning hunters must shoot a lot of deer to keep it in check.

Although this Texas white-tailed buck has only 8 points, it has about a 28-inch inside spread to his antlers, making him a real trophy.

The greatest sacrifice for hunters would be passing up younger bucks. The landowners or members of each club must set minimum requirements for the bucks that can be shot. In many cases, this could be determined by rack size and/or number of points. I know of one club in Texas that allows only bucks with 10 or more points to be taken.

I have my doubts that most hunters, on a statewide basis, would agree to such restrictions. But of course, maybe someday I'll be proven wrong.

Q: I was trying to stalk my first deer today; it was a six pointer in his bed. As I got closer, a squirrel two trees away started screaming and chirping and stayed in plain view of me. It was twitching and jerking its tail like mad. As I tried to get closer to the deer, the squirrel followed me from tree to tree screaming and staying in view. The deer finally jumped off the bed and was gone. Will a squirrel purposely give a hunter away to a deer?

M. S., Cola, South Carolina

A: The squirrel was not deliberately giving your presence away to the deer to help the deer. However, the scolding and chattering was an alarm call

The chirp of the squirrel will often warn deer of a hunter's presence.

that the deer understood: Something that didn't belong in the woods was there. All wildlife is constantly alert to the alarm calls of all other types of wildlife. There was once a book titled *The Night Has a Thousand Eyes;* well, so do the woods. A squirrel chattering or scolding, the clucking of a chipmunk, the putt of a wild turkey, the cawing of a crow, the scream of a blue jay—these are but a few of the myriad alarm calls that accompany a hunter in the woods. Just as often, a sudden halt to all wildlife noises—the absolute silence when the birds stop their chirping and singing, the frogs stop their peeping, and the toads stop trilling—also puts wildlife on complete alert.

The fact that you were stalking very quietly, moving slowly, and probably dressed in camouflage made the squirrel unsure just what you were. If it had identified you as a human, it would not have followed you but instead hidden itself on the far side of the tree.

The next time you attempt to stalk a deer and are discovered by a squirrel, just stop and stand absolutely still. In about 15 minutes, the squirrel should lose interest in you. Most wildlife, like many people, has a short attention span. After a squirrel or other creature sounds an alarm call, it would be a waste of time to attempt to complete your stalk without waiting.

Q: I hunt in Michigan, and we are having trouble getting deer to come out of the cornfields during daylight. They come to bait piles, but only when it's dark. The area has plenty of good buck sign. Any suggestions?

S. C., Winchester, Kentucky

A: I assume you're referring to the early bowhunting season in October. I am amazed that deer would visit bait piles at all, considering the available farm crops. You must be using something sweet like apples, sugar beets, or carrots.

Without making deer drives, there is no way to get them out of the cornfields, and if you're bowhunting a drive won't work. However, by November, the corn should be harvested. That will greatly reduce the deer's food supply and eliminate areas of cover. Chances are that deer will bed in nearby woodlots when the corn is down.

Having the corn down will help, but you'll still have the baiting problem. If deer are too wary to come to the bait pile during the day, this probably won't change once the corn is down. Nocturnal tendencies in whitetails often signal that an area is overhunted.

I suggest you find a few alternative places to hunt to reduce the pressure near your bait station. Move the bait piles to the middle of an open field and use only one pile. The deer will have no trouble finding the pile, and although you can't hunt over the bait pile, you can hunt the trails leading to it. Because they'll have to travel farther to reach the bait pile, the deer leave their beds earlier.

Q: There's been recent talk about introducing elk to parts of Kentucky. Although I would love to see elk, aren't they likely to damage farm crops? More important, would elk spread diseases that might harm our whitetailed deer population?

E. G., Frankfort, Kentucky

A: According to the Southeastern Cooperative Wildlife Disease Study Group of Athens, Georgia, elk can transmit four diseases to white-tailed deer: brucellosis, tuberculosis, the tissue worm, and chronic wasting disease. However, elk are quarantined and thoroughly tested for disease and parasites before they're transported to new areas.

The greater possibility is that whitetails might infect elk with the meningeal worm. As whitetails have expanded their range, they have decimated mule deer populations, along with elk and moose in some areas. About 50 percent of whitetails are hosts to the meningeal worm, but they have developed an immunity so it's seldom fatal to them.

A fine 6-point bull elk.

Following continued exposure to this parasite, mule deer, elk, and moose—after an initial die-off—have survivors that are also immune to the disease. This immunity has allowed the moose population in Maine, New Hampshire, and Vermont to increase and repopulate most of their former range.

Pennsylvania has a viable elk population of 500 animals in its north-central region. The elk coexist with deer with no problems. If the imported elk are taken from areas that also have whitetails, there is a good chance the elk will have already acquired an immunity to the worm.

Elk are direct competitors with whitetails when it comes to winter browsing. And elk usually find more food than whitetails, because they can reach food deer can't. This is part of the reason why mule deer have been virtually eliminated from Mammoth, in Yellowstone National Park, while the elk there are thriving.

Q: Here in Wisconsin the issue of baiting deer is a hot topic. There are strong suggestions that it may soon be illegal in our state.

Many people with whom I've talked feel that if baiting were banned, the deer's physical condition going into the winter would not be as strong; when a hard winter hits, a bigger percentage of the herd would starve. I feel through adaptation and strong genetics, the deer will survive the winter with little or no change. Who's right?

Also, do you think that if hunting over bait were banned, the number of hunters would decline (which would consist mostly of consistent baiters)? If that happened, then the annual harvest would also decline which would leave more deer after the season was over.

And if that also were also true, do you think the trophy potential would be better, especially in the heavily wooded areas that are found in the northern half of the state? M. V., Little Suamico, Wisconsin

A: In my home state of New Jersey, and in Pennsylvania and New York, baiting was strictly illegal—although New Jersey now allows it. I have never seen baiting carried out to the extent that it is in Texas, where they lay down trails of corn for deer to follow right to a blind. Usually they have a feed dispenser out in front of the blind. In my opinion, that's not hunting, that's shooting.

On the other hand, is putting your tree stand on a deer trail leading to a corn- or alfalfa field, where you know they have been feeding, any different? While it is not as important to gun hunters as it is to bowhunters, I always recommend using deer scent. Using scent could be construed as baiting, and I have heard of proposed legislation banning its use.

There is no doubt that deer that have fed heavily on bait will be fatter and go into the winter in better condition; hence they will have a higher survival rate than deer that have not fed on bait. A disadvantage to bait is that it has a tendency to concentrate the deer, which may cause habitat destruction in that area. This is particularly true of winters following poor mast crops.

You are right in believing that the deer have adapted to survive Wisconsin winters. They have been doing it for thousands of years without being fed by man.

If hunting over bait were banned, some hunters might not hunt. Even if they stopped, I am sure the harvest would decline. Many successful bait hunters would be less successful if the deer were scattered, feeding on natural food.

Hunting over bait does not guarantee that a hunter will get his buck because the deer, under heavy hunting pressure, soon change their routines

Mule deer bucks flehmen exactly the way white-tailed bucks do.

Credit: Len Rue Jr.

and come in to the bait only during the night, when no hunting is allowed. Baiting does improve a hunter's chances of success considerably, however.

If food were plentiful, if the carrying capacity of the habitat has not been reached (I'm sure it has), then having fewer hunters would allow some deer to grow older and perhaps get up in the trophy class. If the carrying capacity has been reached or exceeded, though, fewer hunters would mean more deer trying to survive on a limited amount of food. The chances of a trophy animal being taken on depleted habitat are just about nil. The results would be the exact opposite from what you would hope.

Q: I have hunted whitetails all my life and I love it. This coming fall I will have my first opportunity to hunt mule deer. A hunting buddy of mine moved from Michigan to Colorado, and he wants me to come out there and hunt with him. I have no basic knowledge of mule deer. Do they make rubs and scrapes, do they flehmen, do they chase does the way whitetails do? Can you rattle in mule deer? Do grunt tubes work? How about using scent? What would be some good books for me to read? I've got to do some homework before I get out there! P. Q., Ypsilanti, Michigan

A: The answer to almost all of your questions is yes. Let me get more specific.

First of all, you have to realize that the mule deer is much more of an open-area animal than is the whitetail. If you don't have brush cover, you don't have whitetails. Whitetails are much more adaptable than mule deer; you can find them in desert canyons, mountain country, and out on the plains. The mule deer is capable of surviving on much drier vegetation than the whitetail, however. I have seen mule deer eat vegetation so dry it was brittle.

Yes, mule deer do make rubs, but not as many as those of the whitetails, or as conspicuous. A major reason for this is that there are few trees in the plains and desert. In such areas, mule deer will frequently rub on such tall, stiff weeds as mullein. I have seen them rub on aspen and cottonwood trees, but I have also seen them rub on telephone poles, something I have never seen a whitetail do (although I suppose some big ones might). Like whitetails, mulies eat the bark they rub loose from trees.

I have not seen mule deer make the classic scrapes that whitetails do. Whitetails want an overhead branch to chew and rub their forehead scent glands on. Then they paw beneath the branch and urinate in the scraped area.

Mule deer bucks approach the does with an aggressive posture.
Credit: Len Rue Jr.

Mule deer do rub on overhead branches, but I have not seen them chew on those branches. They also rub their forehead and preorbital scent gland on weeds. I have not seen them paw a scrape and then urinate in it. However, they do urinate frequently on their hock or tarsal glands; because they do it so often, they do not deposit as much urine at one time as whitetails do.

Yes, mulies do flehmen, but they do it a bit differently than whitetails. When a whitetail smells the urine of a doe or another buck, he breathes in deeply, curls up his lip to trap the scent molecules inside, and then processes the odor. A whitetail does this only once. A mulie buck does everything the same way but may repeat the process three or four times.

Yes, mulies do chase does. The buck tries to get the doe to urinate so he can check the urine for the pheromones that tell him if she is ready to breed or not. When the doe is in estrus, he will chase her until she is ready to stand and be bred. The chasing always attracts other bucks within sight range. A running doe is very stimulating to both white-tailed and mulie bucks.

The tending buck will attempt to keep all other bucks from getting near the doe. The chase may go a couple of miles.

A major difference between the breeding patterns of white-tailed and mulie bucks is that a white-tail buck, after breeding a doe, usually waits about four hours before attempting to breed her again. On the other hand,

This mule deer buck is checking the doe to see if she is in estrus.

Credit: Irene Vandermolen

a mulie buck will attempt to breed the same doe repeatedly. I saw one buck breed the same doe three times in a half-hour period. Also, whereas a white-tailed buck may mount a doe three or four times before achieving penetration, most mulie bucks mount a doe six to eight times before achieving penetration. I believe this is due to the tremendous size differential between the mulie buck and the doe. The buck may be three to four times larger than the doe he is breeding, and his penis may have a harder time locating her vagina.

I have never attempted to rattle in a mulie buck, but I have had hunters tell me that they were successful doing so. I have never used a grunt tube on a mulie buck, nor have I ever heard one grunt. I imagine that they do but, being partially deaf, I may not have heard them. However, I have heard whitetails grunt many, many times; perhaps they grunt louder. Instead of using regular hearing aids, I always wear Bob Walker's Game Ear. Even hunters with good hearing will benefit from using Game Ears, because they not only amplify all sounds but also shut down instantly to protect your ears when you shoot. Then the Game Ears turn themselves back on.

I am sure that mulie bucks would also be attracted to scents, particularly urine scents, but I have never seen scents that are mule deer specific. (I have been told that Pete Rickard offers them. Rickard scents are good; I used them for years when I trapped.) All of the oceans of scent being offered for sale are for whitetails. I also believe that a mule deer buck would be attracted to white-tailed doe urine. It's a known fact that white-tailed bucks are attracted to mule deer doe urine. Much interbreeding takes place between the species.

My book *The Deer of North America,* while primarily about whitetails, also describes the various types of mule deer and their habits. The definitive book on just mule deer is *Mule and Black-Tailed Deer of North America* by Olaf Walmo, a Wildlife Management Institute book published by the University of Nebraska Press (501 North 17th Street, Lincoln, NE 68588).

Q: This last season at our hunting camp in the Upper Peninsula, the guys got into a rather heated argument about whether you could smell a buck or not. I have noticed a musky smell to a deer carcass after it has been shot and I'm close to it. That's no problem. Some of the guys say they can smell a buck even when they don't see him—they just pick up his scent in the air. Have you been able to smell a deer that you couldn't see?

O. B., Ann Arbor, Michigan

A: Yes, I can smell a deer without seeing it, and have done so hundreds of times. Although I have had extremely poor hearing for most of my life and my eyes are not as good as they used to be, I do have a keen nose.

The more dominant a white-tailed buck, the more frequently he urinates on his hock glands.

The odor of a buck in rut, produced primarily by the tarsal gland scent and the urine mixed with it, is so strong that I assumed everyone could smell it. Perhaps you cannot, but your buddies can, and I'm sure that most people are able to smell bucks.

I do have to say that the strong odor is seasonal, because bucks' tarsal-gland production is testosterone driven. Both the production of the glandular scent and the buck's urinating on his hocks occur primarily during the rutting season. The more dominant the buck, the more frequently he urinates on his tarsal glands; the darker the stains, the stronger the odor.

Q: With all the scent-elimination soaps on the market, how come none claim to include antibacterial agents? Aren't bacteria the leading cause of human odor? T. C., Tallahassee, Florida

A: You are absolutely correct. It is the bacteria proliferating in the sebum given off by the human sweat glands that causes human body odor.

Perhaps none of the scent-elimination soaps can claim to be antibacterial because they aren't. I have always liked Ivory soap, even though the maker doesn't claim it to be antibacterial. Ivory is the only commercial soap I know of that is not perfumed, and that is what I've always liked about it.

CHAPTER
2

Antlers

Antlers have been held in high regard by hunters from time immemorial. You can't eat them; they really serve the hunter no useful purpose. Still, a big set of antlers proves that you have bested a worthy opponent.

Only mature animals sport a crown of big antlers, and only the smartest of the deer become mature. Most deer, about 85 percent, are killed when they are 1½ years old. Such deer haven't lived long enough to get "smart." A large set of antlers indicates that this buck was one of the best at what most deer are good at, survival. The hunter who shoots a buck with a large set of antlers proves that he is one of the best at hunting. Both animal and hunter deserve respect.

We are constantly learning more about antlers, and we're doing many things to ensure that we will have deer with big antlers. There is no easy way to do so, because so many factors are involved: genetics, food, age, soil, fertilizers, management practices, proper culling, and more.

The white-tailed deer is one of the most extensively studied wild creatures in North America, and the thrust of most of the research is to produce bigger, better bucks with bigger, better antlers.

Following are some frequently asked questions about antlers.

Q: Over the past several years I've killed six bucks in one area in New Hampshire. Ironically, the left antlers on each buck were smaller than the right antlers. One of the bigger bucks weighed 180 pounds and sported a rack that gross-scored 129 inches. His final score was 115 inches, because the left antler was smaller and had shorter tines. Is this a genetic trait that isn't likely to go away?   L. M., Hudson, New Hampshire

A: Yes, the antler problem you've noticed is genetic. Normal bucks might have extra tines, but their antlers are pretty much the same size. There might be slight variations, but a 14-inch difference is unusual. If this kind of discrepancy was found in just one set of antlers, I would say it was the result of an injury; when several bucks in one area exhibit the same trait, though, it is no doubt genetic.

Q: On opening morning of the 1995 season, I killed my first decent buck, an 8-pointer. When I first saw him, I only saw part of his neck and chest. When it was approaching, I at first thought he was a turkey because he was black.

After shooting the deer, I was amazed by how much black hair he had. His coat was almost entirely black. In 25 years of hunting, I have killed several deer that varied in color from light brown to brownish gray.

Is black an unusual color for whitetails? What causes this type of color variation in deer?   L. W., Kansas City, Missouri

A: Deer are one of the few mammals that grow two coats each year—in summer and winter. The hair of a whitetail's summer coat can vary from sandy tan to the more common russet red. A deer's winter coat varies from dark brown to dark bluish gray.

The black coat on the deer you describe was probably attributable to genetics—an abundance of melanin would cause this.

I doubt that its source was Gloger's Rule, which states that darker pigments are prevalent in warm, humid climates. Obviously, your area of Missouri does not fit that description.

I believe there's an exception to Gloger's Rule, because I've found that animals living in heavily forested habitats tend to have darker coats even if the climate is not humid.

Q: I am writing in regard to antler shed dates. I raise some whitetails as a hobby and had four bucks during the winter of 1994–95. All were 1993 fawns and sported their first antlers. Flag, my breeding buck, was quartered with three does and had an 8-point rack. The other three bucks were penned together, but separately from Flag and the does, and shed their antlers, as follows: One 8 point buck shed both antlers on February 21; one

The buck on the left still has his antlers, while the one on the right has cast his.

spike shed his antlers on February 13 and 18; the other spike shed on January 23 and February 5.

While all the bachelor bucks seemed to shed by the book, Flag was still antlered on March 26, when the first doe had twin fawns. This being the beginning of my first fawn crop, I worried about their safety. By mid-April, with Flag still holding on to his antlers, I conceived the idea of putting him in with the bachelor bucks. I did think that Flag, with antlers intact, might bully the antlerless bucks, though. On April 22, I decided to try it anyway. I immediately learned that a deer's territorial rights seem to supersede antlers, antler size, and breeding status, and my earlier worries were unfounded. The three bachelor bucks (maybe acting as a small family group?) would not tolerate Flag's presence in their pen. The next 30 minutes or so were quite hectic (for me as well as the deer) and, by the time I got them separated again, Flag was minus both antlers. How long they would have stayed on without this episode I'll never know.

B. C., Annandale, Minnesota

A: Your observations about deer dominance coincide with some that I have made.

While some bucks retain their antlers longer than others—some hold them until April—this does not guarantee that the bucks will be dominant.

This leads me to believe that the testosterone levels of the late-casting bucks dropped when the levels of the regular casting bucks dropped, or perhaps just a little later. It is the testosterone that imparts the "maleness" to the bucks and makes them more aggressive. Early shedding of the velvet makes a buck dominant, no matter his size, because his testosterone level is higher than those of the bucks that have not rubbed the velvet from their antlers. Bucks carrying their antlers into January and February will be dominant over those bucks that have cast their antlers. But bucks carrying their antlers into April are not usually dominant over the bucks that have started to regrow their antlers. To start the new antlers growing, the deer's pineal gland causes the pituitary gland to stimulate the release of gonadotrophic hormones (that is, testosterone) into the deer's bloodstream. The deer with growing antlers have higher testosterone levels than the late-carrying bucks, and they are usually dominant, antlers or no antlers.

Undoubtedly your three smaller bucks ganged up on Flag, but his antlers would not have fallen off if they were not ready to do so. I once saw a late-carrying buck make a tremendous leap; the impact of landing was just enough to jar one antler loose.

Q: My brother owns a dairy farm in upstate New York (Schoharie County) with a good-sized deer population. Over the years, we have noted that the bucks usually drop their antlers in late December or early January.

In 1998, however, a (crotch-horn) buck was observed at the backyard feeder on March 20 still carrying one horn. What would cause this deer to still be wearing one antler so late in the year?

R. F., Greenville, New York

A: Ordinarily, all the bucks in a general area shed their antlers at about the same time. For most of them this is from the last part of December through the last part of January. Some sections are a little earlier, some a little later.

Circumstances can change these regular schedules, of course; milder or colder weather will cause the antlers to be carried longer or dropped a little sooner. Sometimes the key factor is not temperature but snow depth, or lack of it. A superabundance of food, or the lack of it, may throw the schedule out of whack, too.

The winter of 1997–98 was very warm in the northeastern section of the country. We had practically no snow at all. I don't know how the acorn crop was in your area; it was moderate in mine. The lack of snow would have allowed the deer to move more freely and to have better access to whatever food was available.

I'm sure that the forkhorn kept his antlers longer because of the moderate winter and lack of snow. Why didn't more bucks keep their antlers

Bucks seldom lose both antlers at precisely the same time.

longer? Because, despite these external factors, most of a deer's cycle is still determined by the number of hours of daylight in a 24-hour period and by genetics.

Q: In 1997, while I was whitetail shed-antler hunting, I found one side of a 6-point buck. It was broken off down deep in the skull, instead of flush with the skull, like normal.

In 1998, my brother found a larger shed from the same side. It was found in the same bedding area. It also broke off down deep instead of flush, like normal. It may have been from the same deer. Have you ever seen this? What causes this? And how common is it?

T. W., Freeburg, Illinois

A: Yes, I have perhaps a half-dozen shed antlers in my collection that have been shed below the regular pedicle base. However, none have as much bone material on them as your 1997 shed.

I have always believed, and still do, that such antlers have not been cast, or shed, the way antlers ordinarily are. I feel that such antlers have been broken off by fighting; it would not be normal for a section of the pedicle base to be shed also. The pedicle base is an integral part of the buck's frontal skull plate.

You can see that the pedicles on this buck have healed over, proving that his antlers were cast at least two weeks earlier.

I know of several captive bucks that had their antlers broken off by fighting in just this manner and thereafter produced a freak antler on the side that had had a part of the pedicle base broken off.

The antler your brother found in 1998 could have come from the same buck; this would be caused by a lack of calcium in his system. Note that, in both cases the antler is not an impressive growth, and also note that the 1998 antler is a freak with two main beams growing out of the one pedicle base.

This might be a fairly common occurrence. I think it occurs most frequently in areas whose soils are poor in minerals.

Q: This letter is a response to your request to hear from anyone who has seen bucks with antlers in April or later.

During the spring of 1993, my hunting partner and I daily watched five areas, with several bucks in each. We were hoping to search for sheds just after the antlers were cast.

Most of the deer lost both antlers during the second and third weeks of March, but several of the larger bucks carried both antlers into the first week of April.

By this time, we'd begun searching for sheds every afternoon. One evening in mid-April, while returning from shed hunting, we spotted a group of deer on a rifle range. We stopped to look. After a closer look, we noticed that two of the deer still had one antler each. Both of the deer were large bucks. These were the last we saw that spring.

In 1993, I moved to Fort Knox, Kentucky, approximately 150 miles northeast of Fort Campbell. At Fort Knox, I never saw any antlered deer after the second week of March; the majority of the antlers were cast during the first week of March.

In December 1995, I moved to Fort Drum, New York. It took about a month and a half to get my family settled, so I didn't get to start scouting until late January. I saw lots of deer, but none carrying antlers. I'm fairly sure that all antlers had already been shed, but by the end of February I still hadn't found any sheds.

Do you think the different dates for antler shedding in the different areas could be caused by the food available in each area?

R. P., Fort Drum, New York

A: Indeed I do. I don't know exactly where Fort Campbell is located in Kentucky, but I do know that it has to be several hundred miles south of Fort Drum. I also know that the weather has to be considerably milder down in Kentucky than up in New York. This would expose the deer to less cold and increase the amount of food available to them in Kentucky. The deer would-

Cast antlers that have been picked up at a Texas hunting camp. Many of these were found in late spring.

n't expend as many calories to keep warm, and the plants would produce more food because of the longer growing season. Hence, the deer in Kentucky would be in much better condition than their New York counterparts.

Q: I was bowhunting in New Jersey the first week of January, and we saw more than 300 deer between three of us. We harvested five. But all of the deer we saw had no antlers. I spoke with a friend in Virginia, and he said he is still seeing bucks with their racks; in New Hampshire, where I live, we are still seeing racked bucks. Can you explain this?

R. L., Epping, New Hampshire

A: I don't know where in New Jersey you were hunting, but the bucks in Warren and Hunterdon Counties often lose their antlers around the first week of December. The earliest I had seen a buck cast his antlers was November 25, but one of my readers reported seeing a buck without antlers on November 15.

Q: I watch deer regularly during the summer months and have two questions concerning antler growth. First, why do some bucks have considerably more antler growth than others in the early summer? I have seen some with only 2 to 3 inches of growth, while others have grown higher than

This New Jersey buck has just dropped his antlers, as the pedicles are still raw.

their ear tips. I assume the bucks with more growth shed their antlers earlier and then started new growth earlier. Is this assumption correct?

Also, as a buck's rack develops, does the mass increase throughout the growth period or does it remain relatively the same size as when it first grew out? S. J., Surry, Virginia

A: Antler growth is stimulated by photoperiodism, the lengthening of the daylight hours in a 24-hour period. As such, you would think that all the deer living in the same area and eating the same food would start growing their antlers at the same time—but it just doesn't happen that way. Deer are as individualistic as humans, and no two are alike.

Under normal conditions, the big mature bucks start growing their antlers first, peel the velvet off their antlers first, and cast their antlers first, but none of this is set in concrete either. When all other factors, such as food and age, are equal, the difference has to be caused by genetics.

I saw one buck that carried his antlers two months longer than another one, and he started growing his antlers about six weeks after the second buck. Yet both bucks peeled the velvet off their antlers at the same time. I was sure that the late-starting buck would peel later, but he didn't. And he did this for two years running. Of course, his antlers were smaller than they normally would have been, because they had six weeks' less growing time. Even bucks that cast their antlers at the same time don't necessarily start growing new ones at the same time, although the time variation is slight—perhaps a week or two.

The diameter of the growing antlers increases only slightly as they continue to lengthen. Most of the mass base is laid down right from the start, and future growth goes to length.

Q: A few years ago I shot a buck here in Mississippi that had only one antler. I figured that he had already shed the other antler, even though I got him in the latter part of November and most deer don't shed their antlers until the end of January through the end of February.

When I got to my buck and had a chance to check him, I was surprised to find that he had never had two antlers. There was no knob or anything for the antler to grow on. On the one side of his head, he had the regular base with a regular antler growing out of it. The other side of his head was as smooth and rounded as a doe's. That buck had never had more than one antler.

Have you ever seen a buck like this? W. T., Jackson, Mississippi

A: Yes, I saw a buck like that on a recent trip to Texas. I was as surprised as you were. I had never before seen or heard of a buck having only one pedicle, or antler base, and hence only one antler. I have seen a number of bucks with only one antler, but that was because the other antler had been snapped off. But this particular buck had never had an antleror a base to grow one.

When I talked about this with other deer men, one told me about a rancher who had had two bucks shot on his property—and neither had ever had more than one antler.

I have no way of knowing just how often this type of condition occurs.

Q: Enclosed is a photograph of a spike buck that my son killed two years ago in Alabama. The spikes are 17½ inches in length and have 3-inch bases. No points have been broken off.

Do you know of a buck having longer spikes than this one? No one in my area has ever seen a deer with spike antlers this tall.

The deer was about 180 pounds, 3½ years old and lived in an area that was not overpopulated with deer and had plenty of food year-round.

W. J., Rayville, Louisiana

A: My brother-in-law, Dave Markle, shot a buck about 30 years ago that had the longest spikes I had ever seen. They were about 15 inches in length and grew in the shape of a buck's regular main antler beams.

I do believe that your 17½-inch spikes are the longest I have ever seen.

You say that the buck weighed 180 pounds, which is a good weight for a southern deer. You also stated that he was 3½ years old and had access to good food year-round. Yet he still had spikes.

In my writings and my seminars I have done my best to put to rest the theory that spike bucks are genetically deficient. I will be the first to say that there are some genetically inferior bucks, however, and evidently the one you shot was one of them. However, research done all over the country has proven time and again that most bucks that sport spikes do so because they were on an inadequate diet. Most bucks receiving a 16 to 18 percent protein diet will develop from button bucks at seven months to 4-, 6-, or 8-point bucks at 1½ years. Your buck is the exception to the rule. He definitely has to have inferior antler genes.

Q: I recently read a newspaper article that claimed that a spike buck remains a spike throughout his life. Everyone I have asked disagrees. Could you shed some authoritative light on this?

L. D., Moorestown, New Jersey

A: The article you read is a rehash of a controversy that first surfaced in Texas around 1980. Work done at the Texas deer research station proved that some spike bucks were genetically deficient and, in breeding, were begetting genetically deficient offspring that were also spike bucks. Re-

A yearling white-tailed buck with long spikes.

search done at many of the northern research stations, such as Penn Station in Pennsylvania and Delmar Research Lab in New York, proved that spike bucks in these states were the result of insufficient nutrition and not genes. My personal experience and observations have borne out these latter conclusions.

Being very interested in this question—"Nature versus Nurture" or "Food versus Genes"—I visited the Kerrville, Texas, research station, where the biologists graciously explained their findings to me. Then and only then did I find out, as Paul Harvey says, "the rest of the story." None of the articles I read mentioned that for years, spike bucks were not allowed to be shot in Texas.

Any genetically deficient spike bucks were allowed to live out their entire life spans without being shot. In that time, even though the big-rack bucks did most of the breeding, these genetically deficient bucks would do

Spike antlers are almost always the result of a lack of sufficient nutritious food.

some of it, thus passing on their deficient genes to create, within the sub-species, a race of deficient-antlered deer. The Texas researchers found that these deficient-antlered deer remained spikes even when fed a high-protein diet.

In most of the northern states, any deer having 3 inches or more of antlers is legal. If there are any deficient bucks, chances are that they are killed before they can breed and could pass on the genes of their defi-ciency. Here in New Jersey, about 86 percent of our deer are shot when they are 15 to 18 months old, bearing their first set of antlers.

In most of the northern states, it has been found that any deer that has spikes has them not because of its genes, but because he did not get suffi-cient protein to grow large antlers. It has been proven time and again that if a buck has access to a 16 to 18 percent protein diet from the time he is born, he will have four points or more by 15 months. I personally have

If this buck had had a diet containing 16 percent protein, he would not have had spikes.

seen many bucks go from buttons to 6-, 7-, and 8-pointers with their first set of antlers.

The laws in Texas were changed to make spike bucks legal to hunt, and that state no longer has the problem of spike bucks with deficient genes. If Texas now has spike bucks—and it has many of them—it's because there are too many deer in some areas for the bucks to get the nutrition they need. In some areas of the Edwards Plateau in central Texas, for example, there are well over 100 deer to the square mile. There just isn't sufficient nutritious food in that area to allow these deer to produce good antlers. In fact, even the average body size of the deer has decreased dramatically.

Even in the old days of my visit to the Kerrville Station, the biologists told me that while their research had proven that they had spike deer that were genetically deficient, nutrition was still the most important factor in antler development.

If you hunt east of the Moorestown, New Jersey, you will find many spike bucks, because the sandy Pine Barrens area is noted for its poor forage production. If you hunt to the south, on the edge of the rich farmland, you see much better deer.

Q: I was reading an article in *North American Whitetail* (February 1992) called "The King of Shed Antlers" by Mark Schmidt.

Mr. Schmidt made a statement that I've never heard before. I would like to know if you have ever heard about this and what your opinion is.

"If you look very closely at deer antlers, you usually will find one or more tiny 'pinholes' somewhere on them. These holes are the entrances to tiny tunnels within the antlers where tiny insects live," said Mr. Schmidt. "To me, they look like some kind of a termite." I have never heard anyone talk about these creatures before. I am wondering, is this something new?

Also, a friend suggested to me that after some big bucks shed their antlers, they might bleed to death from one or both sites if clotting does not take place immediately. We've found fresh sheds and then found the buck that shed them, usually within a half mile or less, lying dead. This could explain why many big bucks just seem to vanish without a trace, even though their sheds are found and it's assumed they have survived the winter.

D. H., Monroeville, Indiana

A: Your question intrigued me. I am sorry that I did not get the opportunity to read the article by Mr. Schmidt.

I have just checked several sets of antlers that I use for rattling, and on the larger 8-point set I did find two pinholes, one in each antler. Each hole was in the junction of the main beams and third tine. I had never noticed those holes before, and I found them on only the one set. It would have to be a very tiny insect that made them, because I was able to push in the tip of a pushpin only 1/16 inch. I have never seen any mention of these holes in all of the material I have read on antlers. I have never heard anyone refer to them before, but you can bet I will look into it.

Your friend is absolutely wrong; deer do not and cannot bleed to death by casting or shedding their antlers.

When a deer's antlers are growing, there is a tremendous flow of blood from his body to his antlers through the blood vessels and covering that we call velvet. Dissolved mineral salts from the deer's skeleton are carried by the blood and deposited on the pedicle, and then on the growing antler. A system of vascular constrictive "valves" in each of the arteries carries blood to the antler. If the antler is damaged or the velvet is cut or torn, the blood vessels constrict instantly, shutting off all of the flow of blood to the antler until the blood at the injured site coagulates.

I have seen a number of bucks just after they have cast their antlers, yet I have never seen as much as a steady trickle of blood. I have seen some

This buck's antlers are almost fully grown.

drops, yes, but I would have to say that the small amount of blood dripped, not flowed.

When I recently produced a videotape on antler development, I was able to photograph a buck just moments after his antler had dropped off. Actually, this buck had lost one of his antlers several days before; I was trying to get some footage of him with one antler on and one off. It was not to be. I was able to tape him standing there with the shed antler at his feet. The top of his pedicle was red from blood, but there was no bleeding. And later, after the buck left the area and the shed antler, I found that the base of the antler (the spicules) was pure white without a trace of blood.

If the big bucks of your area vanish without a trace, it is not because they have bled to death from shedding their antlers.

The few drops of blood seen on this buck comes from the torn skin around the antler base when the antlers were cast.

Credit: Irene Vandermolen

Q: I hunt New York State's southern-tier counties. I love to bowhunt and spend as much time in the field as I can get. Beginning in August, I really start to do my scouting for the coming fall season. I attended your deer seminar a couple of years ago in Endicott, and you said that the buck's antlers reach full size about August 1 and then started to harden. All the bucks I see are still in velvet in August. I wondered how you knew the antlers were hardening. Most of our bucks in this area rub the velvet off their antlers in the first week of September. Does the time of the velvet peeling vary within one area, and is it different from one area to another? With all the time I have spent in the woods, I have never found a strip of velvet lying around any of the rubs I have seen. Why don't I find the velvet?

A. F., Binghamton, New York

A buck that recently lost his antlers scratches an itch. There is little blood loss when they cast their antlers.

A: Let's get first things first. One of the most important things to remember about wildlife is that while most members of a certain species generally do the same thing at about the same time, there are individual variations in the timing because each creature is an individual.

In your area of New York, and across the northern three-quarters of the continent, most of our bucks start their new antler growth about April 7–15. I have seen some start the last week in March. Most of their antlers will have reached their maximum growth for that year by August 1. Most deer will also rub the velvet from their antlers during the first week in September. And most of them will cast, or lose, their antlers between the latter part of December to the end of January.

Please note that I said "most" of them.

I have seen many deer in New Jersey cast their antlers in the first week in December. The earliest I saw a buck cast his antlers was November 25. I have seen wild bucks, not captive deer, keep their antlers up until the first week of April. There is a tremendous variation in the timing of the casting of bucks' antlers. Many factors help determine casting time.

Usually the biggest bucks will cast their antlers first, because the casting of the antlers is tied to the amount of testosterone in a buck's body. The biggest bucks do the bulk of the breeding and deplete their testosterone levels earlier. Prolonged cold weather has an effect, too, because extreme cold seems to activate actual breeding slightly. In a number of different recent years, a rainy autumn (with less daylight in each 24-hour period) caused does to come into estrus two to four days earlier than usual. The amount of food that is available to bucks in the fall is also critical, because during the rut bucks do not—cannot—eat as much as they ordinarily would; they have to draw on their stored fat reserves. A buck with good fat reserves will hold his antlers longer. A buck that has access to a good food supply after the rut will hold his antlers longer. A warm December will allow a buck to hold his antlers longer, because sudden cold will cause his metabolism to slow down a little sooner. Then there is the simple fact that each buck is an individual; his genetic makeup also influences when his antlers will be dropped.

Bucks that cast their antlers first will start to grow their antlers first. However, through my personal observations, I have to add that even though some bucks start to grow their antlers two to three weeks, or more, after some of the other bucks, the late-starting bucks play catchup so that, by the first part of August, their antlers are almost fully grown, too.

You asked how I know that bucks' antlers were hardening after August 1. The answer is simple: I can see it happening.

When a buck is in velvet, his antlers appear massive because the skin and the depth of velvet is approximately ⅜ to ½ inch. Calculating the velvet on both sides of an antler increases its diameter by almost 1 inch. When the antler is growing, you can readily see the raised blood vessels; these carry the blood that supplies the nutrients that in turn form the antlers. The velvet appears plump, rounded, and smooth. When the antlers begin to solidify, the process starts at the base and works toward the tips. The burr, or coronet, at the base of a deer's antler grows outward, gradually decreasing the supply of blood going to the antler. When this happens, the antler begins to look as if it were shrink-wrapped; the velvet loses its plumpness and is reduced in actual size. Each blood vessel creates a groove in the growing antler itself, and the larger the antler, the larger the groove. When blood courses through the antler, the blood vessels are convex. As the blood flow is reduced and gradually stopped, the blood vessels collapse and retreat into the grooves they made in the antler. Now the area between the grooves is more noticeable, because they actually are higher than the blood vessel grooves. If you get a chance to see bucks up close in August, you can see this shrink-wrapping as it takes place. That's how you know the antlers are hardening; the velvet shrinks in size.

The velvet always makes a buck's antlers appear to be much larger than they actually are. Look closely and you can see the blood vessels in the velvet.
(Credit: Len Rue, Jr.)

Although most bucks shed their velvet the first week in September, some may do so three to four days earlier, and others three to four days later. It depends on the individual deer. Different deer in different areas of the country are on completely different cycles for all of their activities. In the middle of December 1990, I photographed a big buck in Alabama that had just shed his velvet. And this particular buck was not so far out of line. Most of the bucks below the 33rd parallel shed in December.

Despite the fact that we say the velvet "dries," it is not really dried when it is rubbed off. It does have a lot less blood in it than when it was growing; I would say there's about a 90 to 95 percent loss. However, the 5 to 10 percent of the blood that remains is a liquid blood that makes the rubbed-off strips of velvet flexible and bloody. Usually the deer eat their own velvet. What they don't eat is picked up and eaten by the first predator to find it. I have never found dried strips of velvet in the woods either.

Q: I am 15 years old and just completed my first hunting season. Although I didn't get a deer, I saw many, learned a lot, and had a lot of fun. Maybe I'll get lucky next year!

Something is puzzling me. Today I went with my dad and younger brother to the woods where we hunt to look for shed antlers. We hiked about 4 or 5 miles all over the woods, near creek bottoms, swamps, and in open woods, but we didn't find a single antler! There is no snow on the ground, and the leaves covering the ground are not that thick. We saw plenty of fresh deer sign—lots of droppings and a few tracks in the mud. We know that there are deer here, both bucks and does. How come we didn't spot any antlers? Are there certain places to look? Have the mice gnawed them up already? Or were we just unlucky? I would like to know because finding some shed antlers would make up for the 6-point buck that I missed this fall.   R. A., Saddle River, New Jersey

A: Let me congratulate you on your outlook on your first hunting season. Your dad has taught you well and he is to be congratulated, too. You hunted to get a deer and didn't, but you really enjoyed the hunt, you learned a lot, and you had fun; that's what hunting is all about, enjoying the great out-of-doors.

As to your not finding any shed antlers, I can only suggest that somehow you didn't look in the right spots. There is also the possibility that someone else could have looked earlier in the same area that you did.

The area you searched may not have been the same area that the deer were in when the bucks dropped their antlers. Of course, New Jersey had a very mild winter last January and February, so the deer were not concentrated; they were able to roam and to feed wherever they wanted. In severe winters they will move to the area of greatest shelter on their home range—swamps, hollows, and, in my area, copses of rhododendron thickets.

Although the mice, rabbits, and porcupines all chew on whatever antlers they find, there is no way they could have completely eaten the antlers in just a month or so.

Finding antlers in New Jersey under any circumstances is a tough job. Eighty-five percent of all our bucks are killed when they are 1½ years old. That means that we don't have many bucks with big antlers. Small antlers are just naturally harder to find.

No matter how big a set of antlers a buck has when they are on his head, they are never as impressive when they are separated from his skull and you are looking at just a single antler.

I am sure you will find some antlers and that you will get your buck. I wish you the best of luck in both pursuits.

Antlers are soon eaten by rodents, by carnivores, and by the deer themselves.

Q: Please read the enclosed article from my local newspaper. Is it true that a spike buck is a spike all his life? It seems to me that, according to this article, a 4-pointer (forkhorn) will always be a 4-pointer, a 6-pointer always a 6-pointer, and so on.

I live in northwestern Pennsylvania, where many large bucks exist and very few spikes are seen. I find it hard to believe that the 8- or 10-pointers taken each year in my hunting area start out as 8- or 10-pointers. Also many 4- and 6-pointers are seen. Is this article wrong?

C. M., Greenville, Pennsylvania

A: The column you mentioned was written by Wyndle Watson and appeared in the Sharon, Pennsylvania, *Herald* on Sunday, December 2, 1990. I quote directly from the column.

> More numerous than trophy racks are deer carrying a single point on either side—spike bucks.
>
> Spike bucks are often spared by hunters for two reasons: the rack is small and unimpressive and the hunter does not want to use his tag on an inferior animal. Some hunters still believe if they let the

spike buck live, he'll develop into a 4-point and possibly into a trophy 8-pointer later.

Not true; a spike buck will be a spike buck all of his life. The spikes will just be bigger each year until he reaches his peak of maturity, then they will start to become smaller each year.

Male offspring of that buck are likely to be spike bucks also.

End of quote.

To which I have to say, "Not true." Yes, the information in the article is wrong. It's a disservice to all who read the column.

I don't know what Mr. Watson bases his information on. A number of years ago, researchers in Kerrville, Texas proved that some of their spike deer were genetically inferior and, despite being given high-protein feed, remained basically spikes throughout their lives. I say "basically" because most did produce more than spikes with age, but still only about half the antler mass of normal deer. These inferior genes came about because Texas for a time protected all spike deer during hunting season; thus any deer that was inferior could pass on his genes. The Texas law has been changed, and the problem has been corrected.

In my home state of New Jersey, 85 percent of the bucks are killed when they are 1½ years old. Any inferior deer would be killed before he could pass on his genes. Most of the breeding would have been done by the larger bucks prior to hunting season.

The northern tier of counties in Pennsylvania is producing a lot of spike bucks because of a lack of nutritious food.

Spikes are a sign of malnutrition and only rarely genetic. Pennsylvania has been a leader in deer research proving that, given a 16 to 18 percent protein diet from birth, most bucks will develop into 6- or 8-pointers by 1½ years of age. If all the spike bucks in Pennsylvania had access to high-protein food, the vast majority would go from spikes to 6- to 8-pointers within one year.

Not only are many of the northern Pennsylvania deer growing spikes, but they are also becoming smaller in body size and weight. New Jersey has the same problem in some areas; we don't have enough food for the number of deer we have. New Jersey is trying to remedy the situation by reducing our overall deer herd. In New Jersey, given all of the seasons, special permits, and so on, a hunter can now legally take 22 deer a year. A reduction of the population should increase the size of bucks' antlers because, with more food available, fewer bucks will produce spikes.

You evidently live in an area that has plenty of good food and little hunting pressure, because many of your deer are 8- to 10-pointers and very few spikes are seen. The bottom line is the good food. One buck I raised

Many bucks in food-poor areas grow only spike antlers.

Credit: Len Rue Jr.

had 8 points at 1½ years, 11 points at 2½ years, and 14 points at 3½ years. He was fed all of the protein I could grow or could feed him, and he had access to mineral supplementation because I fertilized the land.

I'll close by stating it one more time. A spike buck is usually a spike because of a lack of nutritious food, not because of a genetic deficiency.

Q: I attended your white-tailed deer seminar here in Ohio a couple of years ago and thought it was very good. I don't mean to question you, but I have seen something different from what you said. You noted that the size of a buck's antlers depends upon the food he eats and his age. You also said the shape of a buck's antlers is genetic: The shape of a buck's antlers determines the shape of his son's antlers.

This buck has a high set of antlers. . . .

I have been given permission to go on a large tract of land that allows no hunting whatsoever. As I go there often, I have gotten to know some of the individual deer. Because they are never hunted, I can often get quite close.

Three years ago one deer gave birth to a pair of buck fawns. This doe has really large white circles around her eyes, and so did both of the fawns. It is easy to pick out these three deer because none of the other deer have eye rings. What puzzles me is that the two twin bucks have differently shaped antlers and even different body shapes. One buck has a beautiful wide rack with high tines and a blocky kind of body. The other has a more massive rack in diameter, and the antlers reach up high. This buck has a much longer, leaner body. You said the sons would have the same shape of antlers as their father and yet these two bucks, which I know are twins, have two differently shaped racks. How do you explain this? Also, how do you explain the white eye rings? Both bucks have them and they must have inherited them from their mother.

C. W., Youngstown, Ohio

. . . while this buck has an exceptionally wide set

A: Okay, let's take the second question first.

I have always said that the mother's genetic makeup is as important, if not more important, than the buck's, because many deer body characteristics are passed from grandfather to mother to grandson. Apparently these bucks have inherited the white eye rings from their mother.

Adult does usually have twin fawns. If a single egg is fertilized and then splits, it will produce identical twins, either two bucks or two does. If a doe gives birth to a buck and a doe fawn, it means that two eggs were fertilized and the twins are fraternal. In the case of the twin bucks you saw, where each had different antler shapes, I'm willing to bet that they are fraternal twins from two separate eggs. The difference in the antler shapes could easily have been caused by the doe being bred by two different bucks with two different antler shapes. Each buck fertilized one egg. It often happens that two or more bucks breed the one doe during her 28- to 30-hour estrus period. I have seen it happen on a number of occasions. In my book *The Deer of North America,* I report on one doe that was bred by nine different bucks.

In the case of the bucks you are watching, one may have his father's antler shape while the other has inherited his mother's father's antler shape. Given their different antler shapes, they cannot be identical twins.

The same factors creating the differences in the shapes of their antlers would also be responsible for the different shapes of their bodies.

Q: You wanted to hear from readers having seen bucks with antlers in April or later.

I have been fortunate enough to have seen this twice, and lucky to have had my camera to catch them both on 35-millimeter slides. The first (April 13, 1976) was an 8-pointer carrying both sides. The other time (April 24, 1979) was a 7-point buck carrying both sides. The slides of the latter buck show the time of the year, with new leaf and grass growth, and the buck is shedding so his coat is rough looking. I took these in Knox County in north-central Ohio.

Could a high level of testosterone combined with good physical condition delay antler shedding in some cases?

Here in Ohio, most of our deer go into the winter in very good condition, and I have reason to believe that at least one, and probably both, of these young bucks was the traveling companion of an older, more dominant buck—and therefore had little if any opportunity to breed. Case in point: buck number 1, April 13, 1976. Seven deer were coming

Many yearling bucks, after dispersal, team up with mature bucks.
Credit: Irene Vandermolen

The Deer Hunter's Encyclopedia

out of a woods to feed in the early morning. Five came out the western side of the woods ahead of two (one the antlered buck) that were right together some 50 yards away, coming out of the southern side of the woods. I don't know the sex of the other deer, but this is common buck behavior. In the second case (April 24, 1979) the young whitetail was along side a larger-bodied antlerless buck (large 5- and 3-point antler sheds were found not more than 150 yards from the spot where I photographed him). They were bringing up the rear some 5 to 10 minutes behind the pack. I don't need to tell you that seeing older bucks traveling with, and behind, young yearling bucks is not uncommon.

C. B., Danville, Ohio

A: You have answered your own question. A high level of testosterone, combined with good physical condition, definitely contributes to bucks carrying their antlers longer than normal. However, as I have said in response to previous letters, I believe those bucks having antlers in mid-April owe it more to good physical condition than to high testosterone levels.

Yes, it is common for young bucks to travel with bigger, older bucks. Sometimes young bucks will stay with their own age-level peer group, but teaming up with older bucks is far more common.

Big bucks are never leaders; that's how they got to be big. No big buck will ever stick his neck out when he can get a younger buck to do it. I'm sure they do this deliberately, though it may also be inadvertent if the big buck is more cautious and hangs back.

Q: In Ohio, what is the best time of the year to find sheds?

M. H., Marysville, Ohio

A: The best time to look for shed antlers in the northern states is as soon as the snow is off the ground. Most antlers are bone white by the time they are cast in late December or January, and they are difficult to see against the snow. And of course, deep snow buries them. In my area of New Jersey, most of our snow is usually gone by late February, and that is the time I get out to look for antlers. The longer you wait after the snow melts, the greater the chances that rodents or other critters will gnaw on the antlers. In the more southern states, I recommend that you look for cast antlers by the end of January at the latest.

Q: Several years ago I was doing some spring scouting in late March. I stopped when a deer came crashing through the brush toward me, and was amazed to see a small 6-point buck with bleached white antlers still firmly implanted on his head. Even more amazing is the fact that a much larger

Antlers become lighter in color as they are bleached by the sun.
Credit: Irene Vandermolen

8-point buck was following close behind; he also had a bleached rack that I would estimate had an 18-inch inside spread.

This happened in the Kettle Moraine State Forest in southeastern Wisconsin. Is it unusual to see two bucks running together in spring? And why do you think both bucks had retained their racks so long?

L. P., West Bend, Wisconsin

A: It is not at all unusual to see two bucks traveling together. I have often seen groups of three to four white-tailed bucks together, and rarely six to eight. Mule deer bucks, after the breeding season, often band up in groups of 200 or more.

Except when they are concentrated in winter feeding areas, or yards, and during the breeding season, white-tailed bucks usually keep separate from the does and their young. A doe's fawns stay with her for one year, until she drives them off prior to giving birth to her new fawns. After giving birth, the yearling does usually regroup with their mothers. The yearling bucks, on the other hand, usually leave their natal home range and seek out a home range of their own. It is the movement of these young bucks that causes the whitetail's range to expand into any areas that do not have resident deer. Quite often several of the yearling bucks will band together in a peer group or a yearling will follow after some of the mature

In winter, mule deer concentrate in large herds.

bucks, serving a sort of apprenticeship. The breeding season is not on at this time so the older bucks accept the young ones, because they do not perceive them as competition, although they will be as soon as the rut commences.

Deer cannot reach the ticks and parasites on their own heads and necks, so two of them frequently pair up to groom each other's heads and necks. Mutual grooming causes a strong bonding relationship, and many bucks become "buddies." They will retain that friendship until the rutting season, when they will try their best to beat each other's brains out. When the rut is over, all is forgiven and the friendship is reestablished. So it is not at all unusual to see two bucks together.

Late March is a little late for most bucks to cast their antlers, but not all that uncommon. The bucks you saw must have had access to exceptionally nutritious food. Good food is usually the main reason for late carrying of antlers.

Q: I saw an antlered buck in April. I was scouting for turkeys on the Atlanta Wildlife Area in northeastern Missouri on the weekend prior to opening day of the 1993 season; I'm not certain of the exact date, but it was probably around the 15th. The buck had only one antler remaining, but it was a nice one with at least 4 points and possibly more.

I thought you'd also be interested to know that at the other end of the scale, I found a fresh pair of sheds from a really nice 8-point buck the first week of December 1984 in Southampton County, Virginia. We killed the buck a few days later and he was healthy but very small bodied, weighing only 105 pounds live. We've killed a lot of other bucks up there with similar-sized racks, and they usually ranged from 140 to 170 pounds. Have you seen bucks drop their antlers this early?

R. F., Chesapeake, Virginia

A: Yes. For years many of the bucks in my area of Warren and Hunterdon Counties in New Jersey would cast their antlers the first and second week of December. Our shotgun hunting season usually opened around December 5 or 7, and many of the biggest bucks could not be taken because they had already cast their antlers. We could see that the buck's pedicles were either raw or freshly healed. We knew they were bucks, but we couldn't take them because the law said they had to have at least one antler longer than 3 inches. These deer had no antlers at all.

I've shot bucks whose antlers fell off when they hit the ground. I've also shot bucks whose antlers pulled out when I tried to lift their heads off the ground. It wasn't unique to just the bucks I saw and shot; this was a common occurrence. It must be a genetic characteristic.

The biggest bucks usually cast their antlers first.

Q: I harvested a spike buck with the bow and a last-minute-of-light, last-day 7-pointer with my blackpowder rifle. I found nine shed antlers, six of which were complete sets.

As for shed antlers, I am now addicted. I was grouse hunting off the Appalachian Trail about one week after a 2-foot snowfall we had in December 1995, and I found my first shed antler. It was a 4-point horn with blood drops all around it and on the base. I admired the fine horn for a while, then proceeded along the well-packed snowmobile trail (the snow off the trail was way too deep). Fifty feet ahead I found the match, also with blood drops around it. The second horn had 4 points, although one tine was broken off. I spend every Saturday between January and April in the big woods of Upper Greenwood Lake, looking for horns. I had no luck this spring finding any in the big woods, but I was introduced to some small patches of woods in the southern Passaic County area that blessed me with nine sheds. I didn't find them until April, and I started my quest in February.

Mr. Rue, I have read many articles on deer hunting, finding sheds, and locating deer. They all stress concentrating on feeding and bedding areas. Now, I'm a little confused about what would be feeding and bedding areas in this mountainous region with no farms. By all means, I'm not looking for an easy way to harvest these mountain bucks—just a few tips or reference points from you that I may be able to use in the future. Do deer have one particular feeding area and bedding area? What if I startled one or two deer by walking to my post? Will they return within one day or so?

Note: Where I hunt in northern Jersey, the ridges run north and south, with the distance from the base of one ridge to another being 100 to 200 yards and fairly steep. There are some swamps, 2 to 3 acres in size, up in between the higher ridges. There is an abundance of laurel along with a moderate amount of white oak, red oak, hemlock, maple, beech, and birch. My hunting tactics are 100 percent tree stand in bow season. I post half an hour before sunup and sit until 10:30 to 11 A.M. Most action seems to be around 8:30 to 9 A.M. Then post again from 3 P.M. until dark. During all of the gun seasons I post on ground before sunup, sit until 9 A.M., stalk around for a few hours, go out for a bite to eat, then return by 2:30 to 3 P.M. for the afternoon hunt. I always position strategically with the sun and wind.

S. B., Upper Greenwood Lake, New Jersey

A: For the last 48 years, I have lived at the base of the same mountains that you describe, just a mile or two from the Appalachian Trail, so I know exactly the type of terrain that you hunt.

The main difference between my area and yours is that there are farms in the valleys on both sides of my main ridge. The deer do come down to the

In hilly areas, deer will bed on ridgetops during the daytime.
Credit: Irene Vandermolen

open areas to feed. In our area, the bedding areas are up on the ridges or the top of the sidehills just below the ridges. Deer do not usually go up to the tops of the ridges unless they are pushed during the hunting season. There are two ridges behind my home that are separated by a varying distance of ½ to 1 full mile. There are several lakes in those mountain hollows. Those are good places to hunt after the deer have been pushed up there by hunting pressure, but they are poor spots for deer the rest of the year because of the lack of food. The forests are mature with almost no underbrush, although they often produce a good acorn crop from mid-September to October. Because of the very dense rhododendron and laurel thickets, the deer will go to these mountain swamps to escape hunters and to yard up during severe winters. Those thickets are so thick that they are practically impenetrable.

Except during the acorn season, the deer definitely have different bedding and feeding areas. When the acorns are dropping, they are usually falling in the same hilly areas that the deer bed in; the deer are seldom seen unless you push up to the ridges.

Both bedding and feeding areas shift constantly in response to the seasonal availability of food. Where deer have access to farm crops and open areas, they will use a preferred bedding area almost all the time. In the unbroken forested areas that you describe, deer will shift both their bedding and feeding areas to be near each food source as it becomes available. In these areas, your deer population will be low because there just is no food available over the bulk of the year unless some spots have been burned or timbered. I reiterate a statement I have made over the years: Deer are not unbroken-forest animals. They thrive on edges. The Indians understood this; they set fire to the virgin forests to create the new growth needed to support deer. I'm not saying that you should set fire to the forests—I just want to explain why you don't see more deer in the areas you hunt.

You actually gave the same answer in your letter. You said you found no shed antlers in the big woods, but you located nine sheds in the small patches of woods.

You should have no trouble patterning the deer in the big woods during bow season. Your letter indicates that you are knowledgeable enough to know the different species of trees. No one will ever become a good hunter until he is familiar with the trees and vegetation that make up a deer's habitat.

You mentioned the white oak and red oak trees. White oak acorns are whitetails' most preferred food in autumn. Put your stand in among white oaks and you will see deer. Don't worry about occasionally spooking a deer. We all do it; they will be back, particularly to the white oaks. If the white oak acorn crop is poor, which it is three years out of four, put your stand in among the red oaks.

You also make a mistake that is common to most hunters. Do not leave the woods until about 1 P.M., even if it means delaying your lunch. Deer that are not under heavy hunting pressure get up and feed quite heavily from 11 A.M. to noon, a period that most hunters miss.

Q: I have just been out hunting for shed antlers and was lucky enough to find one. It was not a big one, but still a nice 8-pointer. Evidently the buck had been in a fight, because two of the antler tips had been broken off. I found the antler the third week in March, but the rodents had already been hard at work, chewing off a couple of the tips.

The thing that puzzled me, and the reason I'm writing this letter, is that the antler burr has a jagged piece on the outside edge of the surface where the antler joined the deer's pedicle. It actually looks as if a piece of the pedicle separated from the pedicle and stayed on the antler. It's not a big piece—only about ¼ inch long—but all of the antlers I have ever seen were slightly rounded in a convex fashion. Have you ever seen this, and do you think that this piece was a part of the pedicle? It looks like when you are sawing a board and the wood snaps off just a fraction before the saw can make a clean cut.

T. O., Decatur, Illinois

A: Although it is not common, I have seen a number of antlers that had that jagged edge you describe. In Ohio, I saw three different sets of antlers from the same captive buck, and each year the left antler had the same jagged edge. This edge is a piece of the pedicle and evidently, if it once breaks off in a certain spot, it will continue to break off in the same spot each year thereafter. I saw one large antler that had a jagged piece about ½ inch in length.

Q: I am a first-year bowhunter. While taking my bowhunting education class, the instructor posed this question: "If a deer's first set of antlers are spikes, what will they be next year?" Several in the class thought that the buck could become a 4-pointer in his second year. The instructor told us that, without exception, the buck would never be better than a spike. Is this true?

B. C., Absecon, New Jersey

A: Absolutely not—with one exception. If the buck continued to be on the very poor nutritional diet that caused it to be a spike in the first place, there is a chance that it might be a spike next year.

No buck should ever be a spike. The chances of a spike being a spike because of defective genes are slight. The chances of a buck being a spike because of poor nutrition are all to high. If your instructor's theoretical

Spike antlers are seldom a problem of genetics; they are usually caused by a lack of nutritious food.

buck was given a 16 percent protein diet, I am willing to bet that he would be at least a 6-pointer next year, and probably an 8-pointer.

I appreciate the fact that the instructor is donating his time to a most worthy cause, bowhunting instruction. I hope he knows more about bows than he does about deer.

Q: I shot a buck in late October that had its antler broken below the pedicle. The antler was straight out. It was bleeding but not severely, and the buck seemed in fine shape. I thought it should heal, but only after the antler was shed. I realize that this is assuming it doesn't get infected. If it healed, it would probably be at an odd angle. Am I correct?

B. DeC., Burlington, Wisconsin

A: If the pedicle is broken and the skull heals without infection, the antler will grow at an odd angle for the rest of the buck's life. What makes it even more odd is that instead of being normal shaped but at a different angle, the antler itself will probably be misshapen.

A friend of mine has a buck that broke his pedicle below the burr, and the wound became badly infected. The following spring the buck grew a normal antler on his uninjured side, but a nontypical antler on his injured side. This is not so unusual, but what *is* odd is that the injured side starts to grow its antlers two to three weeks after the other side starts, and it has done this each year since the pedicle was broken. With each succeeding year, the antler on the injured side is less misshapen than it was the year before.

Q: I live on a farm in southern Ohio. One of my neighbors, an Amish man, has raised deer for a number of years. Several years ago, one of his bucks developed huge nontypical antlers and had nontypical antlers for several years in a row. The man sold this buck to a fellow in Missouri who was going to use it for a breeder. What causes nontypical antlers in the first place, and will the buck's offspring also be nontypical?   B. W., Strasburg, Ohio

A: This is an exceedingly difficult question to answer, because I have not had much experience with captive, nontypical bucks. Several biologists with whom I spoke gave me what information they could, but there were a number of questions that they could not answer either.

From what I have observed, I have always believed that nontypical antlers are caused by injury to the antlers or to the pedicle while the antlers were growing.

This buck has two main beams growing from his left pedicle.

I have 11 pairs of shed antlers from a buck that our neighbor raised in captivity. When the buck was a yearling, he broke his right antler, as it was growing, just above the pedicle. The broken antler grew downward for 2 inches, then turned and grew up and out. At age 2½, the right antler grew out for about 1 inch and then grew straight up. At ages 3½, 4½, and 5½, the right antler grew up for about 2 to 3 inches and then bent out and around like a normal antler. Each year the bend became less noticeable. Each succeeding year from 6½ to 11½ years, the bump or bend straightened out even more. At 11½ years, it would not have been noticeable at all if I didn't have the other antlers with which to compare it or unless I was looking for it.

The oddest nontypical antler formation in my personal collection was given to me by my friend Joe Taylor. The buck was killed in Warren County, New Jersey, by an automobile in early September, just after most of the velvet had been rubbed off. He was in excellent condition. He must have suffered a massive blow to the pedicle just as his antlers had started to grow. The pedicle on his left antler is 1¼ inches across, but the antler base is 3½ inches across. The seven main beams have 13 points that grow in all directions. I have no idea what could have caused a blow that could do so much damage yet not kill the deer.

Another friend has a beautiful big buck that is 7½ years old. His first set of antlers, as a yearling, had 8 points. Then he became a 10-pointer, not counting a couple of little sticker points. At 4½ years of age he grew a crazy

This Texas buck has a nontypical right main beam.

The Deer Hunter's Encyclopedia

These antlers are an extreme example of nontypical growth. I believe they resulted from the pedicles being smashed as the antlers started to grow.

tine on his right antler that bent down and up like a 12-inch letter *U*. That point broke off right after the velvet was peeled, and the buck has grown perfect antlers every year since.

Still another friend of mine has a big buck with a damaged pedicle and each year it grows a fresh antler on that damaged pedicle. The first antler after the pedicle was injured was a monstrosity, but each succeeding antler has been close to normal. None of the buck's offspring is nontypical, but then they shouldn't be because their father's nontypical antler was caused by injury, not genetics.

In many wild bucks, we have no way of knowing if their nontypical antlers are the result of injury or genetics, so we don't know what kind of antlers their offspring will have. I have seen some bucks become more nontypical with age, while others become less so. I believe that more bucks become less nontypical with age, simply because such growth is abnormal and antlers do try to go back to what they should be.

The truth of the matter is that we just don't know that much about nontypical antlers.

Q: It's mid-May as I write this and I've just been watching a buck out in my cow pasture that has horns long enough to start to split for the first time. The bases are fat and furry and, through my binoculars, they look to be over 2 inches in diameter. The buck has a big body. If these antlers are over 2 inches in diameter, they will be a big set, won't they? I was also wondering if the horns grow from the base or from the top. Do the horns get all of their nourishment from the velvet? F. S., Sun Prairie, Wisconsin

A: Let's put things straight right from the start. If you are looking at a deer with your binoculars, what you see on top of his head are antlers. If you are looking at one of your cows, then you are seeing horns.

If that buck has antlers that look to be over 2 inches in diameter, hope and pray that you see him in your pasture during hunting season. He will definitely have a big set of antlers when they are fully grown.

The velvet hairs on a growing set of antlers are usually ¹⁄₁₆ to ⅛ inch in length when they stand on end, and most of them do. The skin itself, when it is blood filled, is also about ¹⁄₁₆ inch in thickness. Deduct ½ inch or slightly more for the skin and the hair and you still have antler bases measuring about 1½ inches in diameter. That's the base of a big antler.

The hairs on the velvet are pressure sensitive and warn the deer of any obstacles that may injure the antler.

Antlers grow from new material being added to the tips.

Speaking of cow horns, they are made of keratin, as are your fingernails and deer hooves. Horns grow continuously throughout the animals' lifetime, and all of the growth is nourished from blood vessels in their core. Thus, a horn grows from the inside out.

A buck's antlers are pure bone, the same as its skeleton. Initially the antler is nourished by blood vessels running up through the center as well as some going up the outside of the antler through the velvet. As the antlers get larger, the internal blood flow is shut down so that they are nourished from the outside in.

Antlers grow like trees, with new growth being added to the tips, instead of like grass, whose growth is in the bottom, pushing the entire structure up. If an antler grew in that latter fashion, it would not branch into tines at all but instead be long and thin, like some antelope horns.

Q: Here is a newspaper article I saved for you about an antlered doe. I hope you can use it to educate present and future deer hunters. The more that is learned about deer, the better hunters we can be.

D. R., Gallatin, Missouri

A: The article referred to was an Associated Press release about Tim Groves of Hartsburg, Missouri, who shot a nice 8-point buck in Charlton County on the opening weekend of the 1997 Missouri deer season.

The article quotes Groves as saying, "I saw the antlers first." By the time the big deer stepped into the clearing, just 30 yards away, Groves already had the animal in his rifle scope's crosshairs.

"I thought it was odd there was a fawn hanging with a buck," Groves said. "It was big enough to make it on its own."

After the deer was field-dressed, the conservation agent at the Keytesville check station verified that it was a doe.

The picture that accompanied the article showed a deer with a large, hardened, 8-point rack with the second, or G 2, tines having a length of between 8 and 10 inches.

If this doe was actually the mother of the fawn accompanying her, it is contrary to everything I have ever read about antlered does.

First of all, let me state that I have never seen an antlered doe. All that I know about antlered does is what I have read in the scientific literature or have been told by biologists.

It has always been my understanding that if a doe is producing more of the male sex hormone testosterone than normal, she might grow antlers that would not harden. In this condition, she was still more female than male and could be bred and produce fawns. If the female produces more testosterone than estrogen, she is basically a male and her antlers will harden; the velvet will also peel off, as it had in the doe that Groves shot. But she is incapable of being bred and producing fawns.

If the doe's uterus had been saved, it could have been checked for placental scar tissue, which would have proven whether or not Groves's doe had ever given birth. Because it was not, we can only assume that the fawn seen with her when she was shot was her own. If so, this was a most unusual occurrence, or at least I have never heard of it happening.

So, you see, not only an I trying to help others with what I have learned, but others are helping me learn more, too.

Q: This past hunting season (1996), I shot a buck in Manchester Township, Ocean County, in the Pasadena-Greenwood Forest area in southern Jersey. This is Fish and Game Department property.

The buck I shot was not nontypical, but he certainly wasn't typical of southern Jersey deer either. He was quite symmetrical, and his first two tines were palmated with 2 additional points on each one (all told 12 points). At the checking station, the state biologist considered him a 10-pointer, 3½ years old, and felt that the teeth were different and very interesting.

I took the head to be mounted, and when I went to pick it up the taxidermist said the antlers were exceptionally light in weight for their size. I examined the mount more when I got home; when I tapped the antlers, they sounded hollow (no doubt about it). Out of curiosity, I drilled a hole in the antlers, and they are definitely hollow. This is my reason for writing. I'm really curious to know why the antlers are hollow. So are my fellow hunters. Is this unique or more common than I know of?

K. W., Matawan, New Jersey

A: While it is quite rare, I have seen several deer with palmated brow tines and have photographed one of them. The extra points can only be considered bona fide points if they are over 1 inch in length.

You did not tell me how the teeth were different, so I am unable to comment upon them.

I have never heard, or even read, of hollow antlers; believe me, it is not a common phenomenon.

Horns grow from the inside out, and they are not hollow either. The outer layer will be hollow after the horn has been cut off and the core has dried and been removed.

Antlers grow from the outside in, with bone salts being deposited by the blood vessels in the velvet. The bone salts—calcium, magnesium,

A white-tailed buck with palmated brow tines.

Because each of the projections on these palmated brow tines is over 1 inch in length, they are considered tines.

and phosphorous—are derived from the buck's skeleton. After the antlers have grown, the center—known as the sporangium—is softer than the outer part, but the antler is completely filled. When the antlers are full grown, they begin to solidify from the base to the tips and from the outside in. The bulk of the fighting that bucks do is in October and early November, when the sporangium is not completely solid and the antlers thus have more give when they are crashed together. Applying such pressure to the antlers in December, when the cores are drier, would probably result in breakage. Bucks break off more antler tines and beams later in the season than they do at the start of the rut.

Q: I have hunted deer all of my life and spend as much time as I can looking at them and studying their behavior. This year I saw something I had never seen before. Ordinarily the bucks I have seen shed their velvet the first week of September, just like you said in your book *The Deer of North America.* But this summer (1994), I saw a big buck that had shed his velvet by the middle of August. I saw him on August 15, and his antlers were free of velvet but still had some red on them from the blood. I figured that he had just peeled the night before. This is the earliest I have ever heard of. Have you ever heard of a buck losing his velvet this early?

J. G., Mahwah, New Jersey

A: No, I had never seen or heard of a buck that had shed his velvet that early. However, I noticed that this year all the bucks were peeling in the last week of August, and I did receive a report from a friend who saw a 4-point buck that had started to peel on August 8, 1994.

This past summer was the wettest I can recall. I don't know what the official amount of rain was, but I heard we were 5 inches above normal, and right after that we had a 4½ inches of rain in one afternoon. More rain meant that the sky was much darker than normal for a much longer period of time. Many mornings it didn't get light until after 6 A.M. The many storm days effectively shortened the daylight hours. It's as if autumn came early.

Most wildlife activity is governed by photoperiodism, which means that it is increased or reduced by the amount of daylight in a 24-hour period. The storm clouds fool the deer's glands into responding as though it was later in the year than it is.

The deer's eye acts as a photoelectric cell, gathering the ambient light that it is exposed to each day. The eye sends electrical impulses to the pineal gland located in the brain. The pineal gland then relays an electrical impulse to the pituitary gland at the base of the deer's brain. The pituitary gland sends a chemical message throughout the deer's body.

This year, because of the extensive cloud cover, the message sent in July was that it was August. The decreased amount of light fooled the deer's brains. The animals' testicles consequently descended earlier than normal. Higher levels of testosterone coursed through their bodies earlier, and the antlers solidified earlier. In turn, the velvet was peeled off at least one week earlier.

After the summer, I had expected that the peak of this year's rutting season to be November 6–9, or even a day or so earlier.

But then came October. In this area, October was absolutely fantastic! We had gorgeous fall colors. We had warm days and cool nights. We had crystal-clear blue skies and blue skies and blue skies. What we had was one of the driest Octobers on record; we had a drought.

Although I did not think it possible, once the process had been set in motion, the clear skies seemed to compensate for the dark days of August and September to put the peak of the rut back on schedule. I noticed an extraordinary amount of breeding activity November 9–15.

I have never seen quite the weather conditions I saw this year. The deer's response to it was a real eye-opener.

August 15 is still the earliest I have heard of for a wild buck to peel all the velvet from his antlers, although the one that started on the 8th probably would have been clean by then.

Q: During the first week of November in 1997, one of the members of our hunting camp shot what appeared to be a healthy buck with all the signs of being in full rut except that he had lost both antlers. We hunt the Quinn Lakes area of the Madawaska Highlands in eastern Ontario. This area is several miles from the nearest road, so I doubt the antlers were lost in a car accident. The empty sockets were quite large and still damp. Is it normal for a mature buck to drop his antlers while in rut, or could they have been lost fighting? Thank you.

K. J., Perth, Ontario, Canada

A: From your description of the pedicle, it sounds as if the antlers had not been broken off in an accident but had been cast. I realize that this is exceptionally early; in fact, it is the earliest I can recall hearing about. The earliest I personally know for a whitetail casting his antlers is November 25. I live in an area where many of the bucks cast their antlers around December 5. I once photographed a mule deer buck in Colorado on November 15 that had cast his antlers a day or two before; I knew this because the pedicle had dried but had not yet begun to heal over. This is also exceptionally early, as the rutting season was at its peak. In the case of the New Jersey whitetails, it really didn't matter, because the bulk of the breeding season was already over. In fact, I always felt that because the New Jersey deer herd was so badly skewed in favor of females (about seven to eight does to each adult buck), the breeding season was so intense that the bucks cast their antlers early.

The buck you describe would definitely be at a disadvantage, as your breeding season would be approaching the peak of the rut. Without antlers, your buck, no matter how big or old he might be, would have no chance at breeding. The smallest spike buck could, and would, have driven him away from the does.

Q: A friend of mine shot a 6-point buck that was still in velvet. It was not a big rack, but it looked to be fully formed. In your book *The Deer of North America,* you claim that most deer shed the velvet from their antlers around September 5. Our deer gun season here in Pennsylvania is in the first part of December. I have never seen a buck in velvet during the hunting season before. He sure looked unusual. Why did he still have his velvet when all of the other bucks had shed theirs?

J. N., Shamokin, Pennsylvania

Many different factors affect the exact time that a buck will cast his antlers.

A: The shedding of velvet by deer is the result of photoperiodism. The diminishing amount of light after June 21 affects the deer's pineal gland, which is often called the "third eye" because it works on the light gathered by the deer's two regular eyes. The pineal gland sends electrical impulses to the pituitary gland, which releases minute chemical secretions that cause increased production of the male hormone testosterone, along with enlarging the deer's testicles.

With testosterone coursing through his body, the buck's antlers begin to solidify starting at their bases. This occurs about the first part of August. If you look closely at a buck's antlers in August (or look closely at photos taken in August of a buck), you will see that the velvet has started to shrink. The base of a buck's antler, called the burr or coronet, grows outward, effectively reducing the blood supply to the antler and then shutting it off.

Whereas the antlers and velvet were filled out and rounded when the blood supply was flowing, the velvet looks as if it were shrink-wrapped onto the antler once the supply has been shut off. And basically, it has been. Now you can actually see the longitudinal grooves made by the blood vessels that supplied the nutrition to the antler when it was being formed.

Under normal circumstances, a buck's antlers will have solidified and the velvet dried sufficiently to be rubbed off around September 1. This timing is not set in stone. Some bucks shed the velvet the last week in August, some the first week in September.

The buck you saw that still had his velvet in December evidently had either his pineal gland removed or some sort of injury to his testicles.

Researchers at Penn State University removed a buck's pineal gland—an operation called a pinealectomy—and the buck retained his summer coat and the velvet on his antlers into mid-winter.

Antlers grow at a rate of up to ¼ inch per day.

Credit: Len Rue Jr.

You did not mention the condition of the buck's testicles. Because it's unlikely that anything happened to his pineal gland, some injury to his testicles probably did, in effect, castrate him. Even though he may have still had his testicles, something—and I don't know what—happened that cut off the supply of testosterone. If this happened during the summer, all of the antlers' developmental process would have been halted.

Q: My first question involves antlered does. Do does with antlers get bred? The second question involves white-tailed deer raised in captivity. If a person raised a buck and wanted to get him "fixed" so he could not breed, how would this affect the buck's antler growth? Would he stop growing antlers, or would he remain in the same stage of antler growth he was in at the time he was fixed? J. B., Morrilton, Arizona

A: It varies from one area to another, but Pennsylvania found that out of 38,270 antlered deer killed in the state in 1959, 17 were does. This figure of 1 antlered doe out of each 2,251 antlered animals killed comes very close to the New York State figure of 1 antlered doe for each 2,250 antlered animals killed. Further studies in Pennsylvania showed an antlered doe ratio of 1:4,024. The highest ratio of antlered does comes from Camp Wainwright in Alberta, Canada, which had the unbelievable ratio of 1:65. I personally have never seen an antlered doe or, if I did, I didn't realize it.

Does grow antlers when their supply of the male sex hormone testosterone is higher than normal. There are three different basic situations. It must be remembered that both male and female animals, including humans, have both the male and female sex hormones. In women, the supply of estrogen suppresses any effect that the male hormone testosterone might have in the body up until menopause. After menopause, as their estrogen supply decreases, many older women take on masculine characteristics. Their voices deepen and they get more facial hair.

A doe that has a slightly higher level of testosterone than normal will grow antlers that never harden. Such antlers usually freeze off when the weather gets very cold. These does are capable of breeding, giving birth, and nursing their fawns. One antlered doe, when dressed, was found to be carrying triplets. Except for being antlered, these does are thoroughly female.

In the second situation, a doe's estrogen level is suppressed by the testosterone. She will grow antlers that harden; their velvet will peel off, and they will be cast in midwinter. Does in this condition cannot be bred; they are basically males with female genitals.

The third case is known as hermaphroditism. The doe will not only have antlers but may also have a rudimentary penis and perhaps even a scrotum. The marvel is that all this doesn't happen more often. Fetuses in their first month or so are actually either-or: They have sexual characteristics that could develop into either male or female. Sexuality is determined by a tiny dose of chemicals.

Turning to your second question, the simplest, most positive way to "fix" a buck so that he can't breed is to physically remove his testicles through castration. If the buck is castrated before his antlers start to grow, they will not develop. If the buck is castrated while the antlers are in velvet, they will not harden. If the buck lives in a very cold climate, the antlers will freeze off, and new ones will not develop.

Q: I am an 18-year-old who has just completed high school. I am also an avid bowhunter and spend a lot of time in the woods. I am writing you to pass on an experience that I had in the spring of 1992. It was the opening of turkey season here in northern Illinois and I was, of course, in the woods. Shortly after sunrise, I saw several whitetails coming toward me. There were seven in all, and I recognized the leader of the group as a buck that I had seen the previous fall because of an unmistakable patch of white on his face. They walked right in front of me, only 7 yards away. The interesting thing about this group of deer is that one of the last ones to come by still had half a rack on his head that he had not shed, even though this was the middle of April. I've never seen or heard of any deer that kept a rack this long. I am absolutely sure of what I saw; there was plenty of light and I was close enough (this deer never came closer than 12 yards) to get a good look at him. In addition, I watched him for about two minutes when he was at his closest. Have you ever heard of a deer keeping part of his rack this long? There is one other interesting thing: The farmers in the area all had unusual trouble with running over shed antlers in the fields while working the ground during the spring of 1992. They usually don't have any such trouble but, for some reason, that spring they did. We had a fairly mild winter that year. Could that be the reason bucks kept their antlers longer than usual? Could that also be the reason that the buck I saw still had his rack in April? K. W., Sterling, Illinois

A: I personally saw a buck that kept his antlers until April 15.

The fact that you had a very mild winter may have had something to do with his retaining his antlers so long. Bucks that are well fed have a tendency to keep their antlers longer, though I don't know why. After the velvet has been removed, the antler has no living tissue connected to it, so the availability of food should have no bearing.

Q: I read an article in the January 1995 issue of *Deer and Deer Hunting* called "Chubby, the Buck That Lived with Deformity," by Rusty Metcalf. The story stated: "The buck had an injury to his left hind leg near the hoof. True to form, his right antler's growth had been affected by the injury." I have heard many haunting stories that if a deer grows one very strange antler, when dressed he is often found to have injuries to his opposite side. I would like to know if there is any other information on this phenomenon in articles or publications.

M. K., Pte-Cle, Quebec, Canada

A: The buck Chubby was true to form. I have seen a number of bucks with deformed antlers on one side that were the result of injuries to their lower extremities on the opposite side of their bodies; I have documented this twice. Most times, the injury was to the toes. Please bear in mind that the deer's tarsal glands are on its ankle. Injuries on an upper leg, thigh, or ham, do not seem to cause the opposite antlers to deform as much or as often.

I was very interested in Chubby's foot because I have an almost identical hoof in my collection. The buck had stepped in a piece of hard rubber that went up over the two center toes and caught under the dew claws, deforming the foot in the same way. The buck did not walk on that foot at all; the hooves had continued to grow and were long and curving.

CHAPTER
3

Behavior

I have long said that we cannot understand wildlife until we understand more about their methods of communication. Most animals, and deer in particular, live in a world of scent—a world of chemical communication. As we are constantly learning more about the deer's chemical communication, we are learning much more about the deer's basic behavior. And it is knowledge of behavior that improves the quality of a deer hunt and boosts its chances of success.

I am continually amazed at all the new facts about deer behavior that I am constantly learning, not only from the deer themselves, but from researchers as well.

This is the fifth book I have written about deer. With so much new information coming my way daily, I know it won't be my last.

Q: I was watching a small doe and her fawn feeding in a clover field last autumn when a large doe approached them. Ironically, the small doe chased the big doe out of the field. Isn't it usually the other way around?

V. P., Frankfort, Kentucky

A: Yes, but when it comes to whitetails, nothing can be termed "normal." Still, it is true that in most cases larger deer will chase smaller deer from food sources. In the wild, size and strength determine dominance. The difference in your case was that the small doe had a fawn with her, while the big one did not.

The ferocity of the maternal instinct is well known. Before giving birth, does have a birthing territory, and they drive all other deer from it. After giving birth, they defend this territory fiercely for four to five days.

The fawn you saw was probably 2 months old. At this age, the doe would have given up the birthing territory, but she might have established a protective zone around her fawn. Such protectiveness diminishes as fawns grow older. By winter, the larger doe that was run off would surely be the one running the younger does away from food sources.

A white-tailed doe and fawn.
Credit: Len Rue Jr.

Q: January 1998 had an exceptionally mild winter, and there were quite a few deer out scavenging for corn in a nearby field that had been harvested. The deer also seemed to be soaking up the sunshine. On several occasions, we saw does stand up on their hind legs and beat at other deer to chase them off the corn. I have seen does do this on many occasions, but never a buck do this. Do bucks fight like this with their front feet? Just curious.

P. W., Dubuque, Iowa

A: Yes indeed, bucks do fight by standing on their hind feet and striking out with their forefeet. It always amazes me how long deer can stand upright (about half a minute), and I have seen them cover about 50 feet in distance in this fashion. Bucks get a lot of practice, because they fight with their front feet when they don't have antlers and also when their antlers are soft and growing.

I was on the National Bison Range in Montana one July years ago. There was a baby antelope in one of the compounds, and I asked if I could go in and photograph it. Upon receiving permission, I climbed over the gate and started snapping pictures of the baby pronghorn. Suddenly a mule deer buck with big antlers walked over. It was early July and the buck's antlers were still growing, in velvet, so I paid no attention to him. That was a mistake. That buck stood up on his hind feet and lashed out at me with his forefoot hooves. Those hooves could have cut me wide open. I hit him in the head with my hand, knocking him off balance, and I got out of there . . . quickly! I would hate to be around that buck when the velvet was off his antlers. A captive buck, whitetail or mulie, that has lost his fear of man is one of the most dangerous animals in North America.

You probably have not seen this (fighting) action among bucks because there are never as many bucks as does in areas where deer are hunted. Under all circumstances, bucks are less likely than does to feed early in the afternoon. And if the deer were at a distance and the bucks had cast their antlers, it would be very difficult to tell the bucks from the does unless there was a great difference in body size.

You're also right in assuming that the deer you were watching were soaking up the sunshine, no matter how meager the heat. In late winter, deer move no more than they have to at night. They conserve more body heat by lying still. In cold weather and after the hunting season, if there is no pressure on them, deer prefer to feed during the warmer daytime hours. It prevents body heat loss and, if the day is clear, they will absorb heat from the sun.

Q: I am an avid deer hunter and hunt my own property in Pennsylvania.

Do you think doe are territorial and that a mature doe can control an area? By this, I mean keep other deer out of her so-called turf, especially does not related to her.

For example, I've seen one particular good-sized doe on many occasions. On one of these occasions, she was with what I assumed to be her two offspring. Another young doe came fairly close to her, and she reared up on her back legs and hoofed the young deer, which left immediately.

Deer sightings have declined on my property and the surrounding properties in the past three years, but this past season was the worst. During archery season I usually see 11 to 12 different bucks. This season I saw only six. In my mind, the fewer doe in the area come into estrus, the fewer bucks.

Because of this, I decided to try to take the aggressive doe during anterless season. By a stroke of luck, and by being in the right place at the right time, I was able to accomplish this. Will this somehow increase the number of deer on my property?   R. C., Bernville, Pennsylvania

A: Deer are not territorial in the true sense of the word. A buck does not try to chase all other bucks out of his particular range. A dominant buck will try to drive all other bucks away from an estrus doe and, so long as they stay about 200 feet away from her, he doesn't bother with them. A doe will claim a birthing territory for 2 to 3 days prior to giving birth and 10 to 14 days after. The size and placement of this territory depend upon her rank and size. The older, bigger does get the best territories, while the younger does are pushed to the fringes. The purpose of a birthing territory is to scatter the does over the widest possible area cutting down on fawn predation. This is the only time deer have a territory.

What you have witnessed is very common. Deer have a home range of from 1 to 2 square miles. It is a range they share with many other deer—20 individuals to the square mile is the average for good deer habitat. If a particular doe and her 2 fawns are using 2 square miles, she could be coming into contact with perhaps 37 other deer. In their search for food, deer frequently come into competition with other deer. It is very common for a bigger, stronger, older doe to rear up and slash at other younger does and their fawns if they get too close to the food she is feeding on. In the winter, when food is scarce, the doe will even drive off her own fawns; at this time her own survival is more important, and the maternal bonds have been weakened by time and necessity.

If you are finding fewer deer in your area, it is not because that particular doe was driving them out. It may be that the habitat on your land and the adjacent area has gotten so poor that it will not support the numbers of

White-tailed deer have a home range of one to two square miles, depending upon food, water, and cover.

deer it formerly did. You wrote your letter on February 12, 1997. The winter of 1996 was a very hard one on deer because of all the deep snow. Perhaps you lost a lot of deer to starvation. If so, it will take several years for the herd to build back up. However, this is not all bad, because it will give the habitat a chance to recover.

Q: I have a theory that I'd like your opinion on. It concerns buck rubs. I feel that one reason a buck rubs is to determine the size and mass of his antlers. Bucks don't have any mirrors, so I figure they rub different-sized trees to determine their antlers' width, and brush to determine the overall mass. Otherwise, how would they know which buck to fight and which to run from? R. B., Hill Air Force Base, Utah

A: Being able to see almost in a full circle, a buck has no trouble seeing the size of his own antlers. He does not have to measure them by rubbing a tree, he does not need to see them in the mirror surface of the pond from which he drinks. He knows their size instinctively and by sight.

Bucks also know how their own antlers compare to another buck's the moment they see them. It is not only the actual antler size that determines

Buck rubs are visual as well as olfactory signposts.

dominance, but also body size, weight, and the belligerence shown by body language.

On too many occasions, I have seen bucks that had slightly smaller antlers than their rivals drive off the bigger bucks because they were more belligerent. Perhaps the larger buck was past his peak. It's a little like pitting a 22-year-old man against a 60-year-old man. The older buck will definitely have a bigger body and probably bigger antlers, but the years have robbed him of the vigor of his youth.

Q: I have just returned from a deer hunt on a commercial preserve in Alabama. The club is located on thousands of acres of land, and its perimeter is not fenced in. Extensive food plantings in the center of the holdings keep the deer in.

The Deer Hunter's Encyclopedia

I had been put on a stand while it was still dark. A short time after dawn I could see some deer, one a nice buck, working their way toward me from a clover field where they had been feeding.

Before they even got within rifle range, a herd of feral pigs appeared out of the woods between the deer and my stand. Long before I saw the pigs, the deer had stopped and appeared to be very nervous. Their tails were flared, and several of the does were stamping their feet. When the pigs got within 150 feet or so, the deer just exploded into action, dashing off in all directions. All I could see were white tails disappearing in all directions.

I don't think any of the pigs could have weighed 100 pounds. The buck had to have weighed at least 150 pounds, and he had a nice set of antlers; still, he ran away as fast as any of the does. The pigs weren't even moving toward the deer, just sort of cutting across in front of them. Why are deer so afraid of pigs?

T. L., Youngstown, Ohio

A: I really don't have an answer for your question, although I have seen similar incidents many times, not only with feral hogs but with the smaller collared peccaries (also called javelinas) too.

It might be that deer look upon pigs as predators. Most folks don't realize that pigs in the wild are predators, much preferring to feed upon meat

Deer do not like to be around peccaries or feral hogs.

Credit: Len Rue Jr.

than roots and tubers. Wild pigs will eat every egg of a ground-nesting bird, along with the young birds when they can find them. Pigs are often used to clear an area of rattlesnakes, as they will eat all that they encounter. Pigs seem to be immune to the snakes' poison. They also eat mice and baby rabbits; although I have never seen it, I am sure that they would eat any newborn fawn they discovered. I believe the fear instilled in them as fawns stays with the deer when they grow up and makes them so leery of pigs.

When I first saw deer's dislike of pigs, I figured it was because the pigs' noise made it difficult for the deer to detect other danger. It is this noise factor that deer dislike about wild turkeys. If a flock of turkeys moves into an area where deer are feeding or bedded, the deer usually move off.

Also, remember that pigs are almost always in a herd, and they often fight as a herd. Even though Gulliver was much larger than the Lilliputians, they were so numerous that they took him down; and a herd of pigs would be a juggernaut. However, I once saw a single 60-pound peccary chase a buck deer that weighed 135 to 150 pounds for a distance of about 150 feet. That deer tucked tail and *ran!*

When pigs move into an area, the deer move out.

Q: This year (1993) we had a very wet fall out here in Washington State. So did most of the western and central parts of the United States. I don't believe I have ever seen so many mushrooms as there were this year.

I was bowhunting on the edge of some cut-over land just a little south of Spokane, where I live. The cut land has come back with a lot of blackberry and thimbleberry bushes, which are good deer food, and we are getting some big whitetails here. The area I hunt has a big buck that we saw several times before the season. I have never shot a big buck, and I had made up my mind that this year I would wait till I got a shot at the big guy. I haven't seen him since the season opened, but I have seen a lot of other deer, which gave me a good chance to study them and their behavior. One doe and her two fawns ate a lot of mushrooms. I don't know what kind of mushrooms they were eating, but they did eat several different kinds. I had never heard of mushrooms as a deer food, yet the deer really seemed to like them: They would eat them in the forest even before they would come out in the clear-cut to feed. Are mushrooms an important food for deer? Would it be safe to eat the same mushrooms deer are eating?

T. E., Spokane, Washington

A: I am not the person to ask about edible mushrooms; they are not one of my favored foods. I can recognize a number of them, but I really haven't made a study of them. My advice to everyone is *not* to eat wild mushrooms unless you have an expert with you. Then let the expert eat them first and

Shaggy mane mushrooms are readily eaten by deer.

wait three days. Do not eat mushrooms just because you see wildlife eating them. If you don't know a mushroom expert, and I don't, buy any of the dozen or so good edible mushrooms available on the market today.

I have seen deer, elk, moose, and caribou eat mushrooms. Beavers do, too. I rode a horse in British Columbia on a trip into the Cassiar Mountains for Stone's sheep that ate every mushroom we passed. I just couldn't keep his head up when we passed a mushroom. And he evidently was an expert, because he would pass up some but eat all the others.

I have not been able to learn the nutritional value of mushrooms, but I have always heard it's low. I have found that mycologists (mushroom experts) claim mushrooms are very rich in potassium, phosphorus, and nitrogen. They say that mushrooms have as much as 100 times more of these elements than the browse growing on the same soil, making them veritable "mineral licks" for deer.

Q: I recently read an article by John Phillips in a bowhunting magazine that said to "shoot for the squat." In fact, that was the name of the article. It described a hunter named Pittman who had discovered that most of the deer he had missed with a bow were missed not because he was undershooting them, as he thought, but because he was overshooting them. Or, rather, Pittman was not actually overshooting the deer either, but the animals were squatting when he shot so that the arrows went over their backs. Pittman thus advocated shooting for the bottom of the heart so that, if the deer didn't squat, the arrow would hit its heart. If the deer did squat, though, the arrow would hit the center of the lungs or at least the spine.

I have never heard or read of this theory before and would like to know what you think about it. Pittman also said that the more deer are hunted, the more likely they are to squat. Do you think that's true? How far up from the bottom of the deer's chest is his heart? One last question: There is quite a lot of hunting pressure where I bowhunt. Do you think most of the deer in the area will squat? B. O., Lexington, Kentucky

A: John Phillips is a good friend and probably the most prolific outdoor writer in the business today. His articles are all thoroughly researched, and because John is a very successful hunter, he knows what he is writing about.

I do not know Pittman, but what he is talking about is not theory but fact.

I wrote several years ago about deer squatting when they were startled. I had seen them do this many times, but it was not until I was shooting a video camera that I could actually see just how often deer squatted. Lots of deer, especially does, will actually run off in a squatting position, usually with their tails clamped down tightly. When they run off, they are doing an exceedingly fast trot, not bounding. It's as if they are trying to make themselves as small and inconspicuous as possible.

Bows are not silent weapons, and some make a lot more noise than others. Make sure that your arrow rest is quiet, or the deer will hear the arrow being drawn back. You should also use effective silencers on your strings. Do whatever it takes to muffle any sound the bow might make. Sound travels at 1,128 feet per second. Deer have exceedingly sharp reflexes, honed by thousands upon thousands of years of survival.

I believe deer squat for two reasons. One is to make themselves appear smaller, as I just mentioned. The other is to bunch their muscles in preparation for springing forward. Before we humans throw anything, we have to draw our arm back. Before we jump, we do as the deer do: We squat. Just look at Olympic sprinters as they get set in their starting blocks. A snake has to coil before it strikes; deer squat.

Pittman is undoubtedly right that the more deer are hunted, the edgier they become. Being much more tense, they react even faster to any sight or sound of danger. Nothing departs as fast as a really spooked deer.

Yes, if your area is hunted hard, I am sure most of your deer will squat at every disturbance. You had better follow Pittman's good advice and aim for the heart. The bottom of the heart is located about 2 inches behind the rear point of the deer's elbow and about 2 to 3 inches up from the bottom of the chest. Try for a spot 4 to 5 inches from the bottom of the chest. Under any circumstances, this is an excellent point to aim for.

Q: During the 1991 gun season, I hunted in southern Illinois.

It was about 5:30 A.M. on opening morning when I got to my stand. My ground stand was at the top of a valley.

At about 6, when the sun began to rise, I made my first call. At 6:30 I made a second. Then, around 6:45, I looked to my right and saw a huge 10-point buck staring me down. We stood staring at each other for what seemed to be about five minutes. As he was snorting and stomping, wanting me to move, he never took his eyes off of me.

I had my shotgun facing to the left, waiting for him to look away. The second he turned I swung around, but he turned back at me. At the same time he leaped down the other side of the hill out of my sight.

Do not move a muscle if a deer is looking in your direction.

My question is, what is the best way to handle this situation? Should I have moved fast when I first saw him or waited for him to turn as I did?

A. H., Des Plaines, Illinois

A: When you say you made your first call, I have to assume that you were using a grunt call and not rattling antlers, although you don't specify. No matter which you were using, your timing was about right; most hunters call too frequently.

Also, I must assume that you were not using a blind of any kind, because you said that the buck had spotted you first. By the time you saw him, he had already seen you. By using a tree stand, you could have minimized the possibility of being discovered. Using a tree stand usually allows you to see a greater distance so that you can see the deer coming in.

It is a common practice of deer to stamp and snort in an effort to get whatever it was that disturbed them—in this case, you—to move so they can

A deer's ears never stop moving, even while it sleeps. Deer can also see 310 degrees of a circle.

confirm what, up to that point, they only suspected. Your only recourse was to simply outwait the deer. Don't berate yourself, as there really isn't much that you could have done in any case. The deer was already spooked; even if you had waited, you had little chance of catching him off guard.

Deer can see 310 degrees of a circle, and even if this buck had turned, he still would have kept his eye on you. He would have seen you move even if you had waited until he had turned completely away from you. And, even if he didn't, you wouldn't want to shoot a deer from the rear.

You've evidently got your calling technique perfected. Try using a tree stand, and better luck next time.

Q: On November 20, 1990, the second day of New York's gun season, I was hunting a patch of woods that had a heavy supply of acorns on the ground. I had seen a few rubs the week before and hunted this area on opening day. I spotted three does that morning, and had a chance at a 4-pointer in the afternoon but missed him. This turned out to be lucky, because better things occurred on day 2.

I climbed into my tree stand at 6:30 A.M. in the pale light and began my wait. At about 8 A.M. I saw a large doe approaching. She passed to my left at about 20 yards, well within easy shooting range, but I decided to wait. She then walked out in front of me to feed on the vast supply of acorns.

She stayed within 20 to 30 yards until about 9 A.M. Then she lay down right in front of me and proceeded to relax a little, but still she didn't leave.

At about 10 A.M., the doe stood up and looked out in front as another, smaller doe with two fawns approached. The large doe rushed at the doe and fawns and chased them out behind me at about 40 yards. They walked off, and the big doe walked back toward me. She passed at about 10 yards near a rub and a small scrape. She stopped, sniffed the rub, then deposited a load of pellets in the scrape. She then walked out in front of me and fed on acorns again.

At about 10:30 A.M., the doe and two fawns returned, but the big doe didn't bother them this time. The four of them fed in front of me until about 11:30 A.M., when the big doe suddenly put her ears down and charged the threesome again, chasing them out of the patch of woods, across a powerline opening, into another section of woods, and finally out of sight.

I climbed down at about 12:15 P.M. and walked back to my house. I returned to my tree stand about 1:30 P.M. I applied some doe-in-heat scent to the scrape and laid a couple of trails of scent to the scrape.

I began my wait again, half expecting not to see any deer because I had scared a 4-pointer from the same spot the day before. About 4 P.M., things began to happen as dusk neared. A deer emerged from a swampy patch and headed my way. At first I thought it was the 4-pointer returning, but before long I could see that this deer was larger. I got my shotgun up, pointed it down a shooting lane next to the rub, and waited.

He walked into the lane at about 14 yards and I dropped the 8-pointer in his tracks.

Here's my interpretation of the day's events: The larger doe was older than the smaller one, and was protecting the small patch of woods as her feeding ground. She was in heat and was keeping that area for herself to be bred by this buck.   R. O., New Windsor, New York

A: You have written about the most important factor of the hunt: not the shooting of your buck, but being outdoors to witness deer interaction.

I agree with your first observation. The doe was protecting her feeding turf. I have seen this type of aggression at all times of the year between does, and it is usually over food. The only other cause for such aggression is when a doe is protecting her birthing territory in mid-May or early June. At that time she will drive off all other deer, whether they're bucks, does, or last year's fawns. This is nature's way of dispersing the does and their new-born fawns over the widest possible area to minimize predation.

As far as your second conclusion goes, I have never known a doe to hold a territory in which to be bred. Usually, when a doe starts to come into estrus, she becomes exceedingly nervous and high strung, moving about a great deal. She drips urine and pheromones almost constantly, ad-vertising her condition to all bucks.

I was interested to read that the doe sniffed the forehead-gland scent that the buck had placed on his rub. It was also interesting that the doe defecated in the buck's scrape. On a number of occasions I have seen does urinate in scrapes.

I have also known does to show a preference for just one buck, refus-ing to allow other bucks near.

I do not hold with the theory expounded by some writers that the way to get your buck is to find his breeding territory. A lifetime of experience and observation has shown me that bucks go where the does are, and the does go where the food is. In this case, your little patch of woods contained all the acorns. It was the acorns that attracted the two does and the fawns, and it was the acorns and the two does that attracted the two bucks you saw.

Q: I recently moved to Montana from Englishtown, New Jersey. I am a little disappointed with the white-tailed deer hunting in Montana. Although I have seen three very large deer, the vast territory makes hunting extremely difficult. The whitetails can, and do, go anywhere.

Which part of the country has the best whitetails, considering the quan-tity of bucks and their size—not necessarily record-book size, but big? Most of the bucks I've killed are immature 4- to 6-pointers, and I would like to score on some a little bigger. I was thinking about northern Missouri.

J. S., Condon, Montana

A: Montana has excellent white-tailed deer hunting, particularly around Glacier National Park on both sides of the Rockies. But if you're intent on moving and you're looking primarily for whitetails, I would check out Minnesota. This state has provided more Boone & Crockett record-book bucks than any other. Look in St. Louis, Itasca, and Marshall Counties up north, and Winona County in the southeast.

Minnesota's winters are hard, but the deer are great. Wisconsin is also a great deer state, with Buffalo, Vilas, Ashland, Forest, and Sawyer Counties all tops for hunting.

Missouri is producing big deer, but there is no localized spot producing them in big numbers. St. Louis County produced the current world-record nontypical white-tailed buck in 1981. Missouri is a beautiful state with a good mix of rolling hills, farm fields, and timber. Its winters are moderate.

Some of the biggest deer I've photographed were in the southern Texas region bordering the Rio Grande from Del Rio to McAllen. The deer are on

Both of these Texas bucks are trophy animals, with the one on the left being the better.

private ranches, though perhaps you can get a job on a ranch. But rest assured, the summers can blister your saddle with heat. The area around Kerrville produces a lot of deer; some get big, but most are much smaller.

The area around Peoria, Illinois, is good deer country. The farmland is rich and the weather mild—both important factors in producing big deer.

To the north, the biggest deer are coming out of the prairie provinces of Alberta and Saskatchewan.

Q: How soon after gun season will deer return to their normal patterns? In some states, the bow season extends beyond the gun season. Knowing the answer to this question would be helpful.

J. W., Watermill, New York

A: Your question touches on several points. In New Jersey, our gun season used to be over by mid-December. If our weather was moderate, deer would be back to their normal haunts in one to two weeks, and would feed in the open during the day in two to three weeks. If the weather was cold, deer would stay in the heavy cover they had sought as refuge from the hunters. This kept them out of the biting wind.

New Jersey now offers bowhunting through the end of January. While the early bowhunting season in October does not disrupt the deer's daily activities too much, the late season does. Our deer are subjected to tremendous hunting pressure during the shotgun season, which follows on the heels of our small-game season. Deer that make it through the gun season

After the hunting season is over, the deer will often feed in the daytime during the winter.

are exceptionally wary, or they hide in the rhododendron swamps or the Kittatinny Mountain ridges, where few hunters go. After that intense pressure, deer are wary of the slightest disturbance, even during the January bow season. I used to see deer grazing in fields at midmorning in January. Now I don't see them until mid-February.

So, in short, the answer to your question is two to three weeks.

Q: In September (muzzleloading season in Kansas), I put out a scent line for a bedding area and drew a very nice mature buck to my ambush point, located in a grove of small walnut trees. I shot, but hit a small limb that deflected my slug. What I want to know is, do deer have memories? In other words, can I draw him back to this same area or will he remember and avoid it from now on? I would appreciate an answer; no one here in Cherokee, Oklahoma, can tell me—factually. J. M., Cherokee, Oklahoma

A: Yes, deer do have memories, but I don't believe you will have a problem with this buck just because you shot at him. I have found that deer pay very little attention to a single shot. They may actually have as much of a problem locating the exact direction of a single shot as most humans do. If the deer has not been wounded by a shot in the past, he would not associate a shot with pain. Except for extreme wilderness areas—and there are few left—most deer have heard a great many shots in their lifetimes, at least distant shots. If that buck took off as fast as I suspect he did, he was probably gone by the time you took your rifle off your shoulder. So he probably didn't even see you. The fact that he came in close enough for a shot proves that he didn't smell you. All that this deer heard was an exceptionally loud noise; he didn't know what caused it. He wouldn't leave the area anyway, so I don't think you will have a problem with him.

Q: Small-game season is on here in New Jersey, but bow-and-arrow season is still open also. We don't have Sunday hunting, so that's when I get out and do a little scouting to see just where the deer activity is. We have a good acorn crop this year; the ground is just covered with them.

A saw something this past Sunday that I have never seen in the woods before. As I was checking for deer sign and tracks, I kept seeing little pieces of acorn scattered about on the ground. There weren't a lot of pieces, but a little piece here and a little piece there scattered all over the entire area under the oaks. What animal or bird would crack the nuts and not eat them? T. L., Flemington, New Jersey

A: I have seen this many times before, but it is quite common in years of bumper acorn crops. The small pieces of acorn that you are finding are

Acorns are a deer's top-priority food.

pieces that fall out of a deer's mouth while it is chewing. I see this only in years when acorns are plentiful. Ordinarily, when acorns are scarce, deer just pick up one acorn at a time. When they are plentiful, deer often pick up two or three at a time. Deer are sloppy eaters. When they are eating corn, some of the kernels may fall out of their mouths. When they are eating apples, pieces of the apple and some of the juice often come out of their mouths. When they eat acorns, some of the small crushed pieces fall out of their mouths.

Q: I just came back from a hunting trip for mule deer in Colorado. I got a nice 4-pointer, but that is not the reason I'm writing. The outfitter put me on a stand overlooking a small canyon that he said was a major trail for mulies. It took three days before I got my buck; actually, I got it early on the morning of the third day. The weather was good, I really enjoyed myself, and I got to watch a lot of doe activity through my binoculars.

The thing that I noticed that was so different from whitetails is that when the mulie does urinated, they squatted so low that their rear ends almost touched the ground. Do mulie bucks squat to urinate, too? Have you ever seen a whitetail squat like this to urinate?

B. O., Nashville, Tennessee

A: Yes, mule deer bucks squat just as low to urinate as does do. And you are right, they squat much lower than whitetails ever do. White-tailed bucks do occasionally squat a bit to urinate.

A great deal has been written about how white-tailed bucks rub their tarsal, or hock, glands together and then urinate on them. This is called rub urination and is very common during the rutting season. White-tailed does also frequently perform rub urination. They often balance on their front feet while doing this so that very little weight is on their hind feet; one or the other foot is often entirely off the ground.

What is little known, or at least seldom mentioned in the literature, is that even during the rutting season bucks, including big ones, will often spread their hind feet apart by about 2 feet and squat slightly while urinating.

Mule deer bucks squat much lower than do whitetails while urinating.

Q: I recently read an article in the January 1990 *Southeast Farm Press* by Dr. Jim Byford in which he relates that a doe another fellow had shot, and that they were tracking, hid in a pond. The deer had submerged herself so that only her nose was above water among the vegetation. It was a pond in the middle of a farm field with only pasture all around it and a mud shoreline all around the pond. They tracked the doe going into the pond, but could find no tracks where she had exited. Knowing the doe had to be in the pond, they searched extra carefully, and it was only then that they discovered her nostrils sticking out above the water. Evidently the doe panicked when she picked up the scent of the two men close by. She burst from the water, so startling the hunters that it took a fusillade of shots to drop her.

Have you ever seen or heard of this type of occurrence?

H. F., Ewing, Virginia

A: No, I have never witnessed a deer escaping by submerging itself. I have seen wounded ducks do it, though, and I believe that animals that are wounded, as this doe was, may be more apt to do it than unwounded ones.

I have read a number of accounts of this behavior being seen. Archibald Rutledge, for instance, told of a big buck that he hunted in the Santee delta of South Carolina. He actually submerged himself until the hunters and dogs gave up the chase and left the area. Rutledge had lingered behind for some reason and saw the buck emerge from the water and dash off through the pinelands. I do not remember if the buck had been wounded or not, but I never forgot the incident.

Deer frequently take to water to escape from their enemies.

Credit: Len Rue Jr.

I have to surmise that this behavior is very unusual, though it might actually happen more times than we know about simply because the deer are successful in their attempts to escape detection.

I'd like to add a footnote about deer feeding in water. I have seen, and photographed, deer feeding in water that put their heads, nose, and eyes beneath the surface, but not their ears.

I hate to get water in my ears, because it's hard to get out. I have seen deer that did get water in their ears shake and rotate their heads vigorously in their efforts to get the water out. A deer that has its nose and eyes underwater has only its ears to use to detect danger, and that may be as much a reason for their not submerging their ears as the discomfort that it causes.

Q: I read somewhere that a dominant buck can usually be distinguished at a distance because he walks with his head held high and his tail held out straight behind. I hunt in central Iowa, and we have some pretty good bucks. Quite often there will be two or three bucks together, and it's often hard to tell which buck is dominant, because you don't have the time to check them all out. I don't recall ever seeing a buck walk with his tail held straight out backward. Is it because I'm not seeing a dominant buck? If I see three bucks together, won't one of them be dominant? Have you ever seen a buck walk with his tail straight out?   B. L., Waterloo, Iowa

A: An alert buck usually walks with his head held high, while a wary buck will hold his head low in more of a sneak attitude. If a dominant buck is not alarmed or wary, he will walk proudly, as he should, with his head held high. I have seen them and photographed them with the head high and the tail held almost straight up. I can recall seeing only one walk with his tail held straight out.

Anytime you see two or more bucks together, one of them is going to be dominant over the others, although he may not be the dominant buck in the area. One of any two spike or forked bucks will be dominant over the others. Dominance fluctuates about as much as a thermometer. A buck's status goes up or down according to which other bucks he encounters and whether he is injured, slightly or severely. Anything that may be advantageous to one buck and disadvantageous to another will instantly change the status quo. Even if nothing serious happens to the dominant buck, he may temporarily "retire" from the dominant status because of lack of food or excessive exertion in driving off lesser bucks and herding or tending estrus does, breeding, and so on. He may simply be burned out, in need of a rest. Such a buck may lose interest in the constant competition for a few days or even a couple of weeks. He may actually be marshalling his

The dominant buck walks with a very determined stride, and sometimes with his tail pointing straight out.

internal resources for the second major rut, which occurs a month after the primary rut in November.

Q: I have just purchased and moved to a small farm south of Zanesville, Ohio, and I have always been interested in deer. A number of farmers in the area have their own captive deer, and I am thinking of getting a couple of fawns from them to raise as my own. If I bottle-feed and hand-raise the little bucks, will they stay tame? Should I buy the fawns from different farmers so that the bucks and does will be unrelated, or doesn't this matter? Are there any other suggestions you can give me?   A. C., Zanesville, Ohio

A: I'll start by answering the question you didn't ask. Don't do it.

When I was a kid back on the farm, before artificial insemination made having your own bull for your dairy cows unnecessary, the most dangerous animal in North America was the domestic bull, particularly a Jersey bull. I'm willing to bet that the most dangerous animal in North America today, if statistics were known, is the captive white-tailed buck. He can kill you, and he probably will if the occasion arises.

The most dangerous of all are the little bucks that are bottle-fed, hand-raised pets. They have no fear of man; when they are yearlings, they have antlers, and the hormone testosterone courses through their bodies during the rutting season. They can—and I say "can" because some don't—become instruments of destruction. Like playing Russian roulette with a single bullet in the cylinder, you don't know which buck or which cylinder is going to go off.

This white-tailed buck is showing extreme aggression. His ears are laid back, his hair is standing on end, and he is walking with a stiff-legged gait.

If you do decide to get deer, and you probably will despite what I have written, try to buy a little buck four to five months old that has been raised by his dam and has never been hand-fed or petted. Such a buck is more likely to fear man and stay away from you. Still, *always* be cautious around him. Make sure that the pens you build are at least 8 to 9 feet high and strong and secure enough that he doesn't get out. A buck in captivity, when he is in a pen 2 to 3 acres in size, will spend all of his spare time during the rutting season (and he has lots of it) trying to tear the fence apart.

And don't think just because the "tame" buck has shed his antlers in spring that he is not dangerous. He is less dangerous, but he could still be aggressive with his feet, as I have seen.

If you are going to raise deer, do buy your stock from different farmers to prevent inbreeding. Cross-breeding produces better animals. You will have to introduce new bloodlines every year or two to continue this practice.

Deer are fascinating to have around, but I advise you to plant corn, winter wheat, buckwheat, and the like close to your home so you can watch wild deer come in. This is less expensive, less of a responsibility, and far safer.

Q: This summer, while driving along a lane, I noticed a fawn traveling with two young bucks. I know that artists often draw or paint deer in family groups: a buck, a doe, and one or more fawns. I have never seen deer travel in family groups such as this, however, and have read in your column that they do not. How, then, do you explain the presence of this spotted fawn with two yearling bucks?   L. O., Blairstown, New Jersey

A: Mature bucks usually travel with does and their fawns only during the rutting season or when they are concentrated in areas of food and shelter during the winter. A mature buck is not a "family man."

Just before they reach their first birthday, most young bucks are chased from the area that their mother expects to use for her forthcoming birthing. She chases away all deer, including her own previous buck and doe fawns and any other adult bucks or does that stray into her birthing territory. After she gives birth, she keeps her young hidden and her territory inviolate for 1 to 2½ weeks. When her fawns are strong enough to follow her easily, about two weeks, she abandons her territory and will rejoin her blood-related family group. If she has female fawns from a previous year, they will rejoin her as she rejoins other does that might be her mother or sisters.

At this period of dispersement, yearling bucks either join a peer group of other yearlings or attach themselves to an older buck or a group of older bucks. Occasionally a yearling buck will elect to stay with his dam, at least for another six months. This is not uncommon. The spotted fawn you saw could have been in the company of its older brothers and perhaps also with its mother, even if you didn't see the doe. If the doe was dead, the fawn

Fawns keep their spotted coats until they are four months old.

would have no choice but to tag along with whatever deer would allow it to do so. An adult doe in the wild almost never accepts an orphaned fawn.

Fawns usually keep their spotted coats for about four months, and it takes almost four months for them to be completely independent of the mother, although they stay with her for almost one year. If you saw the fawn with the bucks in August, it probably would survive. If you saw it, as an orphan, in July, it is extremely unlikely to be able to make it on its own. Even under the best of conditions, fawn mortality can run as high as 40 percent.

Q: In your book *The Deer of North America,* you describe the "licking stick": Bucks rub their forehead scent on a limber stick and then lick it off. What is the purpose of their licking their own scent off? It sure must dilute the amount of scent left on the stick.   J. O., Alpine, Texas

A: I don't have a clue why bucks lick off their forehead glandular scent after just putting it on stick. I do know that all of the glandular scents of a buck are attractive, not only to other deer but to himself as well. Bucks also have scent in their saliva, so they may actually be depositing more scent by licking than what they are removing.

I have seen bucks stand and lick each other's foreheads. I have seen bucks lick each other's tarsal or hock glands. I have seen a buck urinate on

Bucks in a fraternal group frequently groom each other.

his tarsal glands and then turn and lick both the urine and the tarsal scent from his entire hind leg, starting at the hoof and continuing right up to the gland itself. I have seen bucks lick the interdigital scent from the glands between their hooves.

The only conclusion I can come to is that this behavior is a stimulant for them as well as for other deer. It must be a means of self-gratification.

Q: I have had enough close encounters with bucks at point-blank range, on ground level, over the past 10 years to prompt me to ask: If a deer cannot smell a hunter, can it recognize a human form as human if this form is stationary? It appears not, from what I have seen.

I have been using a masking system that takes a lot of fooling around to prepare, and I will go out on a limb here and say that I don't think deer smell me. But they will spot movement or hear me, sometimes letting out a snort but always holding their ground. I know if a buck smells me; there is no fooling around, he is gone!

Several years ago, on a cold October morning with an inch of fresh snow, I got caught standing in the middle of a logging road. A buck came out of the brush 200 yards down the road. He stood on the road looking right at me, then walked up the road to the other side. A couple of minutes passed, then he walked back out on the road and checked me out again. At ease, he nearly walked all the way up to me—within 12 yards. He was right on top of me; I couldn't draw my bow, so I just kept still and shut my eyes. When a tiny piece of snow crumbled at my feet, he trotted off to the side at 25 yards, in alder brush, watched me for another five minutes, then started browsing a bit and paid no more attention to me.

I've also encountered bucks, some mature, face to face at ground level—and what happens always amazes me. It certainly appears that if the deer does not smell, see, or hear me, he doesn't seem to recognize my form as human. And if he doesn't smell me but hears or sees movement, he will still tolerate it if it is slight. Applying this to hunting, you might assume all the camouflage in the world won't help you if the deer smells you—and if he doesn't smell you, maybe you don't need much camouflage, providing you are still.

What are your opinions about this?   J. P., Port Wing, Wisconsin

A: Your observation ties in with a statement I have made for years: "If a deer doesn't smell or hear you, and you don't move, it will not recognize you as a human being." Countless times, I have been standing stock still—a couple of times out in a bare field—and had deer look at me yet pay me absolutely no attention. But remember, you don't even blink your eyes. In fact, I've found it better to not look at the deer directly; don't make eye contact.

I always dress in Trebark camouflage when I'm doing my photography and, if I'm not standing in the open or silhouetted, the deer don't even appear to see me. They just don't seem to recognize the human form as human. This is not so with any member of the dog family—the fox, coyote, or wolf. If one sees you out in the open, it recognizes the human form visually at once and is gone. That's why it is extremely important to back up into a bush to break up your form or outline when hunting predators. It's best if you do that with deer, too.

The cold October day you describe was also in your favor, because cold makes it harder for the deer to smell you.

Q: After rattling during the rut, I watched an average-sized doe for almost five minutes proceed with caution, yet she seemed to be looking for something. Do you believe that this doe knew what rattling was? How do does react to it before, during, and after the rut?

Also, what is your opinion on whether or not deer can determine human footprints in the snow as being from humans?

J. R., Leonminster, Massachusetts

A: You bet she knew what rattling was. Does are as tuned in to the sound of antlers crashing together as bucks are—perhaps more so if they happen to be in estrus and are actively searching for a buck.

Most people fail to recognize the fact that a doe often has considerable choice in which buck she mates with. Usually does prefer to mate with the largest buck; they instinctively know that the resulting fawns will have the best chance of survival. Mating with the dominant buck gives the doe the best return on her investment of her time and her life. Almost every wild creature looks for the betterment of the species, not consciously but in actuality.

Even if a doe is not in estrus, she will still be interested in a fight between two bucks just out of curiosity. After all, who can pass up a good fight?

No, I do not believe that deer can distinguish a man's track in the snow by sight alone. I believe they completely ignore human tracks if there is no scent associated with them. It is much more difficult for any animal to detect scent in cold weather, and the colder the weather, the less any scent can be detected. In 10- to 20-degree weather, I believe that a man's track in powdery snow would be scentless in about one hour.

Q: I have had a lot of success hunting scrapes and rubs here in Mississippi. I have several questions about scrapes.

Last year I was hunting a scrape line in a small patch of cedars. It was the first time I had hunted with a muzzleloader. Around 7:30 a spike came into the site and began to work one of the scrapes. I got excited and shot him. Later in the season I went through this area again and noticed that the scrapes were still being worked. I hunted this area a few more times, but nothing happened.

By the time this season opened, I was eager to see if there were still scrapes in this area. When I got to the cedars, I noticed two scrapes within 15 yards of each other. I walked around the area and found six more scrapes, all of them very large. They were the largest scrapes I have ever seen. I have hunted this area eight times and have not seen this buck. Can you tell how big a buck is by the size of his scrapes? Can you tell the size of a buck by the height of the limbs broken off above the scrape? The highest ones are a little over 6 feet up. Do you think this is a nice buck, and how would you go about hunting him?   J. R., Batesville, Missouri

A: No, you cannot tell the size of a buck by the diameter of a scrape, because several deer may be using the same scrape. The largest scrape I have ever seen was about 40 inches in diameter. In my video *Rutting Whitetails,* I show a huge buck on a scrape, throwing the dirt from the scrape at least

A primary deer scrape is almost always under an overhanging branch. You can't tell the size of the buck by the diameter of the scrape.

30 feet. The dirt is just flying in all directions. Later I looked at the scrape itself and found it to be 30 to 36 inches long. If you can see the freshly pawed track, you can judge the size of the buck. However, if a number of bucks are using the same scrape over a period of time, they may not stand in its exact center when they paw the dirt. Over time that scrape will become much larger than normal, even though none of the bucks are big ones. The size of the track is the key, not the size of the scrape.

My video also shows that same buck standing on his hind feet and using an antler to pull down a branch about 8½ or 9 feet above the ground. I taped him doing this three times. Anytime you find evidence on the branches 8 feet or more above the scrape being used, you are seeing the work of a monster buck.

Twigs that are broken or chewed on a little over 6 feet above the ground tell you nothing. A big buck can reach that high easily while standing with all four feet on the ground. A small buck can do so easily by standing up on his hind feet. The average deer browse line is about 7 feet above the ground, and most deer can stand upright to feed that high.

I can't begin to tell you how to hunt this deer. Bucks expand their range from 1 or 2 square miles to 10 or 12 square miles during the rutting season.

Unless the earth is soft, a deer's dew claws do not show in its tracks. The size of the track is a good clue to the size of its maker.

You sat there eight times and never saw a buck. The buck may only visit those scrapes every 10 days or so. Or not at all. Or he may be visiting the scrapes after dark.

You could try covering the scrapes with some dead leaves. This will at least tell you if they are being worked regularly, or at all.

Q: Recently, while bowhunting in my home state of Massachusetts, I hit a large buck. Unfortunately it was not a good hit and, after almost a day of tracking the animal, I was unable to find him. If this buck survives the wound (and I think he will), can I expect to see him in the same area again? Or will the deer abandon the area altogether?

J. McK., Easthampton, Massachusetts

A: Yes, you should find that same buck in the same area, because it is his home range. Deer move about when they disperse as youngsters, usually at one year of age, but once they have settled into an area, they seldom leave it; they can't really be pushed out of it. After all, they are safest in their home range, which they know intimately.

This buck, if he survives, will be a darn sight harder to hunt, because he will be increasingly wary. He may become completely nocturnal, in which case you may never see him again unless someone pushes him out of his bed in his hiding area.

Q: A friend and I hunt a 200-acre piece of property that has acorn-bearing hardwood trees, corn, and alfalfa. Twelve or 13 other hunters hunt the same place.

On the third day of the early bow season in 1997, my friend was hunting in the acorn patch when a big 10-pointer charged him from out of nowhere. After one charge, the buck kept on running out of sight.

Then, about seven days later, I was hunting the same plot, about 200 yards from my friend, and the buck came charging out of a thicket at me. I was able to slip behind a big oak tree. He passed me and kept on going; we didn't see him again through the rest of bow season and shotgun season.

Why would he charge each of us just once in the same area? If he was scraping or rubbing, wouldn't he stay and defend his territory instead of charging and running? Just curious. T. H., Monticello, Indiana

A: Each year a very few hunters are attacked; occasionally, one or two are killed by white-tailed bucks. I'm talking about wild deer, not captive deer. It is a well-known fact that captive bucks are an invitation to disaster; they will kill you, or at least try to.

A five-day-old white-tailed fawn.

A white-tailed doe nurses her week-old fawns. Does commonly give birth to twins.

Credit: Len Rue, Jr.

A brown-with-white-spots camouflage and virtually no odor are the fawn's primary defenses.

Credit: Len Rue, Jr.

An alert doe keeps watch over her eight-day-old fawn.

A whitetail buck flehmening.
Credit: Len Rue, Jr.

A monster buck rubbing his antlers on a tree. Big bucks will rub big or small trees, while smaller bucks usually rub only small trees.
Credit: Len Rue, Jr.

A buck scrape in the woods. Note the typical bitten-off overhead branch.

Credit: Len Rue, Jr.

A Texas buck chewing on an overhead branch at a scrape.
Credit: Len Rue, Jr.

This good-sized buck just made a rub. Bark is still on his antlers.
Credit: Len Rue, Jr.

A white-tailed buck approaches a doe during the rut. Part of his left antler broke off in a fight with another buck.
Credit: Len Rue, Jr.

A white-tailed buck and doe breeding.
Credit: Len Rue, Jr.

*A huge white-tailed buck.
Note antler tip that has
been broken from fighting.*
Credit: Len Rue, Jr.

*White-tailed bucks and
does.*

*Aggressive bucks square off. Note the
angle of the ears, the erected back
hairs, and the swollen necks.*

*An alert buck, at the peak of the rut.
To get a trophy like this, a hunter
must do everything right.*
Credit: Len Rue, Jr.

A buck rubs his antlers on a tree.
Credit: Len Rue, Jr.

A big buck feeding on browse.

A monster buck that any hunter would be proud of.
Credit: Len Rue, Jr.

An alert white-tailed buck during the rut in mid-November.
Credit: Len Rue, Jr.

Tail up, a spooked buck takes off across the snow.

Bucks like to retreat to heavy cover such as this as soon as hunting pressure intensifies.
    Credit: Len Rue, Jr.

A buck stamps his foot at unseen danger.

A white-tailed buck takes off through the brush at top speed.
    Credit: Len Rue, Jr.

*White-tailed buck on a warm
autumn day in New Jersey.*
Credit: Len Rue, Jr.

*A buck grazing near the edge of a
power-line clearing.*
Credit: Len Rue, Jr.

*Mouth open, a Texas buck grunts as
it runs through brush country.*
Credit: Len Rue, Jr.

*Texas doe hides behind some cacti
while surveying its surroundings.*
Credit: Len Rue, Jr.

A buck with doe, in the snow. Deer yard up when the snow deepens.
Credit: Len Rue, Jr.

Whitetail buck in a snowstorm. Hollow hairs in its coat keep it warm.

A buck in the snow. Tracking snow makes for ideal hunting conditions.

This buck has just shed his antlers. There is little blood loss.

Although extremely rare, there have been instances when wild bucks have charged hunters.
Credit: Irene Vandermolen

In the two instances you mention, where the buck charged you and your friend, I believe it was a case of mistaken identity. I'm quite sure that when the buck started his charge, he thought he was charging another deer. Did either of you have buck urine, or even doe urine, on your clothing? Your stepping behind the tree would not have deterred the buck if you were his intended target. He would have gone right around the tree after you. As it was, he evidently discovered his mistake partway through the charge and just kept on going instead of following through.

The buck may have tried a third charge on someone else and been killed for his trouble. It is probably just as well that you did not see him again.

If, as you say, he was rubbing or scraping, he would be interested in chasing off a rival buck, not a human.

Q: Can deer be called?   G. G., Tom's River, New Jersey

A: Yes, deer can be called. And a number of companies are now making very good deer calls.

Deer make many different sounds, vocal ones as well as snorts and stamping of feet. The calls that are being manufactured imitate the snort, the bleat, and the grunt. The rattling of antlers is also a deer call, as it simulates two bucks fighting.

Does and bucks make two different kinds of snorts. The most common snort is made with the mouth open slightly. It is an expulsion of air from the lungs through the mouth. This snort alerts every deer that hears it, but what they do about it is up to the individual animal. This snort often arouses deer's curiosity, causing them to come closer to investigate. This is the sound that the calls are designed to imitate.

The second snort is made by the deer expelling air through both the mouth and the nostrils. This creates a much higher-pitched, whistling snort. No manufactured call wants to sound like this, because it chases away every deer in the area. This is the paramount deer warning call, and it is never questioned. Every deer gets into high gear immediately and is gone.

All deer make a bleating or blatting sound. Fawns have a high-pitched bleat somewhat similar to the bleating of a lamb. Does make a much lower bleating call. Big bucks make a very raspy, low-toned call similar to that of an old ram. The vibrating calls that are manufactured sound like a cross between that of the doe and that of the buck. This call stimulates deer's curiosity.

I have heard bucks grunt; does do it too when they call their fawns. There are only two circumstances in which I have heard bucks grunt: when a buck is trailing a doe, and when one buck is challenging another prior to fighting. In either case, the grunt quickly gets other bucks' attention. If one buck is following a doe, other bucks will also be interested. If the grunting is preceding a fight, other big bucks may want to get in on the action. Grunting will not necessarily scare away smaller bucks because, although they may not want to get into the battle, they are always anxious to see one.

Grunting is an exceptionally good call to use.

Q: I hunt a small woodlot near my home. I do quite a bit of scouting during the summer. There seem to be a lot of deer on the property, with scrapes during the season. On June 20, I was scouting and walking a good, heavily used trail when I found a fresh scrape, complete with deer droppings and an overhead branch worked on. Now it's got me puzzled. Why would a buck make a scrape at this time of the year? Have you heard of this?   E. Y., Park City, Kentucky

A: A scrape on June 20 is unusual but not unheard of. Gentle rubbing and chewing on overhead branches are more common, but seldom noticed. I have video footage of a big buck rubbing his forehead scent gland on a branch in June while his antlers were still growing and covered with velvet. The depositing of forehead scent takes place at all times of the year, but is greatly intensified during the rutting season. We humans don't see this done very often, so we don't realize how commonly it occurs. We really only notice it when our attention is directed to the overhead branch by the scrape pawed into the earth.

Q: We had some really cold weather between Christmas and New Year's Day in 1993–94, and also had snow on top of the ice.

I checked a pond in our area and was surprised to find that the snow was crisscrossed with deer tracks; I mean, there were thousands of tracks all over the place. I always thought that deer avoided ice whenever they could, because they can fall down on it and not get back up. What were they doing out on the ice when there is nothing out there for them to eat? With their sharp hooves, aren't the deer more likely to break through the ice than would a man?   C. R., Skytop, Pennsylvania

A: You did say that there was snow on the ice, and that would have given the deer a little better footing. However, the deer probably would have been out on the ice anyway, even if they shouldn't have been. Deer probably go out on the ice for the same reasons kids do: It's there, they are curious about it, and it lets them go places they couldn't go before.

You have to realize that deer know their home range intimately; they go over every bit of it. Their very survival depends on knowing the terrain and where to run and where to hide when they need to. When a pond or lake suddenly freezes over, there is a piece of unexplored terrain right in the middle of their backyard. They just have to check it all out, and they do.

You are right that the deer shouldn't go out on the ice, because they frequently slip, dislocate their legs, and can't get back up. A number of years ago, your state had a tremendous ice storm and lost quite a few deer that fell on ice-covered ground, dislocated their legs, and had to be shot.

Years ago, when I was chief gamekeeper for Coventry Hunt Club here in New Jersey and also worked as a deputy game warden for the state, I had to shoot several deer that had fallen on river ice. It just wasn't safe to attempt to get the deer, and there was really nothing that could be done for them even if they could have been rescued. I shot them from the riverbank to put them out of their misery; their carcasses were soon cleaned up by the bald eagles that were common along the river at that time.

This doe dislocated her legs when she fell on the ice.

Your question got me thinking about the relative merits of a human's big foot and the deer's pointed ones. Now, I have a big foot. I just measured my Iceman shoepacks: The soles are 13 inches long by 5 inches wide, giving me an average of about 60 square inches of weight-bearing surface per foot, allowing for the narrower heel portion. I weigh about 186 pounds on the scale, but dressed I must be close to 200. With two boots, I put about 1.65 pounds on each square inch of weight-bearing surface.

A deer hoof is roughly 2 inches by 2 inches if the toes are spread apart a bit at the tips, or 4 square inches of weight-bearing surface per hoof, for 16 square inches total. Our deer average about 125 pounds live—some a little more, many a lot less, but let's take 125 pounds as the average. An average of 125 pounds and 16 square inches of bearing surface converts to about 8 pounds of weight per square inch of hoof.

When we walk with two feet, one is lifted off the ground so that all of the weight is put on just one foot, increasing the bearing weight to 3.3 pounds to the square inch. When a deer walks, it lifts just one foot off the ground at a time, which increases the weight to a little more than 10 pounds to the square inch on its other three feet. However, I'm putting a weight of 200 pounds all in a 13- by 5-inch spot. Because of the length of a deer's body, the weight is distributed over a 3-foot by 6-inch area. We know that to walk on thin ice, we have to distribute our weight over the largest area possible. Although the deer is putting more pounds per square inch on a single spot than we humans do, the fact that the total weight is dispersed over such a large area makes it possible for deer to walk on ice that we would break through.

I am also willing to bet that if you looked closely, you would find more deer tracks paralleling the shore than anywhere else. By standing on the ice, the deer can reach browse on the tree limbs overhanging the lake that they couldn't reach before the water froze over.

Q: I read with interest your column about deer walking on their front feet. I have never seen them do this, but I have seen them stand up and walk on their hind feet. They reared up and struck out at another deer for just a few seconds. I wouldn't really call it walking. How far have you seen a deer walk on its hind feet? B. B., Nashville, Tennessee

A: I have never seen a deer walk on its front feet either. Most of the times I have seen deer standing on their hind feet, it was when they were fighting over food. In my *Eye on Nature* tape, a sampling of my best video shots, I show a doe standing up and striking back at another doe, which had just struck at her. The second doe stands for three seconds and moves about 25 feet.

Just recently I saw two yearling bucks that had lost their antlers stand up and strike out at one another. The amazing thing is that one buck was up for eight or nine seconds and walked *backward* while facing the second buck, which was pressing the attack, for a distance of 48 feet. It so amazed me to see the buck stand up and cover this much distance that I measured it. This was a fight over dominance.

Q: On page 317 of your book *The Deer of North America,* you talked about how sawing off a vicious captive buck's antlers made him completely docile. You then went on to say that even the shedding of a buck's antlers may not reduce his belligerence toward other bucks—and that after all the bucks have shed their antlers, the dominant buck will reassert his dominance. Have you ever heard of a buck that had shed his antlers still being belligerent toward people? I was recently told by a farmer who lives in the southern part of our state, and who has several captive bucks, that one of his bucks was still aggressive and belligerent even after his antlers were shed. O. T., Canton, Ohio

A: Yes, I personally know of a captive buck that was aggressive despite the fact that he had shed his antlers. All during the rutting season, this buck tried his best to tear apart the fence of his pen. It was a good-sized pen, but the buck wanted out. He also showed extreme aggression toward any humans who came near the pen. His ears would flatten out along his neck, his chin would be tucked in, all of the hair on his body would stand on end, and his tongue constantly flicked in and out of his mouth and up over his muzzle. He walked with a very stiff-legged gait, occasionally grunting. He would walk perhaps 20 feet, paw the earth with his forefoot, and hook his antlers against what was left of a couple of saplings or against the fence. He was one mean buck. He did not exhibit this behavior as much to the man who owned him as toward strangers. On several occasions the owner had to shoot him with the red-pepper bear repellent known as Counter Assault, which literally blew him off his feet. In fact, thereafter, if his owner made a hissing noise with his mouth, like the aerosol can being discharged, the buck would rear backward.

After he had shed his antlers, this buck showed absolutely no aggression toward the people who fed him, but he still exhibited all the same signs of belligerence to any and all strangers who ventured near the pen.

Q: My hunting partner, Jody Thacker, and I hunt on private property in northeastern Kentucky near the Daniel Boone National Forest in Rowan County. We are the only hunters on this land, which is 180 acres of virtually undisturbed hillsides and hollows. On opening morning of this October's early muzzleloading season, Jody killed a nice 7-point buck, while I was on stand from 6 A.M. to 7 P.M. without seeing a single deer. Jody hunted from a permanent stand, located between known feeding and bedding areas, while I hunted from a permanent stand in an oak ridge between two oak flats. We were pelted by scattered rain showers all day. On the second day, I hunted from Jody's stand because I thought the rain might keep the deer from moving much and his stand was located closer to the bedding area. Once again I saw no deer.

Do you think the deer would avoid the area around Jody's stand because of the gut pile 80 yards away, left from the previous day? Do deer react to gut piles or dead deer?

Also, if the buck Jody killed was the dominant buck in the area—and we think he may have been—will the other subordinate bucks realize that the dominant buck is gone? If so, will they attempt to reestablish a pecking order, or will the next most dominant buck simply move up the chain and so on? And if the other bucks do "miss" the dominant buck, wouldn't it be a good time to rattle? K. V., Belfry, Kentucky

A: I personally do not want a gut pile anywhere near where I plan to hunt. However, the gut pile from your partner's buck was 80 yards away, and I believe that this is far enough to have no effect on your stand.

I do not believe that deer associate a dead deer, or even a gut pile, with their own lives. Wildlife concentrates on living; it doesn't dwell on death. I have seen deer walk right by a deer killed by an automobile without paying any attention to it. I have had other hunters tell me that they have seen deer go right up to a gut pile and sniff at it. Whereas a wise old buck that had been wounded in the past might avoid the smell of blood, I am sure it would make most deer curious. Believing this, I still don't want blood and a gut pile in close proximity to my stand.

Dominance in deer is mercurial, changing constantly according to the conditions of the day. From the moment the other bucks realize that the alpha buck is gone—and they do realize it, because he isn't there to drive them off—the entire hierarchy shifts one step up. This is automatic. The lineup will stay the same because each buck has had to fight, or bluff, his way to the position he holds in the social standing. This standing will also change instantly if one of the higher-up bucks should be injured, no matter how slightly, to the point that it affects his behavior. He will be pushed down the list until he can again dominate those under him. If the injury is temporary, he will be able to work his way back up—and it *will* be work, because he will have to physically prove that he can dominate each buck he encounters. Dominance is in a constant state of flux; the animals are testing, testing, testing each other all the time.

Anytime is a good time to rattle antlers, but you are right: If the dominant buck is taken out, there will be more fighting as the lesser bucks jostle for dominance. If the dominant buck has not been taken out and is in the area, when you rattle he will be just as anxious to see who is fighting as the lesser bucks. Using large, heavy antlers produces a deeper sound and will attract larger bucks but may scare off the younger ones. Rattling with lighter antlers will probably attract the most bucks, even the big ones, because they don't want the competition to catch up to them.

Q: I am writing to see if you can solve a puzzle for me. We have a lot of deer in southern Jersey—so many, in fact, that there is a very distinct browse line along our fencerows and the edges of all of our woodlands. In your book *The Deer of North America,* you state that a browse line is an indication of too many deer being in the area, no matter what the population is. Despite there being a very prominent browse line, I still see the deer reaching up to feed on the trees' leaves. Some of the deer even stand on their hind legs. Why do the deer continue to feed on the browse when it is evident that most of it has already been eaten?   P. O., Vineland, New Jersey

A: Your observation brings up a very good point and reinforces my observations over the years that deer are designed to be browsing animals; they prefer good browse over all other types of food when it is available. The reason deer feed mainly upon farm crops is that the crops are now growing where browse might have been available years ago. It all comes back to my contention that we have more deer now in the eastern half of the United States than we have ever had before, because in pre-Columbian days, most of the East was blanketed with mature forests. Only when lightning or the Indians, the first game managers, set fire to the virgin forests did good whitetail populations occur. A deer is a creature of the edges, not of mature forests. The opening up of the forest for agriculture, and the reduction of predators, allowed the deer to multiply. Overhunting deer for the market extirpated them in many areas. Good game management and properly enforced protective laws, when combined with the opening of the forests, have allowed our deer population to skyrocket to the current 25 million in the U.S. and Canada. Fueling this expansion is the reduction of agriculture

Deer will readily stand on their hind legs to reach browse, which is a favorite food.

A browse line indicates that the area is overpopulated with deer.

on much of the marginally productive land; that land is trying to revert to forest, but is being held in the brushland state by deer browsing.

When you see deer feeding on a heavily used browse line, you are seeing deer feeding on the foods they prefer if available. What they are eating is browse that has been brought within their reach by the weight of new growth. Unless a branch dies from having all of its leaves eaten, it will continue to grow each year. Many of the lower branches will naturally grow downward, and most of them will be bent downward by the weight of their new growth of leaves. This will often bring them within the reach of the deer, which will be quick to browse upon them. You may have noticed that the deer browse such browse lines more heavily after a rain, when the weight of the raindrops bends many branches down even farther.

There are many tartarian honeysuckle bushes growing in my area. Millions of them were planted during the late 1940s and 1950s, in a huge effort to provide more food-producing shrubs for songbirds. They have been a real success story, providing excellent food and cover for many types of wildlife. The seeds have been spread far and wide by the birds. Deer love to browse upon the leaves, and all of the bushes are high-lined with a browse line. This year the bushes have produced a fantastic crop, and the hundreds of pounds of berries on each bush have brought many of the branches down to within deer's reach. The deer are browsing heavily on the branches and berries.

Q: In scouting around, I have pushed deer from their beds in the same area time after time. Do the deer use the same bed each time or are they just using the same general area? Do they change their bedding areas, and if so, how often? P. O., Knoxville, Tennessee

A: Deer use the same general bedding area, but not necessarily the exact same bed unless some topographic feature—for instance, a boulder, cliff face, or large fallen tree—causes them to do so. On a forested ridgetop, they will be in a favored area but not a particular spot.

Deer don't stay in the same bed for more than one or two hours. Then they get up to urinate, turn around, perhaps walk a few steps, and bed down again.

Most animals can defecate while they are bedded. Most of them can't urinate while bedded; they must stand, which is one of the reasons that they get to their feet so often. Researchers have found that the average person rolls over or moves around at least 27 times in an eight-hour sleep period. This is a requirement of the body to keep joints flexible and blood flowing freely, as well as for the bones to retain calcium. The same holds true for animals: It's to their advantage to move frequently.

A deer's home range is usually 1 to 2 square miles, and it knows every feature in that landscape intimately. It's the main reason that deer run in circles when pushed. Bucks, during the rutting season, expand their range to 10 to 12 square miles, most of which they know fairly well, but they will still have a favored core area that is their regular home range. Because their rutting range is larger, bucks make larger circles when pushed than does do.

Within that 1- to 2-square-mile home range, deer will have a number of bedding areas that they may use seasonally according to the weather, availability of water and food, or hunting pressure. At times each factor, or a combination of them, will determine where the deer will bed. When possible, they do have a favorite general area.

Q: What type of relationship exists between wild turkeys and white-tailed deer?

I ask this question because, since the turkey introduction by the Department of Natural Resources, the deer hunting on our 120 acres has suffered. We see far fewer deer (although deer numbers are up), and I think it is because the presence of the birds is disrupting deer movement and patterns. Neighboring landowners were overly successful in their deer harvest this past gun season, which was during the Thanksgiving week of November 1996. However, they had no turkeys. We had between 20 and 40 of them each morning, scattered throughout the 80 acres that I hunt (mostly wooded with brush and marsh), and they were so noisy it was unbelievable! They flapped their wings, scratched in the leaves, putted, clucked, chirped, and gobbled from just past daybreak to nearly 4 P.M. each day. I firmly believe this is why no self-respecting deer would come close to my property during hunting season. What do you think?

T. K., New Berlin, Wisconsin

A: According to research reports from Vermont, Pennsylvania, and Virginia, turkeys do not really compete with deer for food; they eat enough dissimilar foods. In my opinion, in years of a poor mast crops, the turkeys are definitely competition for the season's acorns. I do not believe that this is a great hardship for the deer, but I do know that, in my area, the competition for acorns among the black bears, turkeys, squirrels, and deer is very high.

I have photographed wild turkeys and deer feeding side by side in a grass field in summer with neither paying attention to the other, but then the turkeys were not making a lot of noise.

In autumn, in the dry-leaf woodlands, I would say that deer definitely avoid being in the same area with turkeys for all of the reasons you listed in your letter. The turkeys are just too darn noisy for the deer. Under these conditions, the deer can't possibly hear danger coming; that makes them nervous, and deer don't stay in a place that makes them nervous.

The noise made by wild turkeys scratching for food disturbs deer.

When deer and turkeys are directly competing for the acorns, I have seen deer strike out with their forefeet at a turkey that got too close, and I have seen turkeys flap their wings and jump up at smaller deer. They didn't try this with full-grown deer, but they often did it with five- to six-month-old fawns.

I would say that you are right: You had no chance at the deer because of the turkeys.

Q: On November 20, 1995, I tracked a large, dominant buck through a several-thousand-acre six- to eight-year-old clear-cut in northern Maine. The thickly regenerating area was providing excellent autumn cover for several whitetail family groups of three to six animals each, judging from the sign.

The buck was striding purposefully through the cover, casting like a bird dog, searching for the family groups he obviously knew were in there. When he sensed or encountered other deer, he would without hesitation charge into the feeding or bedded group, drive off (he was literally ready to kill) any lesser buck hanging close to the does, then harass the devil out of the does; upon finding none in heat, he would head off searching for another group.

At one point, the buck got onto some fresh tracks and was checking them out. He led me to a small area that was heavily tracked up. When I stopped for a second to figure out what the attraction at that spot was, or what had happened there, I saw a shed moose antler on the ground, partially covered by snow.

Clearly, there was something about that antler that commanded several deer's attention that day. What was it?

I would rule out the curiosity factor, because moose are not uncommon in this area, and I have run across plenty of sheds to which deer apparently paid no attention. The antler had obviously been there from the previous winter, so it wasn't anything new.

The antler had been subject to some rodent chewing, but I did not take the time to examine it closely for indications that the deer were interacting with it in any way.

By the way, I never caught up with the buck. Only on rare occasions does a hunter have the good fortune to run across a buck with as dominant a demeanor as this one. He was literally afraid of nothing in the woods and was ready to do anything for an opportunity to sow his seed. Thanks.

B. C., St. Johnsbury, Vermont

A: Deer also chew on antlers, although nowhere nearly as often as rodents do. If this buck was as riled up as you say he was, he was not going to stop to chew on an antler.

If another deer had recently chewed on the antler, the buck may have checked out the saliva to see who had done the chewing. Each deer's saliva is individual, and the buck may have been checking for a rival.

If there were any fox or coyote tracks near the antler, one of them might have been using the large projecting tine as a urine scent station. They commonly do so, although I can't see why this would attract the buck; he would have run past dozens of these scent stations in a 24-hour period.

Nope, I can't see why he stopped there either.

Q: What do deer do in a rainstorm to keep themselves dry? Are their coats waterproof? I have seen deer out in some rainstorms and not in others—but maybe they are out in all storms and I'm just not seeing them.

B. W., Charleston, South Carolina

A: I was raised on a dairy farm, and our cow pasture, near the barn, had a lot of big apple trees in it. We could always predict the severity of a coming storm by the cows' reaction to it. If it was going to be just a short, hard thunderstorm, the cows would dash for the shelter of the trees. If it was going to be a two- to three-day rain, the cows simply went on with their feeding. Deer do the exact same thing.

No animals like to get wet if they can avoid it. Wildlife can foretell upcoming weather before human instruments record it, as you can see by the way that deer feed heavily before a prolonged storm comes in.

Most short storms are just that—short. Deer will move under the trees. It ordinarily takes about 15 to 20 minutes before the rain works its way through all the leaves, and even then, nowhere near as much water reaches the ground under a fully leafed tree as in an unprotected spot. And so the deer stay comparatively dry during short storms.

With long storms, the deer know they are going to get wet anyway, so they just stay out in the rain and go on with their feeding. The deer's summer coat is slightly waterproof, but the hairs are so thin that the water gets through to the skin. Deer rid themselves of the water by shaking their bodies and rippling their skin. They also rotate their heads rapidly and disperse the water by centrifugal force. Because their summer hair is so thin, it dries rapidly after the rain has stopped.

The hair on a deer's winter coat is so long and dense that it is basically waterproof; the long hairs act like shingles, passing the water over the top from one hair to another instead of allowing it to penetrate. The winter coat is also slightly oiled with sebum, an oily residue coming out through the hair follicles. The next time you shoot a deer, run your hand over a skin half a dozen times. You will be able to see and feel the oiliness.

Q: I hunt on public land in northeastern Wisconsin. This area consists of hardwoods surrounding a large cornfield. Beyond the hardwoods lies a cedar swamp. I usually set up along different runways in the hardwoods for my morning hunts, hoping to catch deer making their way back to the cedar swamp.

With increased hunting pressure, my deer sightings have dropped through the years, but I still see enough deer sign to keep me coming back. As the season goes on and the deer get the notion of being hunted, I notice that they start to leave the corn and head back toward the swamp in the dark, giving me no opportunity for a chance to shoot.

Does this sound like I'll have to strap on my hip boots and head back into the cedars, or is there something else I can do up on dry land?

C. T., Marinette, Wisconsin

A: You are encountering an all-too-common problem. The more heavily hunted an animal species is, the more nocturnal it becomes.

Prior to the coming of the white man to the continent, deer did most of their feeding in the daylight hours of early morning and late evening. You can still see this pattern in places where the deer are never hunted. With increased pressure, the deer become nocturnal.

Gauging from your reluctance to go into the cedar swamp—and I don't blame you—evidently others feel the same way. In this situation, the deer have a completely safe haven. Unless somebody pushes them out, those deer just aren't coming out of that swamp. You will have to strap on your hip boots and get into the swamp or forget those deer.

Q: Why don't I see more big bucks feeding out in the fields with the does? Some of the alfalfa and clover fields have fabulous food, with the second cutting growing.

B. B., Chillicothe, Ohio

A: There are a number of reasons why you don't usually see big bucks out feeding with the does. Perhaps they just can't stand the kids. No, all kidding aside, bucks usually stay separate from does except during the rutting season and when forced into their company by food shortages in winter.

During the summer, big bucks do not move any more than is absolutely necessary because their antlers are growing rapidly. Growing antlers are soft and easily damaged.

Second, I have noticed that although a buck's growing antlers need a lot of protein, bucks do not compete with does and fawns for food. Whereas does are feeding out in the fields, bucks are staying in the wooded areas. Although there is not a great deal of vegetation growing in a canopied woodland, there is evidently enough to satisfy bucks' require-

Sumac is a highly nutritious food for deer.

ments. Because of a buck's larger size, he can reach more of the new growing browse than does can, and spring and summer are when plants and trees are growing the fastest. The growth rates for many plants and trees is phenomenal.

Some biologists claim that a buck's larger size allows him to more efficiently metabolize coarser vegetation. I'm not sure about this, but I do know that bucks feed more in the woodlands while the does feed more in the fields.

Q: I have your video *Rutting Whitetails*. One thing that you showed that I had never seen before was the drooling of the bucks.

I have been bowhunting for years and have never seen bucks do that. I guess I never noticed it before. Since I got the tape and saw the bucks drooling, I have been watching deer more carefully.

Last week I was hunting an old orchard. A doe and her two fawns were picking up some of the dropped apples. There weren't many applies on the ground because the deer come in there all the time and eat them. The place is full of tracks and trails. Every once in a while an apple would fall from the tree, and although this never made a sound that I could hear, the deer would run right over to the spot and search until they found the apple.

Just before sunset, a good buck came into the edge of the orchard and, like the buck in your video, he actually drooled strings of saliva. He didn't drip as much as the buck you showed but, because the sun was behind him, I could see him dripping.

I have several questions. Where do all the drips come from, and what is the purpose of his doing this? Do does drip, too? Do other animals drool the way the deer do?

C. D., Amherst, Massachusetts

A: Yes, many hooved animals drool during the rutting season. Elk drool quite a bit, though not as copiously as deer. Even within the species, some bucks drool more than others, but they all drool. I have seen cape buffalo in Africa drool huge strings of the stuff. Notice I said "stuff," because I don't have a technical name for the liquid being discharged.

We have to assume that the liquid we see dripping is a type of saliva. I had convinced myself that the liquid was saliva that came from the bottom of the deer's mouth, but then I got a video clip of a buck with his mouth open, and there was dripping coming off the top of his mouth. I was puzzled. In such a situation, when I need technical knowledge beyond my field experience, I call my good friends John Ozoga (a deer researcher from Michigan) and Larry Marchinton (a deer researcher from Georgia). They both agreed that, at this time, no one is sure what the liquid is, but both felt it was probably saliva.

Then I posed the question of whether the drool could come from the vomeronasal organ in the top of the deer's mouth. No, that was a scent organ and, to the best of everyone's knowledge, it was not the source of the drool. Larry suggested that the one time I got the video clip showing the drool coming from the roof of the mouth, the deer could have had his mouth closed and, when he opened it, some of the drool from the bottom of the mouth could have dripped off the top. I can tell you this: As I review my video footage from time to time, I'll be watching carefully for open-mouthed bucks.

Also, if the drool is saliva, it will contain the scent of the individual buck doing it. Because they drool only in the rutting season, the behavior is definitely sexually oriented.

Different bucks drool varying amounts, but I have photographic evidence of some of them drooling eight or more big drops per minute, almost constantly. Some drool long strings, which have a mucous cohesiveness and contain many drops at one time.

I fully realize the size of the opening in the dropper affects the size of the drop. An eyedropper makes smaller drops than a meat baster. However, I found that my sink faucet creates water droplets approximately the same size as deer drool drops. I counted the drops as I caught them in a cubic-centimeter test tube. It took 86 drops to give me 29.5 cubic centimeters, which measures 1 fluid ounce. If the buck dripped 8 drops per minute, and many do, that would make 480 drops per hour, or 16 fluid ounces—1 pint. There are 2 pints to the quart and 4 quarts to the gallon, so a buck could conceivably drool 3 gallons per day.

They probably don't drool that much, however, because they may not drool while sleeping; even during the rut, bucks do sleep, no matter how sporadically. And even during the rut, bucks eat occasionally, and the food would probably absorb some of the moisture. I think it would be safe to say that a dominant buck drools between 1 and 2 gallons per day.

Please note that I said "dominant buck." From my observations, bucks drool in relation to their age, which correlates with their status.

I have never seen buck fawns drool. Yearling bucks drool occasionally. Two-and-a-half-year-old bucks drool frequently, but the big drippers are the bucks in the 3½- to 7½-year age class—the big dominant bucks. The drooling of those big bucks is not only anticipation but another declaration of dominance, another means of communication, in this case through the depositing of scent. All other deer are aware of it, but we humans don't know about it unless we actually see a deer drool. But then, it is a message intended for the other deer and not for us.

Q: From reading white-tailed deer books and articles, I have noticed that some authors say that a whitetail will travel with the wind at its back to smell things from behind it, while other authors say that they travel with the wind in their faces. Which is most often true (I have seen both cases occur while afield)? This may help me set up better tree-stand positions in the areas that I hunt.   D. R., Mercer, Pennsylvania

A: When a buck is traveling, he usually has a destination in mind; he's not out there just wandering about. Because he is going to a definite spot, he goes there no matter which way the wind is blowing. Like you, I have seen bucks traveling no matter which way the wind was blowing during bow season. And during gun season, at least in my area where the hunting pressure is high, the bucks don't take the wind into consideration at all when they are pushed. When they run, they can't smell properly anyhow, and their aim is to get as much distance between themselves and the hunters as is possible.

Deer usually lie down facing their back trail.

Once a buck gets into his bedding area, he usually heads into the wind and then turns and lies down with his back to the wind so he can watch his back trail with his eyes. He relies upon his nose to detect danger upwind, and his eyes to detect danger downwind. I have seen this countless times by following deer tracks in the snow.

Q: I am 21 years old and an avid deer hunter and outdoorsman from southeastern Minnesota.

Various types of wildlife abound here, and white-tailed deer are no exception. We have many big bucks, and I study everything I can on them to help me become a better hunter. I read many books and magazines all year and take notes from each, jotting down helpful hints and strategies that I may use during the hunting season.

One point you brought up in your book *Whitetails* on dominance in bucks (and does and fawns, for that matter) was that a dominant buck will sometimes mount a lesser buck to show him that he is more dominant. I have never heard of one buck mounting another. I am not doubting you one bit, because you have a photograph of this very occurrence in the book.

When a dominant buck mounts a lesser buck, does his penis actually enter the lesser buck's anal cavity, and if so, does the dominant buck ejaculate?

I realize you state in the book that you haven't seen the dominant buck's penis being "unsheathed," but your picture clearly shows the penis of the dominant buck. I was wondering if you had seen or heard anything supporting or denying this since your book went to press? Do you think that the dominant buck could be taking out his sexual frustrations on the lesser buck? Maybe the does had not yet become ready to breed, or perhaps they had all been bred.　　　　　D. V., Spring Grove, Minnesota

A: I am glad you enjoyed *Whitetails,* and that you learned from it. It was written expressly to pass on the knowledge of deer I've gained over the past years.

Many male animals of different species will mount lesser males of the same species as a form of dominance. It is common among dogs, but I have also seen it in wolves, deer, wild sheep, and elk. It is basically a form of forcing the lesser animal to admit that it is subordinate.

Yes, you are right in saying that it is also the result of sexual frustration. Bucks are capable of breeding from the time they peel the velvet from their antlers in early September, although their sexual urges are sublimated by the need to put on body fat before the actual rut begins about October 15. No doe is capable of accepting a buck until she comes into estrus; for most does, that's about November 9 or 10 up to November 21. These dates are not cut in stone—a few does may be a week earlier or later than this—but the peak of the breeding season occurs around November 9–12. To take out his sexual frustrations, the buck will masturbate, make rubs, paw scrapes, look for fights, or dominate other bucks.

In the photo you referred to, the buck's penis is hanging loosely from its sheath. I have never seen a buck's penis fully extended or rigid when he mounts another buck, though I have seen this during masturbation.

A buck's penis is composed of a tendon- or sinewlike material curled into an elongated S-shaped curve, known as a sigmoid loop. In breeding, that S-curve straightens out and the penis becomes rigid.

Because the penis does not become rigid when one buck mounts another, it could not penetrate the second buck's anus. There is no ejaculation. In both masturbation and breeding, at the time of ejaculation, the buck makes a mighty jump forward to drive his penis in, or forward, as far as possible so that the sperm is delivered deeply inside the female. The sperm will then have less of a distance to swim to reach the egg or eggs, so that fertilization can take place.

Several years ago I watched a big buck repeatedly try to mount a six-month-old buck fawn. The little buck either ran off or slipped out from under the big buck when he rose up on his hind legs. At no time did I see the big buck's penis. This was definitely a case of sexual frustration, but I fail to see how there could have been any gratification.

Q: I have found eastern white-tailed deer on mountaintops, with the nearest water source a mile away in the valley. Have studies been made of deer in captivity to determine their daily water requirements? How often do they drink? When do they drink—day, night, end of feeding cycle, midcycle? How far will they roam from their water source?

J. D. V., Springfield, Virginia

A: Many factors determine how much water a deer will drink in a 24-hour period, including the time of year and the vegetation being eaten.

Basically a deer will drink 3 to 4 quarts of water twice a day. A captive deer being fed dried hay and feed in summer may drink an additional 3 quarts.

Deer in the wild have varying needs for water, because a lot of their requirements are met by the water content of the vegetation they are eating. In spring, when vegetation is putting out its first growth, the plants are very succulent with a high water content. If raindrops or dewdrops are on such vegetation, the deer may not have to drink at all.

From mid-May on, lactating does will drink water regularly to meet the demands of milk production. Most does have twins, and each fawn will drink 8 to 12 or more ounces of milk three to four times a day.

Most vegetation has reached its seasonal growth potential by the end of July. From that time on, as the plants mature, they will contain less moisture and begin to dry out. August usually has the hottest days. This heat, coupled with dry vegetation, causes deer to drink more at this time of the year than any other. Most does will be weaning their fawns, but they will still produce some milk.

Acorns begin dropping by the end of September, and they are a moist food. The leaves start to fall shortly thereafter, and the deer eat those leaves with the highest residual sugar content (the brightest-colored ones) and the most moisture. The weather has turned cool and most fawns are completely weaned now, so that a doe's requirement for water returns to about 8 quarts daily. Big bucks require a couple of additional quarts because of their larger body size. They also need additional water during the rut because they drool so much.

In wintertime, deer metabolisms slow drastically, causing their food and water needs to decline as well. As many of their regular water sources will have frozen into ice, deer get their water by licking ice or eating snow. They may require no more than 2 to 3 quarts of water per day.

In summer, deer will go to water two to three times per day.

In March, when deer metabolisms speed up, the animals need more water, the ice melts, and the first new green vegetation is sprouting.

A deer's home range is 1 to 2 square miles under normal conditions, and a part of that range must have water in the form of a brook, pond, lake, or river. For a deer to travel a mile to water is not a great difficulty, although most deer can find water much closer than that. I shot a buck once that had corn in his paunch, and I know the nearest cornfield was at least 2 miles away.

In my area, water is common; I doubt if any deer has to go more than ¼ mile to find some. Under such circumstances, deer usually drink as they cross the water on their way to feed. In Texas, where I have done extensive deer photography, the only water in many areas is at man-made tanks or windmills. In these areas, deer usually feed first and then go to water.

Q: This winter (1996–97) in Fargo, I was watching deer. I saw one buck that had 10 points. Then I didn't see him the rest of the year. I saw many does, and they saw me, too. I would go back the next day and they would be there again. This is all in one place. I was wondering if this was strange activity, since I left human scent everywhere and the does also saw us.

J. N., age 14, Fargo, North Dakota

A: You didn't tell me if the deer were in a protected area or not. And I'm not sure if the only buck you saw had 10 points, or if you saw only one 10-point buck.

Bucks don't usually associate with does unless it is the rutting, or breeding, season, so it is understandable that you didn't see them as often. When the fawns are born the ratio is about 50 percent does and 50 percent bucks, but the buck mortality is always higher because they are more adventurous and get in more trouble. Also, more bucks are shot in the hunting season, simply because more hunters would rather shoot a buck—the bigger, the better.

If deer are in a protected area, they soon become habituated to seeing people, providing the people are in the same spot each time and don't try to approach the deer too closely.

If you saw only one buck in a year, that is most unusual. If you saw a number of bucks but only one that was a 10-pointer, that is not unusual, because 8-point antlers are the norm for even mature bucks.

Q: I keep reading stories about why deer squat when there is a sudden noise or when they see danger. The answer is simple. The muscles in a deer's legs need to be stretched in order to spring forward. It's something like pulling back the hammer on a revolver; you're stretching the spring so it will slam the hammer forward. Have you ever seen a deer leap forward without first cocking its spring? In 45 years of hunting, I never have. They are not dodging the arrow, they are just getting the hell out of there the fastest way they know how. Many thanks to you for getting it right.

J. S., Ann Arbor, Michigan

A: It is all so commonplace that most people don't notice it, but the basic fact is that "for every action there is a reaction." A pitcher or quarterback can't throw a ball without first bringing his arm back. A golfer has his backswing. A bow must be drawn, a gun cocked—some sort of action has to be made before the reaction, the release, can take place. Sprinters draw their bodies into a compact, tensed mass that is released into action when they start. Watch a horse when it starts to run; it really squats as its muscles tense and stretch prior to its springing forward. A deer's squatting may cause the arrow to pass over its back, but the squatting was not done to cause the arrow to go over its back; it was done, as you put it, "to get the hell out of there."

Q: I have been hunting a particular wildlife management area in north-western Florida for about two years. It is predominantly covered with pines and small oaks except by the creek bottoms, where the cover is extremely dense. Although the hunting for me this past year has been fair and I only managed to get a doe during archery season, I was puzzled by the fact that whenever I did see a deer, I had always seen one or more turkeys about 20 to 30 minutes before. Do deer and turkeys travel together? Is it possible that deer are smart enough to use turkeys as an advance scouting party? If the turkeys get scared by something due to their acute vision, do the deer then avoid that particular area? This could be just a coincidence, so I wonder if anyone else has reported this same type of activity. Possibly this could be another effective tactic—hunt where turkeys are known to be, because deer travel and feed with turkeys. Just don't let the turkeys see you or you may never see the deer.   J. C., Tallahassee, Florida

A: I am afraid that your seeing turkeys before deer is a matter of coincidence. From my experience in not only my home area of New Jersey but Virginia and Texas as well, I know that deer and turkeys do not like to feed in close proximity to one another.

Both deer and turkeys feed upon many of the same foods, such as acorns and beechnuts, so they will often be found in the same general area. I have actually witnessed deer striking at nearby turkeys with their feet, and I have also seen the turkeys flap their wings at nearby deer to chase them off. They are competitive when they feed together.

Turkeys don't stay in one spot to feed if food is plentiful. I have seen turkeys come into food and walk off after 20 minutes, even though they hadn't finished feeding, and I believe that this is their pattern. By moving almost constantly, the turkeys force any stalking predator to also keep moving. The more the predator moves, the greater the chances that the turkeys will spot it.

Deer don't like to be around turkeys because of the noise the birds make while feeding. They give out an almost constant low purring sound that keeps each bird in touch with the rest of the flock. Also, turkeys' constant scratching in the leaves and forest duff masks any sounds of potential danger. Deer count on their ears too much to tolerate such noise.

I walked across a piece of forested hillside the other day. It's about ¼ mile from my house. I was amazed when I saw that acres of the hillside had been torn up by feeding turkeys. I know there is a big flock back there, but they must have spent the entire last month on just that area. I have never seen such a large area so thoroughly turned over. It is also a great area for deer, and I saw many tracks crisscrossing the hillside.

Deer and turkey concentrate on acorns when they fall.

So deer and turkeys do cohabit in the same areas. The deer do pay attention to the sharp warning puck of the wild turkey. It's just that the deer don't like to be in the exact same spot as turkeys at the same time.

Q: On November 5, 1994, I downed a full-grown doe with a neck shot on a woods road at about 8:30 A.M. She fell some 50 yards from my box tree stand, which is about 25 feet high on the edge of the road. About 15 minutes later a 3-point buck came out on the road, saw the dead doe, and immediately went to her. For some 50 minutes he stayed beside her and did some unusual things.

On approaching the doe, he immediately began licking her ears, nose, mouth, and neck. He then proceeded to lick her practically all over, moving to her feet, belly, fluffy tail, and female parts. After touching her female parts, he straddled her as if trying to mount her with his penis exposed. This action lasted only a moment or so, and then he resumed licking her. He stopped finally at the neck wound and stayed there a long time, licking the blood oozing from the wound.

The buck was so engrossed in his activities that my attempts to scare him off only caused him to look around. I grunted, whistled, coughed, talked loudly, clapped my hands, and stomped and kicked the stand. At no time did he see me in the stand. Only when he saw my son come into the road some 100 yards away did he lift his tail and trot down the road.

Have you ever seen such activity, especially the attraction to and apparent taste for the doe's blood? Would the doe being in estrus have caused his actions?

J. T., Macon, Georgia

A: What you witnessed was unusual. I have never seen a deer lick the blood of a freshly killed deer, nor have I ever heard of it.

As you assumed, the doe was probably in heat, which attracted the buck to her in the first place. I have had other correspondents tell me about seeing bucks trying to mount does that had been shot. What is far more common and has been witnessed by many people, including me, is for an injured, wounded, or freshly killed buck to be attacked by other bucks. The competitive drive for dominance is so powerful that, when a big buck is badly injured, even the smallest buck will gore him. It's the little buck's first step up the ladder.

This young buck's licking of the doe's ears, nose, and mouth is part of the deer courtship ritual, as is the licking of her genitals. Licking blood is a new one for me.

I know bucks do crazy things during the rut, but this young buck was really dumb. I sure hope he doesn't pass on too many of his genes.

Q: In your book *The Deer of North America,* you state that the rutting season in Pennsylvania starts about October 15. You said it starts when the bucks' necks begin to swell. I was out on October 1, 1994, doing a little preseason scouting, and I saw two small bucks and one pretty good-sized one. It looked to me like the neck on the bigger buck had already started to swell. Was this an indication that the rutting season had started or was going to be early? I was surprised to see the deer out much earlier than usual.

J. N., Pittsburgh, Pennsylvania

A: Under normal conditions, the rut for most of the northern three-quarters of the United States starts on or about October 15. But 1994 was unusual in that the summer was excessively rainy and dark. Darkened days fool a deer's pineal gland into thinking that it is later in the year than it actually is. The start and peak of the rut should have been three to four days earlier than usual. And I did in fact see bucks peel the velvet from their antlers earlier than ever before. I also saw their necks start to swell earlier than before.

If the rainy conditions had continued, the 1994 rut may have come three or four days early. We'll never know, however, because an October drought put the rut back on schedule.

Q: When deer go to a traditional yarding location, is this instinctive or is it a learned behavior? If, for some reason, all of the deer in one locality were killed, would the deer that eventually restocked that area go to the same yards?

L. C., Syracuse, New York

A: This is a very complex question and I'm not sure that I, or anyone else, can give you the correct answer.

Valerius Giest, a man I admire for all his work on wild sheep, claims that if all of the big adult rams are killed, there will be no rams with a memory of where the traditional breeding grounds are or that can lead the young rams to them. I know that he is referring to a breeding range while you are referring to a yarding area, but it's the same concept. It relates to a particular spot on the map that has been used traditionally by a particular species for a particular purpose. It is Giest's contention that going to the traditional breeding ground is a learned behavior, just as the learning of oral traditions and customs is with humans.

I don't say that he is wrong but, in rebuttal, let me point out that one of the main sheep breeding ranges in Yellowstone National Park is the cliffs and benchland lying between the town of Gardiner and the Mammoth Campground. These breeding grounds also happen to be the sheep's winter range.

What makes this spot a favorable winter range? The lower hills get less snow than the higher summer ranges do. The hills are located so that the prevailing winds blow a bit of the snow away; the sheep don't have to dig through deep snow to find food. The close proximity of the cliffs offers the sheep protection from predators. These cliffs also allow the dominant ram to keep rival rams away from his ewe by keeping her on a cliff face.

For deer, the top priority in winter is to get out of the wind. Adult deer can tolerate all the cold in the world; they just can't stand wind. The deer's metabolism is greatly reduced in winter, so its need for food is greatly reduced; hence, getting out of the wind is more important than food.

Most deer wintering yards are located in stands of conifers, usually of white cedars in the northern swamps or on red cedar hillsides in my area. No matter how much snow falls, there is always less snow on the ground beneath conifers because they catch so much of it and hold it aloft. Having less snow makes it easier for the deer to move around.

Red cedar is not a very nutritious food, but white cedar is. In the northern swamps, where deer yard far more frequently, white cedar provides food as well as shelter.

If all of the deer in one area were wiped out and then the area was restocked, I believe that the new deer would go to the same traditional yards that the original deer used. I believe the deer would instinctively seek out the same set of conditions that prompted the first deer to use the wintering

The darkened trail of droppings and the heavily browsed cedars show that this winter yard has been overused by deer.

yards. In other words, they would be seeking exactly what the first deer had been seeking.

To further buttress this theory, I would like to point out that researchers once held young blue-wing teal captive until all of the adult birds had migrated south. When the young teal were released two months later, they flew instinctively to the same locations as the adult birds. They didn't just fly south, they flew to traditional wintering areas, even without older birds to guide them.

Adult herring gulls don't migrate south; the young birds almost always do. How do they know where to go?

I have pondered all morning on what tests could be made to prove or disprove my theory and I can't come up with any. All I can offer are the analogies given above.

Q: I am a 16-year-old deer hunter. I love deer hunting and I want to make it my career. I think deer are the most amazing animals there are. I have one question for you. I would like to know when deer in my area shed their antlers. I live in Culpeper, Virginia, in the Piedmont region. This previous muzzleloader season, I saw two nice bucks. One was an 8-point, the other was an 8 or 10.   S. S., Culpeper, Virginia

A: I can understand your love of deer hunting. There are about 16 million other hunters, and most of them feel the same way.

You said you wanted to make it your career. The only place I know of that has professional deer hunters is New Zealand (and I am not sure that this is still the case). Deer and red deer were imported there and became so numerous, due to the lack of predators, that they destroyed the vegetation, causing erosion.

If you meant that you intend to make deer research and management your career, I advise you to take all the math, biology, and science courses you can while still in high school. More deer research is being done through computer analysis and simulation than is actually being done in the field.

The bucks in your area should drop their antlers between the end of December and mid-February. It will probably be easier to see the bucks themselves, as you have done, than it will be to find their antlers. Finding antlers takes a lot of time and a lot of luck.

Q: I am an avid outdoorsman, and my passion is white-tailed deer. I hunt many beautiful places in North America, but equally enjoy my home in northern Virginia.

I have a brother-in-law who has 60 acres that I hunt every fall. Much of the area is open hardwoods with small thickets containing greenbrier, honeysuckle, and mountain laurel. I have tried to enhance this with two food plots planted with clover and grasses. The areas grew well and are quite beautiful. I would expect that the deer would be quite attracted to these green fields, which still look very good even midway through January. But for some reason, the deer are not so tempted. Trying to enhance the rack-building process, I have supplied this area with year-round food sources, mineral supplements, and am doing my best to create a good habitat. All to no avail.

I just thought maybe you would have a suggestion or helpful hint. Perhaps I'm missing something in the process and you could help.

M. K., Sumerduck, Virginia

A: This is a puzzlement.

I can understand the deer not staying in 60 acres without protective cover, but you did say you have small thickets of greenbrier and honeysuckle, and these should give deer cover. Both greenbrier and honeysuckle also make good deer food.

I can't imagine why the deer don't at least feed in your clover patches, even if they don't stay. Is the surrounding area so ideal that it supplies everything a deer needs?

You say you hunt the land each year. How many others hunt it? Could it be overhunted? You must be seeing deer there or you wouldn't hunt it.

Are there dogs running loose on the property? That would keep deer away.

Is the land more than a mile from water? I can't imagine that it would be but, if it were 2 miles from any water, you are unlikely to have deer there.

You are doing everything right. You are doing what I would suggest to make it a haven for deer. There must be some outside influence keeping the deer away that I can't find without being on the spot. Continue what you are doing while you search for clues.

Chapter
4

Anatomy

Familiarity with white-tailed deer anatomy is critical to the hunter, because only by knowing the vital areas can the hunter be sure of where to place his shot. All hunters owe it to the wildlife they hunt to make the quickest, most humane kills possible. Hunting means killing, and it must be done without causing suffering whenever possible.

The knowledge of anatomy is also important so the hunter knows how his quarry functions, and how and why the animal does what it does. Looking at a track and being able to guesstimate the size of the animal that made it is based on anatomy. Looking at the height of a browse line or at a rub on a tree and knowing the size of the deer that made either is based on anatomy. And if you are to dress out your deer properly, if you are to do your own butchering and prepare the meat, it is essential that you know anatomy.

Q: I have been deer hunting for nearly 60 years, and usually "never looked past the antlers." That changed on December 9, 1996, when I killed a yearling buck that had ½-inch spikes. However, even more strange was that this buck had extremely long eyelashes. It had 46 lashes more than 2 inches long, with the longest measuring 6½ inches.

Is this unusual?   D. S., Escanoba, Michigan

A: With the exception of the 6½-inch eyelash, your buck sported typical lashes.

Unlike humans, deer have eyelashes on just the upper eyelid. A deer eyelid has about 46 hairs, so your buck was also average in that respect. A deer eyebrow has two rows of hair. One row includes about 18 hairs that are about 3 inches long, with some 4 inches long. In addition, the eyelid includes about 18 hairs scattered below the eye that are 3 inches or longer. The rest of the lashes measure in the 1-inch range. All of these hairs are sensory devices, like a cat's whiskers, that warn deer of brush or other vegetation that could harm the eye.

Q: My brother and I were scouting our hunting land in West Virginia in July when we spotted a large buck easing along a ridge. We were shocked when we noticed that the buck's antlers were already hard and polished. Is it possible that this buck never shed his antlers from the previous year? He appeared healthy, and showed no signs of injury.

J.M., Woodbine, Maryland.

A: What you saw was very unusual. Under normal conditions, a buck's antlers are fully grown in velvet by the end of July, and they begin to harden by the first week of August. Most bucks rub the dried velvet from their antlers by the first week of September.

I know of two situations in which bucks don't shed their antlers.

The first scenario involves a buck's pineal gland. This gland, located in the brain, is often referred to as a deer's "third eye." It is the receptor for electrical impulses generated by optic nerves. If removed surgically, through a pinealectomy, the gland can be prevented from signaling the pituitary gland to increase or decrease the amount of testosterone produced and distributed throughout a buck's body. It is the increased levels of testosterone in August that causes antlers to solidify. A decrease in testosterone leads to antler shedding.

A buck could also keep his antlers if he were somehow castrated, by accident or gunshot, and the injury occurred after the antlers had hardened.

Q: During the rut, my son and I found 5 scrapes along the edge of an old farm field and 12 scrapes just inside the edge of the timber. Each of the scrapes had an overhanging branch. What's odd is that the timber strip is only about 40 yards wide by 150 yards long.

What did we find? Is it a scrape hub, territorial scrapes, or breeding scrapes? In many years of bowhunting, I've never seen so many scrapes in such a small area. W. J., Bethany, Illinois

A: Seventeen scrapes in such a small area is a lot for any part of the country, and almost unheard of in the North. In both Texas and Alabama, I have seen scrape lines with a scrape every 50 to 75 feet. I couldn't believe it when I first saw it in Alabama, but my friend the late Ben Rogers Lee said that was common in the South. On some Texas ranches, scrapes are even more plentiful.

I don't classify scrapes into categories, as many people do. First, bucks don't really have a territory, they have a home range. Their breeding area is where the most food is, because that's where the does will be.

A scrape is an advertisement of billboard proportions. By using scrapes made by other bucks, a buck can try to cancel out messages left by other bucks. This also allows bucks to monitor the presence of competitors in the breeding chase. I guess you could say that scrapes are the closest thing to a singles bar that deer have. They literally reek, "I'm here to take on all challengers."

When making a scrape, the buck first chews and rubs on the overhead branches.
Credit: Len Rue Jr.

Then he scrapes, using both of his front feet alternately.
Credit: Len Rue Jr.

Stepping into the center of the scraped area, the buck then rub urinates using his tarsal glands.
Credit: Len Rue Jr.

Q: How long do deer sleep? From my stand I have watched deer bed down and chew their cuds, but I have never seen them sleep. Deer do sleep, don't they?   A. K., Hampton, New Jersey

A: You pose a couple of good questions. Yes, deer do sleep. I have no way of knowing what they do at night, because I can't see them. What I can tell you is based upon many thousands of daylight hours of personal observation.

A question I'd like to have the answer to is, can deer sleep with their eyes open? I ask because they seldom close their eyes for more than 10 to

20 seconds at a time. In my lifetime of deer observations, I can't recall ever seeing more than three or four deer actually stretch their necks out on the ground and fall into a deep sleep. And even then, their ears didn't stop moving. The muscles in deer ears must be the animals' most highly developed muscles for their size; they just never stop moving. The slightest sound out of the ordinary jerks deer wide awake. Apparently, deer are able to screen out the common sounds made by the wind, flowing water, dropping leaves, and so on. The alarm call of a squirrel, jay, or crow gets their instant attention. The sound of anything walking through the woods, even another deer, also gets an instant response.

I have often seen deer hold their heads erect with their eyes about half closed for three minutes or more, which leads me to believe that they are dozing off, even though their eyes are not fully closed. But again, their ears never stop moving.

Although I have seen deer stay in one bed for three or four hours, I have also seen them get up and change their beds several times in that length of time. Many times they move no more than 100 feet and then lie down again. I have also noticed that small groups of deer, elk, pronghorns, wild sheep, and goats usually lie down with each individual animal facing a different direction, which makes it more difficult for a predator to sneak up on them. Although all of these animals can see over 300 degrees of a circle with monocular vision, they have some overlapping binocular vision and will look directly at anything that disturbs them. They also face a disturbance so that any sound the disturber makes comes into each ear equally, allowing them to pinpoint the source precisely.

Q: This past December (1989) was the coldest on record for Pennsylvania, and January was the second warmest we have ever had. Does that mean deer hunting will be better this next fall?　　　　P. V., Scranton, Pennsylvania

A: I believe it does.

In the fall of 1989, the acorn crop was spotty across North America. Here in New Jersey only some of the red oaks produced acorns, and the white oaks did not bear any acorns at all. Still, the deer in our area went into winter hog fat because our farm crops were good. Most of our deer depend on crops, not on browse.

Winter came in with a bang in December and, although the snow was not deep, it stayed powder dry because the temperature did not get above freezing for over three weeks. The wind driving that cold air down out of Canada was fierce. If those conditions had continued, deer losses would have been very high across the northern part of the United States.

Fortunately for the deer, and the deer hunter, the weather changed. Warm winters generally mean that deer survival rates are high, more fawns are born, and fawn mortality rates drop. The result is heavier-bodied, larger-antlered bucks the following fall.

Q: On an extremely frosty morning after two days of rain, the frozen leaves made a noise like glass breaking every time I put my foot down. Under the mature white pines and hemlocks, however, was a different world. I could walk on leaves blown under these trees without making a sound, as they were just wet, not frozen. Why hadn't the leaves and needles frozen under these evergreen trees? C. W., State College, Pennsylvania

A: All trees give off an infinitesimal amount of heat, even during cold winter nights. During the winter days they absorb heat, melting the snow around them, with the darker trees absorbing and giving off a greater amount. Evergreen trees produce a microclimate as much as 8 to 10 degrees warmer than the surrounding deciduous forest.

You have discovered why evergreens are so crucial to deer habitat in the northern half of the United States. Evergreens, being dark, absorb more of the sun's rays during the daytime, and their branches slow down the

Evergreens are important to northern deer because they provide shelter from the wind and hold the snow off the ground.

heat loss at night. In addition, evergreens present a much more effective wind barrier than deciduous trees. During snowstorms, evergreen branches often hold most or all of the snowfall aloft. In a dense stand of conifers, almost no snow reaches the ground and, unless a strong wind dislodges the snow, it may melt from the branches, keeping the ground beneath snow-free. The dark forest duff (the dropped needles) absorbs the sunlight instead of its being reflected by the snow, raising the temperature substantially. To deer on a starvation diet, the difference of 6 to 10 degrees in temperature can mean the difference between survival and death. The slightly higher temperatures beneath the evergreens means the deer expend fewer calories to keep their body temperatures normal.

Evergreens are often critical to deer survival. If there are no clumps of evergreens on the land you deer hunt, plant them.

Q: I have located a trail used regularly by a large white-tailed buck. There are two trees along the trail that could be hunted from. One is directly above the trail (I would have to shoot straight down) and the other is off to the side (I would have to shoot broadside). I believe I could easily hit my mark from either tree. Which tree would offer a deadlier shot with bow and arrow?   D. I., Menomonee Falls, Wisconsin

A: I recommend the broadside shot. A large white-tailed buck, as seen from above, has a rib-cage width of about 12 inches. From that width you have to subtract about 3 inches for the hair, skin, and ribs on each side of the lungs. It is true that a shot through the deer's spine will drop him in his tracks, but at best that is a 1-inch-wide target.

Shooting at the deer broadside will give you a target at least 12 inches high by 18 inches in length. A shot through the heart, lungs, or liver would be fatal, though the buck would run off when hit. If your arrow goes high, it might hit the spine, dropping the deer in his tracks. Go for the broadside shot.

Q: I was turkey hunting last spring when I saw a unique doe. She was feeding on grass when she ambled within 50 feet of where I was set up. When she looked my way, I noticed that she had big white rings around her eyes.

Is this common? If so, what is the purpose of the white rings?

O. B., Staunton, Virginia

A: Most whitetails have varying amounts of white hair around their eyes. I've seen deer with no white markings around their eyes, and I've seen deer with circles that were nearly ½ inch wide.

The amount of white around a deer's eyes, muzzle, and throat patch is highly variable.

Many creatures of the night have white markings around their eyes, particularly owls. Barred, great gray, and barn owls all have large facial disks; in the case of the barn owl, they are pure white. The purpose of these discs is to reflect light into the eyes so the animal can see better in the dark.

Evolution might be the reason some deer have white eye rings and some do not. In centuries past, deer have fed primarily at dawn and dusk when there was enough light to see, even in low-light conditions, so eye rings weren't always necessary. However, where deer are hunted heavily, they feed almost exclusively at night. Therefore, eye rings might show up more often as times change.

Of course, to prove this theory I would need evidence of these markings (or lack thereof) on deer that lived here hundreds of years ago. Unfortunately, this information isn't available.

Q: The past two or three years, while hunting in the morning, I've seen many large bucks, but they never come within bow range. I've tried just about everything to outsmart these deer, but nothing has worked. I believe they sense my presence and stay clear of my stand.

How can I approach my stand unnoticed?

B. M., Mendenhall, Mississippi

A: You did not indicate where your stand was in relation to the prevailing winds, but that's probably the source of your problem.

In most areas of the United States the prevailing wind comes out of the west, unless it's preceding a storm front. The scent from your entrance trail is most likely blowing to the deer's primary bedding area.

To improve your chances, take a new route to your stand. You must enter the area with wind direction in mind. The more you play the wind, the more you improve your chances of going unnoticed.

You also didn't mention what time you get out to your stand. If the deer can see you, you are getting to your stand too late.

Q: I live in the farm country of southwestern Wisconsin and have seen bucks keep their antlers as late as mid-March. Our winters are relatively mild compared to the northern part of the state, and our farmers grow a lot of corn and soybeans, which are deer magnets. Therefore, deer seem to make it through winter in excellent shape.

Which leads me to several questions:

Typically, how many deer can a piece of land support? Also, of the bucks killed annually, what percentage are yearlings?

Some people say our bucks keep their antlers longer because of a high doe:buck ratio. Their rationale is that the surplus of does means some won't be bred until December, which in turn means that bucks' testosterone levels stay elevated until late-estrus does are bred. Is this true?

If does come into heat late and no adult bucks are in the area, will yearling bucks or buck fawns breed them?

Also, if does don't get bred in December, will they continue their estrus cycles in January and February?

Finally, do yearling bucks move away from their home range by instinct to prevent inbreeding? I've been told that inbred bucks have smaller antlers and lower body weights, and inbred does are more susceptible to disease.

What are your views on these issues?   J. K., Platteville, Wisconsin

A: I did some research and learned that the yearling buck kill in southwestern Wisconsin is similar to that for other farmland states. Most states claim that 85 percent of their yearling bucks are killed each year. However, in expansive northern forest areas the percentage is lower, because bigwoods deer do not receive as much hunting pressure.

Ordinarily, 15 to 20 deer per square mile is considered the capacity of most forested deer range. However, in good farm country where deer have access to highly nutritious crops, the deer capacity is virtually unlimited, so it is determined instead by how many deer the farmers can accommodate without financial losses.

It is true that bucks with access to good nutrition usually hold their antlers longer than bucks living on overbrowsed land.

To answer your other questions:

Bucks don't need their antlers to breed, but there is a correlation. Bucks lose their antlers through decreased testosterone levels, which also affects their sex drive. However, they're still capable of breeding during this time.

For some reason, the bucks where I live in northwestern New Jersey often shed their antlers in late November and early December. I know they can still breed because I have seen them do it. They can breed until April.

As for young bucks breeding, yes, this happens all the time, because many areas hold a lot more yearlings than mature bucks. I don't believe that an adult buck in the wild will breed more than 8 to 10 does in a season, because most don't have the time. An adult buck will stay with a doe for up to four days, including her pre-estros and estrus periods.

Buck fawns that have small, polished, button antlers are physically developed enough to breed. In fact, Helenette Silver of the New Hampshire Department of Game has documented several cases of buck fawns that bred and impregnated doe fawns.

It would be rare for a buck fawn to impregnate an adult doe, however, because most buck fawns aren't tall enough to mount mature does.

Few does breed in October. Most of the does in your area, as is true for the northern three-quarters of the continent, breed around November 10. A doe that is not bred during her first estrus period in early November is capable of re-cycling every 28 days up to six additional times.

Inbreeding can and does occur, but it's a negligible factor as far as body characteristics are concerned. Genetic flaws from inbreeding are possible in the first generation, but are almost impossible in succeeding generations because few bucks live beyond two years and most yearling bucks disperse to about 5½ miles away.

Although yearling bucks move away from their birthing range, an adult buck could breed his daughter or granddaughter without ill effects on the offspring. Constant inbreeding, however, as is seen in captive herds, can have deleterious effects on the offspring. Such occurrences are nearly impossible in the wild.

Q: I read in one of your books that animals shed their coats from the head back toward the tail. Do deer shed their coats the same way?

P. T., Alpine, Texas

This doe is changing from her worn winter coat to her cooler summer coat.

A: No. Deer seem to shed all over their bodies at one time. Squirrels and rabbits have distinct hairlines, shedding from the nose on back. This is most noticeable when the hair change gets back to the shoulders. Foxes usually shed their flank hairs first, then shed from head to tail. With deer it seems that the shedding process starts on the spine and works down toward the belly behind the front shoulders. At no time is there the distinct hairline seen on other animals.

I find it interesting to watch fawns change from their spotted natal coats to their winter coats. With fawns, the spots start to disappear in the middle of the body and work toward both ends. This change is due to both hair replacement and a wearing off of the spotted ends of the hair. Around September 1, you can see fawns that have no spots at all on their rib cage, flanks, and back—yet their shoulders and hams are still heavily spotted.

Q: A friend of mine reported seeing a deer flick flies from its eyes with its ears. The deer was one of a herd of seven feeding in an alfalfa field. My friend was watching the deer through binoculars so he could actually see what was going on. The evening was warm and there was no wind so the flies and gnats were out in full force. All of the deer had flies on the bridges of their noses, which they would occasionally dislodge by rubbing their noses against the alfalfa or by reaching up with a hind foot and rubbing them off. One deer in the group, and only one deer, would flap its ears forward to chase any flies that got in the corners of its eyes. Have you ever seen or heard of deer being able to do this? If one deer could do this, why didn't they all?   S. C., Newton, New Jersey

A: I have never seen a deer flick flies from the corners of its eyes with its ears. And when I read your letter, I started wondering whether a deer's ear was long enough to reach its eye.

By actual measurement, a big white-tailed buck's ears are about 8 inches in length, measured along their outside curve. If the ear was bent forward, it would extend ½ to ¾ inch beyond the forward portion of the eye. Thus the ears are long enough to do the job.

And my friend Joe Taylor recently told me that he had been watching his captive white-tailed buck use his ears to flick the flies away from the forward corners of his eyes. Joe said that the flick was exceedingly fast, unlike the leisurely flapping of the ears by a cow. Joe is one of the keenest observers of wildlife of all kinds, and deer in particular, that I know. When he talks about deer, I sit at his feet and listen. If he said he saw it happen, it did.

I must also add that Joe is now 85 years old and doesn't recall ever seeing another deer do this.

In regard to your second question of why the other deer didn't flick the flies away with their ears, perhaps they were not able to.

Q: You once answered a question in your column concerning whether or not a blind deer could survive in the wild. You related a couple of instances in which you had read of adult deer surviving, although blind. As you said, you had no way of knowing how long the deer you had read about had been blind.

I was hunting up here in Maine this past year and shot a respectable 8-point buck that was in good condition. I would guess that his live weight would have been between 150 and 175 pounds. The rack was not a big one, but it was nice. The thing that surprised me was that after I shot the deer, I found that one of his eyes was opaque; it was a milky white. I have no idea how long the deer had been blind in one eye, but it did not seem to handicap him in any way.

Is this condition a rare one?   R. B., Bangor, Maine

A: Deer being blinded in one eye is quite a common occurrence. I usually see at least a couple every year as I travel about, concentrating on deer photography.

The thing that amazes me is that it does not occur more frequently. How many times in walking through the woods have you had a twig jabbed into your eye? I have had it happen a number of times. And I'm usually walking along a cleared trail, while deer are bounding away into the thickest, densest brush possible. I have read of a number of instances where deer have been killed by impaling themselves on a dead snag. Only the good Lord knows how many deer lose their sight by having a stick or twig jammed into their eye.

Many deer must also lose their sight while fighting. Ordinarily only equal animals fight, but that doesn't mean their antlers are equal in length or in number of tines. When a deer fights, he usually catches his opponent's antlers squarely on his own antlers—but not always. And because each deer is trying to catch his opponent unawares, he may drive his antlers into the other's face before the rival is able to lower his antlers.

Q: I recently read in *Newsweek* magazine that forensic scientists can tell a female skeleton from a male skeleton by the width of the pelvic girdle. A woman's pelvic bones are built wider than a man's to allow for the passage of a baby during birth, and this extra width causes the female's feet to be farther apart than those of a male. Would this also be true of deer? Can we tell a doe's tracks from those of a buck because the hooves would be wider apart in the stance? I'm always looking for ways to tell the sex of the deer tracks I see. Do you have any comments on this, and any suggestions?

W. T., Detroit, Michigan

A: I read the same article and found it fascinating. You are being a forensic scientist yourself every time you try to ascertain whether the deer tracks you are looking at were made by a buck or a doe.

I have really never noticed whether there is any difference in the width of the pelvic girdle of bucks and does, and I certainly have handled hundreds of each. I will definitely start to take some measurements to see what I can come up with. Offhand, I don't believe that you would be able to determine sex by the distance between the hooves. Usually bucks have an overall body frame large enough to overcome any slight difference there might be in the actual width of the pelvic girdle itself. In fact, I think a big buck's hooves would be farther apart in the stance than would the hooves of a doe.

It is extremely difficult to tell the sex of a deer by its tracks. If you are in a remote area that is not heavily hunted, where the bucks can live to maturity (four, five, and six years old), you will find that their huge tracks cannot be confused with those of a big doe. Many big bucks get to weigh 300 to 400 pounds, and I can find no record of a doe that weighed as much as 250 pounds. Because such big bucks will be twice the size of the doe, it stands to reason that their hooves will also be twice the size. There should be no mistaking the tracks of a really big buck.

In my home state of New Jersey, most bucks are killed when they are 1½ years old. Many does reach four or five years, old, though, so they will be larger and have more body weight than the young bucks. Hence, their tracks will be larger.

A normal stride for a white-tailed buck, from toe tip to toe tip, is 18 to 19 inches. However, a big doe would have about the same stride length as a small buck.

In a big buck's tracks, the toe tips will tend to point slightly outward from the direction he traveled. A doe's tracks point nearly straight ahead.

If there is a slight snowfall—less than ½ inch—a buck's toes will leave drag marks at the front of the tracks as he takes the next step; a doe's tracks will lack these drag marks. Once there is ½ inch or more of snow, *all* the tracks will show drag marks in front; there will often be a mark behind the hoofprint as well, where the hoof touched the snow before the foot was thrust through. These same marks will appear in soft sand or mud.

Most animals have a tendency, when walking, to place the hind foot on approximately the same spot on the ground where their front foot had been before it was moved to take the next step. All members of the cat family; the red, gray, and arctic foxes; and the coyote all place their hind feet precisely in the tracks made by their front feet. Other animals do not. The tracks made by the hind feet of does and young bucks, while they are walking, usually come down on the front part of the tracks made by their front feet so that the tracks of their hind feet are slightly ahead of their front feet. In other words, they overshoot the tracks made by their front feet. Big bucks' hind

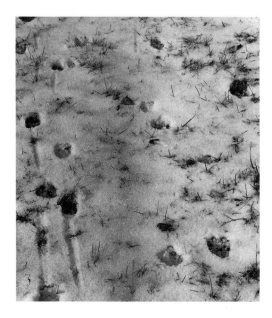

In less than ½ inch of snow, only the buck's tracks show drag marks.

When walking, a deer's hind-foot track is placed on top of the track made by its front feet.

feet tend to land on the rear portion of the tracks made by their forefeet—they undershoot the mark. There are two explanations. Usually a mature buck has a longer body length, which would cause the apparent shortstepping. Also, during the rutting season, bucks walk with a very stiff-legged gait, almost as if they were crippled. This too would cause shortstepping.

Here's one more hint: The tracks of a doe's feet would be spread apart and in front of the spot where she urinated, while those of a buck's would not.

Q: My 87-year-old mother is interested in madstones. She remembers hearing stories of their use when she was young, and her father had one of the stones.

Her research on the subject prompted her to buy your book *The Deer of North America,* and the brief bit of information she found there on madstone formation was of great interest to her.   N. D., Pelham, Alaska

A: Here is the passage referred to in your letter from my book *The Deer of North America:*

Like other ruminants, small children and Indian fakirs, deer habitually swallow indigestible material. I have found stones, a .22 caliber cartridge case and even a piece of melted glass in the deer stomachs I have examined.

Occasionally a hair ball forms in the stomach. Deer frequently lick themselves to help remove their old coats when they are shedding, and they often lick hair from one another. Usually this hair passes through with the food being digested. Sometimes a mass of it does not. The action of the stomach, combined with food material, puts a coating on the hair mass, creating a ball that lodges in the stomach if it becomes too large to be passed on.

On very rare occasions, a "bezoar stone" is found in a deer's stomach. I have never seen one in the many deer I have examined, but I own a bezoar given to me by a Masai hunter who took it from an African antelope. A bezoar—also called a calculus or madstone—is formed by layers of calcium or resinous material, built up around some indigestible object in much the same way that a pearl is formed in an oyster. Some bezoar stones have reached a length of more than two inches (50.8 mm). At one time they were highly treasured, as they were supposed to neutralize poison. These foreign objects are usually found in the reticulum.

I am sorry that I have no new or additional information to pass on to your mother. I imagine that madstones or bezoar stones are quite common, but usually overlooked; no one I know regularly goes through a deer's stomach looking for them.

Q: I have just come back from a caribou hunting trip up on the Ungava Peninsula in Canada. As my trip took place in mid-August, I was surprised to find that some of the caribou still had not shed all of their previous year's winter coats. Most of them had thin new coats, but some were still ragged, with patches of the old hair sticking beyond their new coats. The velvet on their antlers was still very tight, and it took a lot of work to pry it off. Our guide said that in a couple more weeks, the velvet would have just slipped off in long strips. Why hadn't the caribou shed their winter hair sooner? Do they only have one coat of hair per year? In my area I am used to seeing our whitetails in their red summer coats as well as their darker winter coats.

B. O., Syracuse, New York

A: The white-tailed, mule, and black-tailed deer all shed their coats of hair twice a year; the elk, moose, and caribou do not, having only one coat of hair each year.

For years, I have said that deer are southern animals that moved north. This is based on the fact that they shed their hair twice a year, while the other members of the deer family shed only once. The deer's summer coat has hair that is thin, short, solid, and intended primarily for protection against insects; there are about 5,200 hairs to the square inch. There are about 2,600 hairs to the square inch in their winter coat; each is long, crooked, hollow, and filled with air, giving the deer wonderful insulation. As southern animals, they did not need the insulation feature in their hair during the warm months. Also, enjoying a long, warm summer gave them time to go through two hair changes, a luxury denied animals that live farther north. In Canada, Alaska, and the higher reaches of the Rocky Mountains—home to moose, caribou, and elk—summers don't really get warm, and the threat of cold and snow at any time is very real. These latter animals shed each year because their hollow hairs are brittle and break, lessening the insulation qualities.

Further evidence of the deer's southern beginnings is that they don't use freshly fallen snow to good advantage. Whereas elk, moose, and caribou will bed down in the deep snow so that it envelops as much of their bodies as possible, deer do not. Deer paw holes in the snow and lie in the holes, thus losing the insulating quality of the snow.

A deer bedded in the snow here.

White-tailed deer usually paw a hole in the snow before they lie down.

One fellow contested this with me, saying that he had found deer beds that had not been pawed. I replied that the snow had fallen after the deer were already bedded. In this case, the snow does envelop the deer. In the thousands and thousands of hours I have spent watching and photographing deer, however, I have never seen one lie down in snow without pawing a hole first.

Several scientific papers have just been written proving the deer's southern origins.

Q: I live in a subdivision that surrounds a golf course and adjoins a small patch of woods. This spring, while searching for sheds, I came across deer carcass (just bones), and in the middle of the pile of bones was a golf ball. Since the location of the carcass was too far from the golf course for the ball to have been hit there, I'm wondering if the deer could have ingested the ball and either choked on it or had the ball block its intestines, which caused the deer to die. I could find no other evidence as to what might have caused the death of the deer. J. M., Steubenville, Ohio

A: There is a very good chance that the deer swallowed the golf ball. It would have had no difficulty doing so, because the cud, or bolus, that the deer regurgitates, chews, and swallows is about two times larger than a golf ball. Because of the ease with which an object that size could be swallowed, the deer is unlikely to have choked on the ball. And although the ball could have passed through all four stomachs and blocked the intestines, I don't think that happened either. I base this on my experience with cows.

Cows are notorious for swallowing all sorts of things. They have been known to swallow old-fashioned pocket watches, pieces of barbed wire, nails, screws, bolts, pieces of glass, a man's vest, and a variety of other objects. None of these objects did the animals any harm unless it was sharp enough to puncture the stomach. I once found some empty .22-caliber brass hulls and a marble in a pheasant's gizzard. Why these creatures swallow all these oddball items I just don't know, but then ask a pediatrician about the things that kids swallow.

Did the golf ball show a lot of wear? Were the dimples on the surface worn smooth? The bones of the deer were bleached by the sun, so the golf ball would be, too. But only being in the stomach a long time would make the ball smooth. Most swallowed items stay in the bottom of the rumen, or paunch—the first part of the stomach—and so don't get passed through the other three stomachs. Thus they are unlikely to ever reach the intestines.

I just don't know why that deer died. Perhaps it died of other causes that had nothing to do with a golf ball in its stomach.

Q: While shining for deer on our land in the Sheboygan County Marsh, my friend and I saw an adult doe on the side of the gravel road that we use to get to our hunting land. The odd thing about the deer was that she was missing three-quarters of her left hind leg. The leg looked as though it had healed over and was now a stump. When the doe walked across the road, she still tried to use the leg, but obviously could not. She did have noticeable difficulty walking and running.

During the early part of our bowhunting season my father made a poor shot, hit a doe in the left hind leg, and broke the bone. If this was the same doe, would the leg have been able to heal over that quickly? How could the bad part of the leg have fallen off?

Second, if the deer manages to make it through the winter (which so far has been very light), would it be possible for her to have any fawns? Would the bucks in the area reject her because of her missing leg?

J. R., Fond du Lac, Wisconsin

A: You did not say when you were shining for deer or how much time had elapsed between the time that your father shot the deer and your glimpse of the crippled doe.

Deer that are missing part of a foot or leg still move the injured leg in the proper sequence with their other legs, even if the injured limb does not touch the ground. Not only is it instinctive for them to do so, but it helps them keep their balance.

I have seen a number of deer with part of a foot or leg missing, usually as a result of being struck by an automobile. All of these deer were very much handicapped when they walked; none of them showed any sign of the loss when they ran. Therefore, I was surprised to read that the doe you saw was also severely handicapped when she ran. Usually the remaining fore- or hind leg quickly gains more strength to compensate for the missing leg.

Yes, the crippled deer should have no trouble making it through the winter and leading a fairly normal life.

During the time when I was chief gamekeeper for the Coventry Hunt Club here in New Jersey, we had three different deer that had lost a part of their foot or leg to a height of 8 to 10 inches above the ground. None of the deer ever stood on the stump of the foot. On this page is a picture of two bucks; one has lost part of his forefoot, the other a part of his hind foot. The picture was taken in January, and both bucks had lost their antlers. I never learned how they had lost portions of their feet, but both of the wounds had completely healed. This leads me to believe that the loss was

These bucks have each lost one foot through accidents.

probably due to automobile accidents; bowhunting had not become popular when the photo was taken, and our shotgun season had ended only about one month prior to the photo.

The buck with the injured hind foot was shot the following hunting season. The buck with the injured forefoot made it through two more seasons.

In 1960–61 we had the most horrendous winter I've ever experienced in New Jersey. We had 63 inches of snow, and 4 feet lay on the ground all winter. Despite the snow depth and the loss of hundreds of deer, one buck with a missing hind foot made it through the winter. He could not have been able to stand upright on his hind feet as so many of the others had to do to reach food, but he survived when many of the others didn't.

Ordinarily, if the foot or leg bone is broken so that the leg flops around, the portion of the leg or foot below the break is lost. If the bone is broken, but not to the point where it flops, the bone has a good chance of healing itself, because the deer will not walk on it. If the lower part of the break flops around, there is no chance for the bone to set, as it cannot be immobilized. A leg that flops usually receives a restricted blood flow and this, in a short time, produces a type of gangrene that causes the skin at the break to disintegrate; the lower broken part drops off. I do not know why, but there seems to be no putrefaction of the flesh at such a break, as there would be in an untreated human.

Yes, I believe that the doe you saw would be perfectly capable of having fawns. If her injury did not restrict her food intake, her reproductive capabilities would not be affected. I say this based on how well the bucks with missing legs have been able to cope.

And, no, I do not believe that any buck would reject her because she has a missing leg. When she comes into her estrus period, a buck doesn't care whether she has three legs or four, so long as her good legs can support the buck's weight long enough for copulation to take place. And because the copulation process in deer is only a matter of 10 to 15 seconds, I do not believe that this would be a problem either.

Q: On the evening of December 4, 1997, a local TV news station reported that a Prince Georges County, Maryland, deer hunter had killed a buck with six legs. It was also reported that this was not an uncommon occurrence. From the picture of the deer, it appeared that the deer could have been 1½ to 2½ years, based on the size of his rack.

My question is: Have you ever heard of a deer having six legs, and if so, is this common? C. F., Freeland, Maryland

A: Despite what the TV reporter said, six-legged deer are virtually unheard of—or at least I have never seen or heard of one. In a carnival I once saw a six-legged chicken, and I've seen pictures of a six-legged calf. A six-legged deer? Never.

Q: I hunt on leased land in Osage County in Oklahoma. I don't know if you have ever photographed in Oklahoma, but the deer are rather large. Each year I see plenty of 8- and 10-point bucks.

I have a couple of questions for you. Last year my father killed a nice 8-point buck. When we took him to the check station, the men said he was 9½ years old. I know that the teeth wear with age; I was wondering if this is due to food, or if the teeth are just brittle and chip. If it is caused by food, would the deer in less populated areas have more worn teeth because they eat more? I would think that deer in overpopulated areas, which don't eat as much, wouldn't have as much tooth wear.

Also, when I was at the Bass Pro Shop in Springfield, Missouri, I saw albino deer. I was wondering what caused this, and if you have ever seen one and photographed it. They have to be very rare.

B. L., Tulsa, Oklahoma

A: You and your dad must hunt in an area that does not get much hunting pressure. Nine and a half years of age, while not impossible, is most unusual. Only about 1 percent of white-tailed bucks ever live to be five years old. In my home state of New Jersey, about 85 percent of our bucks are killed when they are 16 to 18 months old.

The teeth wear down; they seldom chip and break. Deer teeth are so hard that they will knock the edge off the finest steel knife if you hit them while skinning.

The most common method of aging deer in the field is by gauging tooth wear on the bottom jaw's rear molars, the method used at the check station to which you took your deer. This method was developed and refined by Jack Tanck and C. W. Severinghaus of the New York State Conservation Department. Using known-age deer that had been fed natural browse allowed them to develop the tooth-wear charts that are now used by most game departments. It was exceedingly important that the deer were fed natural browse; if they had been fed the softer commercial foods, the tooth wear would have been less pronounced and the charts inaccurate.

Although there are flaws in this system, it is still the best available for field usage and can be done by laymen, you and me. The most obvious variable permitting flaws, besides the care the worker takes in making his measurements, is the composition of the soil. The deer in southern Jersey wear their teeth down faster than do the deer up here in the northwestern part of the state. The southern Jersey soil is almost all sand and every wind stirs it up, depositing it on the vegetation. When the deer eat the leaves of the vegetation, they also eat the abrasive grit, which causes their teeth to wear faster.

If all other factors are equal, the deer in less populated areas would show less wear on their teeth than would the deer in overpopulated areas. A deer ordinarily eats 8 pounds of green vegetation per 100 pounds of body weight in each 24-hour period. Deer in less populated areas would not eat more food than those in overpopulated areas. In cases of starvation, the overpopulated deer would have less available to eat. However, the deer in less populated areas would have more tender, more nutritious food to eat because the vegetation would not be overbrowsed. In overpopulated areas, the deer would be forced to eat larger-diameter, less nutritious, and less palatable foods. The coarser foods would cause more tooth wear

Yes, I have seen and photographed two albino deer. The phenomenon is caused by a genetic deficiency that does not allow for the production of the pigments that create deer's proper coloration. No, I do not know what causes the gene to be faulty.

Q: In reading your book *Deer of North America,* I noticed that the buck pictured on page 71 has whiskers under his chin. I have looked carefully at all the other photos of deer in the book, and I see that some of the deer have these chin whiskers, while it appears that others do not. Do all deer have these whiskers? Why don't they show in all of the photos? What purpose do they serve? Although I have killed a number of deer, I have never really paid attention to these hairs. You don't mention them in the book either. Thanks again for giving us such factual information on deer in such a readable fashion. B. T., Orono, Maine

A: I thank you for the kind words on my work. My entire life has been devoted to the gaining of knowledge that I could pass on to others.

All deer have the chin whiskers, or vibrissae, that you see so clearly on page 71. They are noticeable in some of the other photos, as well. The reason they show up so well in the photo on page 71 is that it is a close-up, and most of the other photos are taken at a greater distance. The conditions under which I took the various photos also have a bearing on whether the whiskers show prominently or not. I usually use a long telephoto lens when photographing deer. Long telephotos have a very shallow depth of field—the actual area that is in very sharp focus—and because I usually focus on the deer's eyelashes or the hair in its ears, the chin whiskers may be slightly out of focus and so less noticeable.

If you look on page 184, you will see a photo of a maned deer taken by my good friend Richard Smith. Forget the mane for a moment and look at the deer's chin whiskers, which are touching the ground. Chin whiskers serve as sensory organs for deer and for all animals. For example, a cat's whiskers stick out as wide as its body width. At night, or even in total darkness, any member of the feline family can stalk quietly through underbrush; the whiskers tell the animal if its body can fit between the brush being encountered. Members of the canine family—dogs, coyotes, foxes, wolves—don't have whiskers long enough to do this because none of them use the stealthy stalking methods of the cat, hence they don't have the need for their whiskers to be that long.

The deer's chin whiskers tell it how far its head is above the ground and when it is going to come in contact with some object. The photo on page 184 shows this clearly.

Q: Last October I took my first deer with a bow, a 123-pound doe. The shot was from a tree stand from 30 yards. It was a perfect broadside shot and, as the doe ran off, I could see the feathers protruding from her chest, a little far back and high for a heart shot, but a good solid lung shot—or so I thought. I waited half an hour, then got down to track her. When I got to where she stood at the shot, I found lots of blood, but it had food in it. After 50 yards I found the front half of the arrow and 50 yards further, the other half. Both halves were covered with food, and nearly every drop of blood had food in it. I was amazed! I have hit many deer in the same spot with shotguns and muzzleloaders and never had one go farther than 40 or 50 yards. I found her three hours later, bedded down on an island in a small lake and wheezing loudly. A 35-yard shot about 2 inches in front of the initial hit finished her almost instantly.

I have tried to figure out why such a lethal shot produced such poor results. The only explanation I can come up with is this: It was early morning when I shot, and perhaps she had just finished gorging herself all night. Her full belly may have displaced her lungs, much the way a person has to loosen his belt to feel comfortable after eating a huge meal. Would the diaphragm stretch enough to allow this to be an accurate explanation? I know deer anatomy fairly well and I am certain that a shot like this would not normally be a gut shot.   D. M., Terre Haute, Indiana

A: When we overeat, we loosen our belts to allow our bellies to expand outward. The same thing would happen to a deer; its belly would expand outward.

The wall of the diaphragm would not allow the stomach to press forward and compress the lungs. If there was food on both parts of the arrow shaft and food in the pooled blood, the deer was gut shot. A lung shot is only 2 or 3 inches away from a gut shot. You did the right thing by tracking the deer and dispatching her. There is a good chance that she would have died and been lost if you had not persevered as you did. You did an excellent job on a bad situation by staying on her trail for three hours.

Q: I shot a doe during New Jersey's late bow season. The deer was not unusual in any other way, but the hooves on just her front feet were striped vertically. They were basically the same brownish color that all deers hooves are, but these had ¼-inch white stripes running down to the hoof tips. Do you have any idea what might cause this?

M. B., Lincoln Park, New Jersey

A: Yes, I have seen this before. It is not a common occurrence, but I have seen it. In my collection I have a pair of hooves (they were given to me) that are all white or pinkish white, with none of the usual color at all. All-white hooves are more common than striped, which I have seen on two occasions.

I have no idea what causes the lack of pigment in the hooves, or why it may affect just two of the hooves instead of all four. Stripes are an even greater puzzle. Frequently, if some part of the body is injured, the hairs that grow back in will be white, but this is caused by nerve damage. It does not appear to be the case with white hooves.

I believe it is a genetic condition, because when you spot one deer with such hooves you're likely to spot others in the same area. I just don't know what causes the white hooves in the first place.

Q: This past season I encountered a reaction from a whitetail unlike any other I've had from gunshot deer.

Carrying a .35 caliber Marlin with a 4X scope, I was apprehensive about shooting at a buck that stepped into full view 110 paces from my standing position. The advantage of a sturdy sapling on which to steady the gun, the fine 7-point head peering straight at me, and the circumstances of having the animal present a broadside shot against a background of snow were enough to overcome my apprehension, and I took the shot. The distance enabled me to hear the strike of the 200-grain bullet. The deer did not flinch, hunch up, or falter, but simply turned his head forward and bounded away in the direction he was previously traveling, with his tail held high and flagging.

My immediate reaction was that I had missed. Because of the snow, however, and the sound I had heard, I trailed after the deer. It was more than 70 yards before I noticed that the prints were becoming sloppy, in contrast to the crispness they originally had. Another 40 yards allowed my first glimpse of blood and the realization that the deer was indeed hit. Although sparse at first, the blood drops eventually led me to the dead buck many yards beyond. Upon field-dressing the deer, I discovered very extensive internal tissue damage. I shuddered when I realized that I would have lost a deer if I had followed my initial thoughts.

Except for those hit along the spinal column, very few deer I've ever shot with gun or bow have dropped on the spot. Because it is more usual that deer will flee, sometimes apparently unharmed, I've come to rely on one sign to determine a hit—the tucked or lowered tail. Although I have seen deer that were unhurt make their escapes with lowered tails, I have never before seen a wounded deer run with its tail up and flagging.

Have you ever known of a seriously injured deer to keep its tail up in flight? R. C., West Islip, New York

A: I have done a considerable amount of thinking about your question, and I cannot come up with a concrete answer.

I have shot between 55 and 60 deer with guns and 5 with a bow. For the life of me, I cannot recall ever seeing a wounded deer run off with its tail held erect. Some of the deer I shot may have done so but, like you, all I can recall clamped their tails down tightly to their bodies.

I commend you on following up your deer to make sure that you either hit him or else missed him completely. I urge all hunters to make every effort to ascertain whether they actually hit the deer or not. All too often, when a deer doesn't drop in its tracks, jump like a bucking bronco, or clamp its tail down, the hunter assumes that he missed *and doesn't check it out*.

When possible, a deer that has been shot at should be tracked for at least ½ mile. I fully realize that it is very difficult to do so, but we must retrieve more of the game we hit.

I have lost wounded deer. I lost the largest deer I ever hit with an arrow when a cloudburst moved in right after I hit him. At the time I was a ranger at a scout camp and the next morning I combed the area with the help of three scout troops, about 60 boys, all to no avail. So I know from personal experience how easy it is to lose deer, but I also know the effort must be made. We owe it to the game we hunt.

The average deer has 7 pints of blood and must lose 3 pints before it will collapse from blood loss. That's a lot of blood, and it takes a large hole to facilitate the blood flow.

Q: Enclosed you will find a portion of the New York State *Big Game Regulations Guide*. It describes how to tell the difference between a doe and her fawns. Most of this article is very informative. However, I question the statement that a doe is usually the lead deer in a group and that fawns usually follow her!

I bow- and gun hunt in the southern-tier portion of New York and have found that about 70 percent of the time, the button buck leads the family group, particularly during bow season. The doe seems very content to follow her offspring. Thank you.   T. C., no town given

A: The information given on the New York State tip sheet was very good. The characteristics for an adult doe are as follows:

1. Body longer than tall (rectangular shape)

2. Long neck

3. Eyes and nose look small

4. Muzzle looks long

5. Usually lead deer in group

Here are the characteristics for a six- to seven-month fawn:

1. Body about as long as tall (square shape)

2. Short neck

3. Eyes and nose look large

4. Muzzle looks short

5. Usually following doe

I'm sorry, but I have to go along with New York on all points.

The body being longer than it is tall will also be a good characteristic for distinguishing an old buck from a young one if they don't have antlers. Not only that, but an old buck's body will look longer and also deeper than that of a young buck.

The long neck is something I really hadn't considered before, but it stands to reason that the adult's body proportions are correct while the fawn's are still growing. This is particularly true of the muzzle. A six- to seven-month fawn's muzzle is very short because it hasn't lengthened yet to accommodate the last two molars. The first molars are erupting through the skin, but the rear two are not even in place. The second molar is about ⅜ inch long, while the third molar is about ⅞ inch. The fawn's jawbones have to lengthen another 1½ inches.

I would say that about 90 percent of the time, the doe is in the lead. It is true that buck fawns are more precocious and run about more than female fawns do. When the deer are feeding in a field, the button buck may run about and feed wherever he wants to. But when they are on the move, it is Mom who decides where they are going to go and leads them there.

Note the difference between the length of the doe's muzzle and those of her six-month-old fawns.

Q: Could you shed some light on what happens after a deer is shot (especially bow shot), but not mortally wounded? Obviously, many variables will affect the deer's response but, generally speaking, what do you feel are some of the things that take place? For instance, do they bed down for long periods of time? Do they go off on their own? Will they be seen in the same areas again?

I know this question doesn't have any cut-and-dried answers, but it is a topic I have never seen discussed in any publications. Thank you.

B. Z., Middletown, New Jersey

A: The controversy over whether to follow a wounded deer or to sit and wait a spell is one that has raged for years. There are different circumstances in every case, but I belong to the school that believes in following the wounded deer at once.

As I have noted, deer have basically the same amount of blood as we humans do, 7 pints. It takes a loss of 3 pints for the deer to bleed to death. Blood begins to coagulate, or clot, upon hitting the air. A deer that is kept running will be farther from where you shot it, but it may go down for good sooner if those 3 pints get pumped out.

The old idea of waiting 15 to 20 minutes or more for a deer to stiffen up just doesn't work. Deer that are wounded severely often bed down because they are sick from the shock of the wound and the loss of blood. The usual treatment for shock is to stop the flow of blood and keep the patient still and warm. When a deer beds down, it is basically doing the same thing. By not moving, it gives the blood a chance to coagulate. By lying down, it is keeping still; it will also be warmer, as less of its body is exposed to the air. The deer is instinctively doing what we are taught to do.

A deer reacts differently when hit in various parts of the body, but nothing is set in stone. A deer with its heart blown apart may run flat out for several hundred yards, or it may drop within a few feet. I have found that it makes a tremendous difference whether the deer was calm and still when shot or if it had been spooked and pushed. An alarmed deer will have adrenaline coursing through its system, and this will allow it to keep moving even after it is clinically dead.

Many deer will jerk their tail upright when shot, but then clamp it down tightly if they run. A deer that is knocked off its feet by the shocking power of the missile will often bound up and run into trees or heavy cover before dropping again. A deer that has been hit in the paunch area may hump its back when hit and then take off. Unless some vein or artery has been severed, a paunch-shot deer will probably recover.

A lightly wounded animal may keep to trails because it is easier going; a badly wounded animal will just try to get away in a more direct line. In hilly areas, most wounded deer will head downhill, because it requires less exertion. Wounded deer often head toward water—not to drink, but because the cover is usually more dense in wet areas, giving them a better chance to hide. Wet areas are also usually at lower altitudes.

If not pushed, a deer will get all the "bed rest" possible. When it does move it will be to drink, because any wound inflames the body, and drinking will help cool the deer. Most wounded deer will not move to feed, but this is usually of little consequence: Deer generally have enough body reserves to go without food for a considerable period of time.

A deer that has been wounded may avoid the actual spot where it was wounded for as long as its wound reminds it. Deer seldom leave their home ranges once they have established them, because only on familiar terrain do they feel safe. Even if it has been wounded, over time, the deer will return to its old haunts if no additional danger or pain reinforces its memories.

Q: This past Easter weekend I was walking in the woods near my home in Hawley, Pennsylvania. I saw a number of deer, but one old doe looked like she had a bad case of the mange. Most of the hair from her neck was gone, but the skin did not look crusty. She was apparently otherwise in good shape physically. Her belly was swollen from the fawns she was carrying. We have had a fairly easy winter here in northeastern Pennsylvania, and although we had a couple of cold spells, there was almost no snow; the deer could move about freely. Did that doe have a case of the mange?

T. O., Hawley, Pennsylvania

A: I have gone through several dozen deer books and nowhere did I find any reference to mange in deer. I can't say that deer do not get mange, I can only say I have never seen it. I have, on many occasions, seen deer with gobs of hair missing from their necks and bodies, but this has always occurred in the spring, just prior to the annual shedding of the winter coat.

Many times the dead hair seems to be an irritant to the deer and they pull it out. However, when the hair is missing from a deer's neck, it must have been removed by another deer, because a deer can't reach its own neck. Deer frequently engage in mutual grooming, licking and removing ticks from each other's necks. Deer will also eat the hair that they remove from their own or from other deer's bodies. They actually may be getting some sort of trace minerals from the dead hair that are beneficial to them. On rare occasions the deer form hair balls that are smooth, compact masses called bezoar or beazle stones. These stones seem to result from the action of the stomach. Whereas the bulk of the hair is indigestible, the stones continue to grow slowly.

Occasionally deer will have a heavy infestation of lice on their bodies and, in their attempts to get rid of the itching insects, will eat or scratch the hair from their bodies. However, you said that this doe was in good condition, so I doubt that her hair loss was caused by lice. Usually, such parasites as lice become rampant only on emaciated, weakened deer. It is thought that a healthy deer keeps the numbers of lice low by exuding a sort of repellent through the skin with the hair.

I believe the deer you saw had just started her annual shedding of her winter hair early.

Q: I found a deer leg in a state park whose hoof was curled and overlapped. Is this a characteristic of old age, or is it an abnormality? Can a deer walk with its hoof in this condition? C. M., Wilmington, Delaware

A: From the photo you have enclosed, I would say that the deer's upper foot or leg was so badly injured that the hoof was carried entirely off the ground. I can see no sign of wear to show that the hoof was making contact with the ground. It seems to be the result of a severe traumatic injury.

Deer hooves, like our finger- and toenails, grow constantly throughout the animal's life. Constant contact with the ground keeps them worn down.

The ski-tipped hooves of this white-tailed buck are caused by the buck not walking on the tips as he should.

Credit: Marilyn Maring

A more common occurrence, one found primarily among older animals as a result of age or in young animals as a result of injury, is for the deer to walk upon the sesamoid bones at the rear of its toes instead of on its distal phalanges. When this occurs, it allows the forward tips of the hooves to turn upward. As the hoof continues to grow, the bones take on a ski-like appearance and may grow to be 5 or 6 inches in length. Deer with this condition walk with a very stiff, crippled gait.

A friend of mine had a penned buck with this condition. On several occasions, I helped him hold down this buck while he used brush cutters to remove the long, dead hoof material. The removal of this extra hoof growth improved the buck's walking ability for only a short time, though. Because we hadn't corrected the basic condition, the hoof would grow back again.

One animal, the sitatunga of the African marshes, has hooves that grow to be 4 inches long. Here the elongated hooves provide additional support for the animal's weight, allowing it to walk in the soft mud without sinking in as deeply as would a sharp-hooved creature. These antelope seldom, if ever, walk on solid ground, so their hooves are not exposed to wear.

Q: I have often wondered if deer are able to see better than humans during foggy weather. I know that the rods and tapeta in their eyes allow them to see better than we can at night. Do they also help them see better than us during fog?　　　　　　　　　　　　　　　　　　　　D. W., Wise, Virginia

A: Deer are able to see better than we do under any conditions; they just don't see the full color spectrum. A deer's eyesight in the middle of the day is better than most of ours because they don't read or watch television constantly.

Many people believe that, because deer can see so much better at night than we can, we must be able to see better than deer in the daytime. Not true. And the deer definitely see much better than we do under foggy or any other low-light conditions.

Q: I was hunting late December in the eastern panhandle of West Virginia. The last day of muzzleloading season I came upon a gentleman with a nice-sized doe. I noticed that the area under her jaw was very enlarged. It appeared that the musks were swollen or extremely overdeveloped. Do you have any explanation for this?　　　　E. G, Fredericksburg, Virginia

P.S. Are there any glands that could taint the meat once you've gotten a deer?

A: The condition you saw is known commonly as lumpy-jaw. Scientifically it is called elaeophorosis, associated with the arterial worm called *Elaeophora schneideri*. It is caused by the impaction of food below the gum line on the outside of the deer's jaw. The deer cannot get the food out and, as more food accumulates, the skin of the jaw is stretched even larger, so more food impacts.

This can occur in deer of any age but it is more common in older does. Most bucks are shot before they get this old.

Many deer, as well as elk and sheep, are infected with arterial worms, but they do not seem to be a great detriment. The relationship between the worms and the impaction is not clearly understood, but it seems to be that a heavy infestation of worms weakens the arterial walls in the deer's jaw, allowing the skin to stretch slightly. This then sets up a vicious cycle of allowing impaction, which causes more stretching, allowing even greater impaction. Older deer have more parasites than younger deer.

I do not know of any fatalities to deer caused by this condition. I do know that it is not transmittable to man, and that the meat of the infected deer can be eaten.

The parasites are transmitted from deer to deer by the common horsefly, which also acts as an intermediate host.

There are a number of glands that must be removed from a deer's carcass so that they don't taint the meat. Care in dressing out your deer, and in the butchering process, should eliminate all of these problems.

The largest external gland that may taint the meat is the tarsal, or hock, gland. When I first started deer hunting, some old-timers cautioned me to make sure I removed the hock gland as soon as I shot my deer. It soon became obvious to me that if the gland doesn't taint the meat while the deer is alive—and it doesn't—it isn't going to taint the meat once the deer is dead. What probably gave rise to this belief is that if the tarsal gland is handled in skinning or butchering the deer, some of its scent can be transferred to whatever meat is handled.

In dressing out the deer, try to avoid breaking the bladder. If you do break it, just wash out the pelvic region; the urine should cause no problems.

In butchering, I always bone my meat, removing all fascia, bones, fat, glands, and so on. If you leave the bones in the meat, make sure you remove the prescapular gland that is buried in the fat right in front of the scapular, or shoulder, blades. On the hind legs, right in front of the hams and just above the joint between the femur and the tibia is the popliteal gland. Both of these glands are about 1 inch in diameter and grayish green in coloration. If not removed, they will impart a bad taste to the meat.

Q: I am a pretty successful deer hunter. I shot a doe in Wisconsin in 1990, and that deer's hide was light brown. I shot a spike buck in 1989, and that buck's hide color was a dark grey—like a swamp buck. My first buck, in 1981, was a 6-pointer. His hide was a dark brown. What causes a buck's hair to be a certain color? Second, does a buck's or doe's hair color change from year to year? In other words, if a doe or buck is dark gray this year, can it be (say) light brown next year?   K. M., Kenosha, Wisconsin

A: Basically, a deer's color is the same from year to year at the same time of year.

There is a wide range of deer colors, even in the same area, and part of this is due to genetics. On the average, deer found in more open country tend to have lighter-colored coats than do those inhabiting dark conifer forests and dense cedar swamps. Gloger's Rule states that, among warm-blooded animals, dark pigments are most prevalent in warm, humid habitats. I must add that dark coloration also tends to prevail in forest regions. This holds true for most species, not just deer. Just check the conditions under which you find red or gray ruffed grouse.

The winter coat of all deer becomes lighter in color just before it is shed in May. Exposure to the sun bleaches the color out of the hair, and deer lie out in the sun at every opportunity during the cold days of winter and early spring.

A whitetail's summer coat doesn't fade much at all, because the deer give it very little exposure to the sun. To escape the heat of summer, the deer usually remain hidden in the shade all day, coming out only after the sun has set and lost its strength.

Q: On page 55 of your book *Whitetails,* a fellow asked a question regarding the spots of our North American deer compared to those of the deer in Asia. I recently saw a documentary on the zebra of Africa that commented on the stripes. It seems that they act as a camouflage of sorts. When a lion or other predator tries to single out one zebra in a herd, all those striped animals running together makes it nearly impossible for the predator to pick out one specific prey. I was thinking that maybe the spots of the fallow and axis deer could serve the same purpose.

A: Since I wrote about the spotted deer in *Whitetails,* I have had the opportunity to do a lot more research on deer and zebras.

Concealing coloration is known as cryptic coloration, and one of the best examples is the spotted pattern of fawns. When fawns are hiding in the leaves of the forest floor, the sunlight coming through the trees casts a dappled pattern on the ground, and the fawns' spots match that dappling.

Getting back to the zebra, I have always been amazed at how black-and-white striping allows an animal to blend in with a brown background in the early-morning and late-evening light. The striping loses its effectiveness in the middle of the day, but it's not as important at that time because most predators don't hunt then. Biologists claim that zebras' striping also makes them more difficult to see at night, but I can't prove this.

Your theory that the striping makes it difficult for a lion to pick out a single zebra from the herd is absolutely correct. This is the basic premise of herding. As the herd animals run, they try to get into the center of the herd. The animals are constantly changing position within the herd, making it more difficult for a predator to concentrate on an individual.

Both axis and fallow deer are more apt to be in herds than are our native deer. It is true that our deer may concentrate in food areas, but basically the females stay in small family groups, while the males may be with one or several companions. The spots on the axis or fallow deer may play a part in their defense, as they run from danger in a herd.

Our white-tailed deer is as much a creature of the woodlands as the axis deer is, and you would think that a spotted coat would be advantageous for both for the same reason that fawns are spotted. However, the natures of the two species are quite different. Whereas the axis deer is more inclined to run when danger approaches, the white-tailed deer is a skulker and prefers to remain hidden unless forced to run. Biological studies have proven that most whitetails escape from hunters by merely staying put—they hide and let the hunter walk by.

Our white-tailed deer have the advantage of having two coat changes a year. In summer all whitetails have a light russet red coat that blends in well with the ripening grasses and other vegetation. They only keep this red coat for about three months, June, July, and August; their winter coat starts growing in late August. For five to six months out of the year, from October through March or early April, most vegetation has shed its leaves. Brushland and woodland are a basic gray, which matches whitetails' brownish gray coloration. Although you may see a wide variety of color shading in just one deer herd, basically the deer of the dark forests will have the darkest coats, while the deer of the more open areas will have lighter shades of gray and brown.

Q: I need to know more where the deer's vitals exactly lie in the rib cage. I bowhunt, and sometimes I make direct, downward shots; if I don't hit the spine, the deer is usually lost. The broadside shot is the best, but not always possible. Some deer get way too close, and I wind up shooting at them and missing. This upsets me very much. I practice and practice with my bow and I'm very confident in my shooting and hunting, but my biggest problem is when the deer get within 10 feet of the tree I'm in. I am usually about 12 feet high, and I can't seem to figure out this type of shot. I don't know what is going wrong; sometimes I hit the spine and drop them. Other times I hit right between the shoulders and lose them.

L. F., Carlyle, Indiana

A: When you are shooting straight down on a deer, you only have about a 10-inch target to hit. Your best shot is hitting the spine which, as you say, drops the deer in its tracks. If you are hitting the deer between the shoulder blades, you should also be hitting the lungs. You say that you lose the deer when you hit them there, and the only thing I can think of is that your arrow is not coming out through the bottom of the chest cavity, so you are not getting a blood trail to follow. If you are missing the spine, but hitting the rib cage, your arrow has only two ribs to go between or to cut off. It may be that you are not using a strong-enough bow, and I would recommend a minimum of 50-pound pull. With the fantastic broadheads available today and a 50-pound bow, you should be able to get that arrow to come out the bottom side of the deer to leave a blood trail. Whether you can track the animal or not, a deer hit through the lungs is going to die.

CHAPTER

5

Management

The concept of wildlife management, and in particular the management of deer, is constantly changing as circumstances dictate. In the first part of the 1900s, all efforts were directed at bringing deer back to areas where they had been eliminated. In the middle of the 1900s, with deer gaining toeholds in much of their former range, management objectives switched to increasing the number of deer in those areas. Better law enforcement, more research, and more funding were the orders of the day. Building the deer herds up to the carrying capacity of the land was the goal.

By the latter part of the 1900s, researchers had come to realize that deer are far more adaptable than was previously believed. In many areas, the carrying capacity of the land had been exceeded. In fact, many areas had too many deer. A new phrase, *cultural carrying capacity,* was introduced into the mix. As more deer came to reside on private land than on public land, the factor that determined how many animals could be supported on that land was how many deer private land-owners would tolerate. Many states have consequently had to liberalize both their hunting seasons and their regulations. Biologists know how to manage the wildlife they have; they now have to educate the public so that proper management can be implemented.

Q: We have a hunting camp in north-central Pennsylvania. Like other hunters, we are interested in getting the biggest bucks possible.

However, food for deer is scarce in this area because there aren't many farms.

We figure our only alternative is to provide mineral supplements. Is it better to use mineral blocks or granulated minerals?

Have you had any experience with supplements? If so, what do you use, and where do you get it?

B. W., State College, Pennsylvania

A: I cannot compare the granulated mineral supplements to the mineral blocks because I have never used blocks.

For the past 13 years, I have purchased and used granulated supplements. I use Deer-Lix, which is manufactured by the Martin Manufacturing Company (Hephzibah, GA 30815; call Keith Stroud at 706-592-9004 for details). I add red salt to the supplements and simply pour the mixture into holes in the ground.

I prefer granulated supplements because they provide more minerals than a single block and, when dissolved, saturate the soil, which the deer also eat.

No matter which method you choose—granulated or block supplements—any mineral supplement you can provide the deer will help them.

Several companies offer mineral supplements. To find out more about their products, look for their advertisements and write to them.

Q: I returned from the air force seventeen years ago to the house I was born in. Coyotes have taken over the area. I cut wood part time in the winter. I take a walk in the woods every Sunday afternoon after church. I have more than 400 acres that I wander and hunt over. I've built a few miles of truck roads. I can drive them all and see almost no tracks except coyotes. Sometimes I see a deer or two, but I almost never see a rabbit or small game. The coyotes have cleaned up all the small stuff.

One winter I found the hair from five different deer that were killed by coyotes in the small area where I cut wood.

I also haven't found a deer antler in 10 or 12 years. I guess the coyotes must eat them, too. I used to find several a year and some old mouse-chewed ones, but nothing anymore.

I live on Frenchman's Bay, across from Acadia National Park, and I've seen coyotes on the lawn and coyotes after deer on the mud flats out front.

What's going to happen to the deer?

Last fall I shot the 10th deer of my lifetime but only after 3½ weeks of hunting every day.

J. D., Ellsworth, Maine

Coyotes are major predators on white-tailed fawns.

Credit: Len Rue Jr.

A: The coyote controversy is a pot that constantly boils. I read every report that I can find by the state game departments. The conclusions are both pro and con. I talk to men like Joe Taylor and Bob Avery, who have lived with, studied, and hunted deer all their lives and whose opinions I greatly value. I spend considerable time afield myself.

My conclusion is that the eastern coyote and its western counterpart are the most intelligent wild animals in the country today. In areas where the coyote population is high, their predation can have a limiting effect on the deer herd. In areas where the coyote population is high and the deer population low, the coyotes will further reduce the deer population until the coyote population has to decrease because the lack of sufficient food will cut down litter size or inhibit reproduction completely. By the time this happens, the deer population will be extremely low and most of the buffer species, such as rabbits, hares, and grouse, will be almost wiped out. I personally have seen red fox populations decline drastically whenever coyotes move into a new area. In areas where the deer population is high and the coyote population low, the coyotes may take enough deer to prevent the destruction of the deer's range.

Do I think that the coyote is or will be a major predator of deer? You bet I do!

My friend Joe Taylor has a 400-acre tract of land up against the Blue Ridge Mountains here in New Jersey. Joe leases the land to a hunting club each year. He has seen the deer herd decline in his area since coyotes have moved in.

Bob Avery has several thousand acres of land up on the edge of New York State's Adirondack Mountains. For years his family operated a large hotel that catered to hunters during the hunting season. Since coyotes have become numerous, the deer herd has plummeted. I fully realize that the deer herd had to decline in the area naturally, with or without coyotes, because there is very little lumbering going on and the forests are going back into the climax stages.

But Bob also has a 500-acre fenced-in area in which he feeds a captive herd. Because of the quantity and quality of the feed he provides for the deer, the stages of forest regrowth should have no direct bearing on his herd. Coyotes have gotten into his pen and, in some years, killed his entire fawn crop.

I want to see no animal exterminated and, in the case of the coyote, that would be an impossibility. For the past 50 to 60 years, federal predator control men have killed 80,000 to 100,000 or more coyotes annually with no apparent reduction in their numbers. I do believe that, in some areas, more hunting and trapping of coyotes should be encouraged to help control their population.

You mentioned that you are finding fewer shed antlers than previously. You also stated that you had to hunt 3½ weeks before you killed your buck. Obviously you are finding a lot fewer shed antlers because there are fewer bucks in your area now that coyotes have moved in.

You tell of cutting wood on your land, and I don't know if it's just for firewood or if some goes for pulp or timber. At least you are constantly opening up some of the forest to regeneration, which will provide good deer habitat—and every little bit helps. Because you control your land, it is not being overhunted.

I am convinced that your problem is the coyote.

Q: I was introduced to hunting by tagging along with my father at the age of seven. I shot my first deer this year in our peach orchard. It was a large, four- to five-year-old doe.

I've read your books *The Deer of North America* and *The World of the White-Tailed Deer*. I've been very interested in hunting since I was introduced to it.

I've learned a lot from your books, like the feeding patterns in our area. That is unfortunate for us since we own a farm with 15 acres of apple trees and vegetables. It seems like the deer never stop eating our apples.

Deer know where every fruit tree is located in their home range.

Last year, my father shot a very nice 9-pointer in our apple orchard. He was close to 200 pounds.

I've got one question. Do deer eat peaches if they're hungry enough?

R. R., Blairstown, New Jersey

A: *Yes,* and the deer don't have to be very hungry to eat peaches. All they need is the opportunity. However, they do not eat peaches as readily as they do apples; nor do they browse the trees the way they do with apples.

Q: In your excellent book *The Deer of North America,* you refer to aspen as a poor deer food and don't include it in the list of seasonal food preferences.

It is my understanding that, in Michigan at least, aspen is an extremely important deer food. Which is correct?

Also, I have read in several publications that the largest bucks will be found at the highest elevations in a given area. This seems to be true in the area I hunt, even though the difference in elevations is only 200 to 300 feet over a distance of several miles. Is this due generally to higher elevations being less accessible to hunters (not the case where I hunt), or do bucks change their home range after age 1½ to 2½? We seem to have far more spikes and crotch-horns at the lower elevations where there is seemingly better habitat, and we often pass up these deer in the hope they will stick around and grow; yet this does not seem to be happening. Thank you.

R. S. C., Milford, Michigan

A: Back in 1959, the Michigan Department of Conservation put out an excellent little book titled *Michigan Whitetails* by David H. Jenkins and Ilo H. Bartlett, illustrated by Oscar Warbach.

I'm quoting from the book now:

There are three classes of deer food—preferred, good and stuffing. The preferred foods are those that sustain deer better than all others. Ground hemlock, white cedar, red osier dogwood and red maple are good examples of this class.

Some second choice or good foods are hard maple, aspen, jack pine and white birch. These will not sustain deer as well as the preferred species.

The "stuffing" or "starvation" species—balsam, red oak, cherry, spruce, tag alder and tamarack—will not keep a deer going unless they get some of the better foods, too. A deer will starve with a full belly of pine, balsam or spruce. In fact, most starved deer have a full belly—of the wrong food.

I did not list aspen as a seasonal food preference because it is not a preferred food. Jenkins and Bartlett listed the aspen as a good food; some research has listed it as a poor food. It is not a stuffing food. The deer in my area eat very little of it.

Aspen often figures prominently in a deer's diet not because it is a preferred food but because the preferred foods have been exterminated by overpopulation and overbrowsing. This is what skews so many research reports in which observers list the foods they see deer eating. The deer being watched may eat a lot of aspen because there is little else available. Aspen has another factor on its side: It is a pioneer tree, one of the first to reproduce itself and to start reforestation after a fire, clear-cutting, or farm abandonment. This is particularly true in Michigan, Wisconsin, and Minnesota. It is an important deer food in Michigan because you have so much of it.

Much caution must be taken with food studies. In my area of northwestern New Jersey, I have never seen a deer browse on the twigs of spicebush. It is a known fact that the aromatic oil that gives the spicebush its name reduces the production of bacteria and protozoans in deer's

Large bucks like this are extremely wary, and seek out areas where hunters and predators generally don't go.

paunches. Yet one report I read from Massachusetts listed spicebush as a good deer food.

Yes, in general I would say that the larger bucks will be found at the higher elevations (southern swamplands are an exception). Larger bucks are found wherever something prevents hunters or predators from being there. Only by having a chance of living longer will they have a chance of getting bigger.

The smaller bucks that you see, and take, in the more accessible areas haven't been exposed to hunting pressure; they haven't gotten enough smarts to get out of such areas. They were killed before they moved (or realized they should move) to the more inaccessible areas.

Q: You have mentioned deer eating tartarian honeysuckle bushes. There are two types I know of—pink and white. Does the color matter? And would it be worthwhile to plant them for the deer? Are you familiar with another type called Morrow spreading honeysuckle? I would like the spreading type better than the bushes. Plus, can you recommend any other types of bushes or fruit-bearing plants besides apple and pear trees? I've already planted a good many of those. Any information will be greatly appreciated. R. H., Aberdeen, Mississippi

A: It really doesn't pay to plant shrubs for deer. If it is something they like to eat, they will overbrowse it and kill it. I planted hundreds of tartarian honeysuckle bushes on my property so birds could eat the berries. The deer killed all but a dozen or so. You have to fence the shrubs to let them grow higher than a deer can reach or they will be wiped out right from the start.

Tartarian honeysuckle produces such loads of berries that the weight bends the bushes down. Then deer decimate them. This is true with all types of shrubs or trees that deer favor.

Rather than plant shrubbery, you would get far more food value for the deer by planting bird's-foot trefoil, a legume. Check with your county agent to see which variety will do best in your area. This trefoil is very high in protein, reseeds itself, and stands up well to heavy deer usage. I can think of no better deer food for the months of March through September. It is a good deer food year-round, but the deer do need the carbohydrates of corn or acorns from October through February.

Q: I hunt 160 acres of private land. There are lots of mature oak trees but, in the last few years, they have not produced as well as they did in the past. We have tried lime and fertilizer, but with little success.

What I would really like to get my hands on is information on how to manage this land better for wildlife. I know that cutting mature poplar trees might help, and also that creating more understory through planting would be beneficial.

I enjoy these projects as much as hunting. Could you offer some resources that could benefit the wildlife and land management? Thanks.

W. L., Harrison Township, Michigan

A: An oak has to be about 15 years old before it begins to bear acorns. It is considered a mature tree when it reaches 30 years of age.

You did not mention what kind of oak trees you have on your land but, if they are white oak, the deer's favorite, they usually produce a good crop every third year. Black oaks are more productive, and red oaks produce a good crop almost every year. A wet year often causes all oaks to produce better crops.

With your use of both lime and fertilizer, you are doing just about everything you can to feed the trees. You might want to take an iron bar or pipe about 1 inch in diameter and make a circle of holes about 6 to 8 feet

The acorns and leaves shown are: upper left, red oak; right, white oak; lower left, chestnut oak.

out from, and around, the trunks of the trees. Then fill these holes with fertilizer. When the fertilizer is scattered on the top of the ground, a certain amount of it may wash away in heavy rain. All of the fertilizer in the holes will go down to the trees' roots, though. I heat my home with wood and use the ashes as fertilizer for my oak trees.

I would take out all of the mature poplars, because they are contributing nothing to the deer. Opening up the canopy will allow the sunlight to sprout a lot of new vegetation, most of which will be excellent deer food. You won't have to plant understory; it will grow in naturally as soon as you let in the sunlight.

Again, I suggest you contact your local county agent for more advice on managing your woodland for wildlife. Many of the state game departments also have experts who can advise you on the best way to optimize the deer-carrying capacity of your land.

Q: Why is it that when the snow had established itself on the ground (December 1992), the deer suddenly stopped eating out of my feeder filled with corn?

I am somewhat alarmed since this is the first time this has occurred in years.

I sometimes spike the corn with molasses, which they seemed to love before. I like molasses because it its energy-boosting properties, perfect for deer at this time—or is it?

I don't hunt them here; it's my backyard. How can I attract them back to stay? What options do I have?   P. F., Plover, Wisconsin

A: You didn't mention how much snow you have in your area, but deer greatly curtail their travel when there is more than 12 inches on the ground. Eighteen inches of snow will be up to the brisket on young deer; 24 inches makes it difficult for even adults bucks to travel.

However, snow is probably not the problem. Here in New Jersey, December 1992 was the coldest December in a long time. The temperature dropped to 10 degrees on many days, and hard winds created a windchill factor of −25. The cold was not the major factor either; the wind was.

If you have cold temperatures and strong winds with or without snow, the deer will not come in.

A deer's hollow winter hair can allow it to withstand extremely cold weather with no loss of body heat. However, strong winds blow the cold through the hair to the body below. No matter how much the deer need food, they will seek shelter rather than food when the weather turns cold and windy.

If you have been having that kind of weather, there is nothing short term that you can do to keep the deer coming in. Long term, you could get the deer to come in if you would plant an area of (say) 200 by 200 feet with a solid mass of evergreens to give the deer shelter. You can create wintering areas for the deer that they will utilize. Then by putting your feeder on the edge of the shelter or just inside, you will hold the deer.

Summer deer hair is on the left, winter hair in the center, and unusually woolly winter undercoat hair on the right.

Yes, adding molasses is a great idea. Deer get to love it, and they do benefit from it. See what you can do about creating shelter.

Q: My father and I hunt a small piece of land in Tioga County, Pennsylvania. We are looking for ways to make the property more beneficial to the white-tailed deer in the area. Our ground is only about 8 acres and consists mainly of oak trees. We have tried supplements, salt blocks, and planting small patches of clover with pretty much no results. Could you give me any information or tips on how we could better our land for the deer herd?

W. T., Ben Salem, Pennsylvania

P.S. Our ground is pretty rocky, so planting is tough.

A: The average deer's home range is 1 to 2 square miles, depending on how much food and shelter is available in that area. As there are 640 acres to the square mile, a deer will roam between 640 and 1,280 acres. On good deer range, 20 deer to the square mile is considered the optimum number. On a lot of land there are more deer than that; on a lot of land you'll find far less. That comes out to one deer for every 32 acres on good deer habitat. Tioga County, being in the northern part of the state, is primarily a mountainous, wooded area with a few scattered farms. It is deer country, but it is not the best of habitat.

What I'm saying is that your 8 acres would be just 1/160 of a deer's home range, figured on a square-mile basis; your 8 acres would provide just one-quarter of one deer's diet figured on 20 deer to the square mile. As your area is not the best of deer habitat, these figures are probably too high. What you do with your 8 acres, then, probably won't make that much difference to the deer.

However, that's not saying you shouldn't do anything. Every little bit helps, and you are doing a number of things right. Continue to put out mineral blocks or supplements; the deer need these.

You say that you have planted clover, but you don't say how big an area you have. Instead of clover, which I have always recommended, the latest research from Cornell University in Ithaca, New York has shown that bird's-foot trefoil is a much better planting for deer. It has high in protein, withstands heavy grazing, and lasts longer.

What I suggest is that you contact your county agent for advice on your soil types to determine the amount of lime and fertilizer you should apply. All too few folks take advantage of the expertise of their local county agent. You can produce 20, 30, even 50 times more food for deer on cropland than you can in woodland. Fertilizer and lime will greatly improve your crops and, in turn, your deer. Deer really can't get too much lime.

Having oaks on your land is a godsend. Place fertilizer and lime around the base of the oaks to improve their production as well.

Although you won't see the results for 10 years—or longer if your land has open areas—you might want to plant a copse of evergreens. One hundred Norway spruce trees planted 10 feet apart will cover a piece of ground 100 by 100 feet and provide excellent cover in future years. Plant the evergreens in any hollow you have. Most folks don't realize how important protection from the wind is to a deer in the wintertime.

Keep up the good work; every little bit helps. I hope this book prompts other landowners to also do a little something for the deer we love. Can you imagine the impact if 5,000, 10,000, or more of my readers all put out mineral supplements, lime, fertilizer, crops, and evergreen trees on the land they hunt?

Q: I have two questions about an article I read called "The Antler Pheromone" by Greg Gutschow. In his last paragraph he said, "I try to tell my students the right thing to do is to take fawns. In order to manage wildlife effectively, you have to take from that age group." My questions are: Is this true? And why?   F. D., Bartlesville, Ohio

A: For years I have stated that, if in the fall the predictions are for a bad winter, then bowhunters (in particular) should fill their tags with fawns.

My basis for this is that during a hard winter, with the ever-present specter of starvation, the fawns will be the ones to die first. Even as their body growth slows in fall, fawns will not be able to accumulate as much body fat for winter as adults can, even if they have access to ample food. Because of their shorter legs, fawns will not be able to travel in as deep a snow as the adults, nor will they be able to reach as high to feed upon browse as the adults. Harvesting fawns will save them from the lingering death of starvation and make good use of the meat.

If, through overpopulation, deer have decimated their range, then it is a good game management practice to harvest fawns, does, and bucks right across the board. Only by drastically reducing the total population will the vegetation have a chance to recover. In many areas where the deer population is high, there is absolutely no new forest growth. The trees cannot possibly reseed themselves, because deer nip off each sprout as soon as it leafs out.

In areas where the deer population has not exceeded the carrying capacity of the land, I would not harvest the fawns. You can tell when the carrying capacity has been exceeded because such an area will have a large number of spike bucks. Spikes are a sure sign that there are more deer in the area than there is nutritious food to feed them. Don't shoot the spikes to improve the herd; instead, harvest the fawns, does, and bucks across the board to improve the range, which will improve the herd.

Q: I attended one of your white-tailed deer seminars here in Ohio a year ago and I really enjoyed it. I thought I knew a lot about deer because I have hunted them all of my life, and I am now 56 years old. One thing you said stuck in my mind and I've puzzled over it. You said that in New Jersey a hunter could legally take 22 deer a year. Here in Ohio we have a lot more land and a lot more deer, yet we are only allowed to take one deer. How can a little state like New Jersey, which is largely urbanized, allow so many deer to be taken by just one person?   W. C., Youngstown, Ohio

A: There are a number of different goals in wildlife management, particularly of deer, and the ones that are implemented are chosen to fit the situation.

If a state is trying to reintroduce or build up a deer herd in an area from which they have been extirpated or shot off—or where they never traditionally lived—then all hunting must be banned or only a harvest of bucks allowed. In the past, this has been the basic policy of most states, because the deer were eliminated from most of their former range by the early 1900s.

When a deer herd is well established, it is paramount to remove both bucks and does to keep the herd slightly under the carrying capacity of the land. The taking of bucks only would allow for the herd expansion and, depending on how long it continued, the reduction or even elimination of the deer's food supply. This is what has happened in many states, which is why the laws have been liberalized and the taking of does permitted. Unfortunately, in states whose game departments are run by political appointees or the decisions of professional game managers are subject to approval by such appointees, the best game management programs cannot be instituted. Uninformed public opinion puts pressure on the politicians, who nullify the good the game managers are trying to do.

If you have a good healthy herd that is in balance with your food supply and you want to produce trophy bucks, you must reduce the ratio of does in your herd and protect the younger bucks so that they can grow old enough to produce the large antlers desired. The reduction of the does is imperative, because it takes an abundance of food to produce trophy bucks. Extensive habitat management and improvement may also be needed to increase the food supply.

Even though there may be adequate food, if there is extensive crop damage or a high mortality on the highway because of deer-car collisions, you will have to reduce the entire deer herd across the board regardless of sex or age. The same solution must be implemented where you have extensive damage to homeowners' shrubs, flowers, and gardens in suburban areas. Such aggrieved people don't want more deer, they want relief, and it's spelled *herd reduction.*

No one game management program is ever going to be a solution to all problems, nor will any single program be satisfactory to everyone. To some people, no management program is satisfactory; they prefer to let nature take care of its own problems. This attitude is the most unrealistic and damaging of all. It will lead to both destruction of deer habitat and the decimation of the deer herd. Such people will cause countless deaths through starvation, disease, and stress to the very creatures they profess to love, but know nothing about.

Legalized sport hunting is one of the best game management tools available but, to be used properly, requires extensive education of both hunters and nonhunters. Everyone must realize that a reduction in total deer numbers is a prerequisite to the production of trophy deer. You simply can't have large herds of deer and expect to produce trophy bucks unless

Automobiles kill hundreds of thousands of deer each year in the U.S.

The Deer Hunter's Encyclopedia

you have a superabundance of food. Even if you do have an abundance today, within a year or two the herd numbers will increase, causing the food supply to decrease.

The numbers of the deer on the land must be compatible with the game management program that is instituted.

That is what my home state of New Jersey is trying to do, and I believe is doing very successfully. I know of no hunter who has ever taken 22 deer in one year—or even half that number. It is not realistic to think that every hunter would have the chance to take 22 deer in one year; many of the permits that would be needed are very limited in time and access. New Jersey does produce some trophy deer each year, although 85 percent of the bucks taken are yearlings with minimal antler development. New Jersey does provide sportsmen with more than 100 days of deer hunting per year if they are so inclined. That's more than 100 days to be afield enjoying the out-of-doors, and that is a priceless commodity.

Because of excessive roadkill, crop damage, shrubbery destruction, and deer overpopulation, New Jersey's Game Division is being forced to reduce the number of deer in the state by the means that will be the most satisfactory to all concerned.

Regulated sport hunting is the best management tool that wildlife biologists have to control the deer herd.

Credit: Len Rue Jr.

Q: My question is whether the white-tailed deer has ever been successfully introduced to any continent outside its native North America. Also, could any alien deer introduced to North America displace the whitetail from its current range? M. O., Walled Lake, Michigan

A: Yes, the white-tailed deer has been exported to many other parts of the world successfully. It has had outstanding success in Europe, but that is to be expected because the forest habitat is quite similar to what we have here in North America.

It has done so well in New Zealand—which also has a climate similar to our North Temperate Zone—that it has become a nuisance. The same thing has happened with the red deer that were introduced from Europe into New Zealand. The government employs professional hunters to shoot as many of the deer as possible to prevent the destruction of the habitat by overbrowsing. The deer have prevented natural reforestation of some of the native trees and, by denuding the vegetation, have caused erosion.

There are no counterparts to the white-tailed deer anywhere else in the world because the whitetail is native to just our hemisphere, evolving here.

No, it is exceedingly unlikely that any alien deer could ever be introduced into this country that could displace or replace the whitetail. The whitetail population is now estimated to be more than 25 million animals; the species is constantly increasing and spreading its range. The whitetail has already filled just about every inch in which a deer could survive. Introduced deer just could not stand the competition for the available food.

Q: How many deer can be taken statewide each year without it being detrimental to the herd? B. J., Indianapolis, Indiana

A: Indiana has extremely rich soil and moderate winters. With the exception of a few isolated parks in which no hunting is allowed, there is no overbrowsing. Although snowstorms may be common, the snow does not stay on the ground for extended periods of time, so the deer are not concentrated into yards. The chief limiting factor to deer herd expansion is the lack of protective cover due to the extensive clean farming practices throughout the state. After the standing corn has been harvested, vast areas have no cover at all.

What follows is applicable to most areas of most states where the deer range has not been destroyed by overbrowsing.

A seven-month-old fawn is capable of breeding if it has had a good diet of 16 to 18 percent protein. The percentage of the fawns that breed at seven months varies from almost zero in Vermont (because of the lack of food) to 60 to 80 percent in good feed areas such as Indiana and Illinois. A doe usually gives birth to only a single fawn during her first birthing period, whether she was bred at seven or twelve months of age.

From that time on, if the doe has been on an adequately nutritious diet, she will give birth to twins. Not every doe gives birth to twins, but the average is 1.9 fawns per doe. For practical purposes, then, let us say that she will have twins.

Fawns are born in a ratio that slightly favors the buck, being about 105 males to 95 females. This ratio occurs because, from birth on, buck mortality is naturally higher than doe; hunting increases it further.

Fawn mortality varies greatly from one region of the country to another due to localized conditions such as scarce food resources, bad weather, and heavy predation. Indiana should have very low fawn mortality because none of those three factors is prevalent there.

It has been determined that 25 to 30 percent of a healthy, expanding deer herd can be removed each year without cutting back on the total herd population. Such a removal actually enhances the herd by reducing the competition for food. This allows the remaining deer to breed to their fullest potential, reduces the possibility of overbrowsing, reduces fawn mortality, and will actually allow the herd to expand slightly because annual replacement of deer in such favorable areas will be about 40 percent.

A doe nurses twin fawns.

It was estimated that there were 270,000 deer in Indiana in 1996. Let's use the figure 270,000 just to keep things simple. If you were to take 30 percent of the deer, that means 81,000 could be taken every year. I don't say that 81,000 could be taken by hunters. The figure of 81,000 has to account for the total reduction of the herd by *all* factors.

We have to factor in fawn mortality. As I said, this should be low because of all the favorable conditions in the state.

We have to add in the number of deer killed on the highways, as determined by the actual warden count. A percentage of at least 25 has to be added in to the actual warden count, because at least that many more deer will be hit by cars but not be picked up. Many deer stagger off the roads to die in the fields or woods, where they are not found. Many deer are picked up by people who take them to eat their meat. This practice is now being legalized in many states—as it should be, so that the animals are not wasted. A few deer will also die from natural accidents.

We also have to add in predation, which is hard to substantiate. Predation should not be a big problem in Indiana, although there are some coyotes. Dogs—both household pets and feral—probably account for more deer than coyotes do. There are no other predators in Indiana except man.

The combined hunting take in Indiana in 1996 was 117,729 deer. Those are deer that have been accounted for. The missing numbers are the deer that are killed by poaching. I don't have the estimated numbers on poaching, and I know the state doesn't have the actual figures either. In some states as many deer are taken by poaching as by legal hunters, and in some areas it is even higher. If the legal hunters would do everything they could to prevent poaching, they would be allowed to harvest more deer. Join the Indiana Deer Hunters' "Turn in a Poacher" campaign.

Different states allow their hunters to take different numbers of deer per hunter, based on the estimated deer population and the actual number of hunters buying licenses. Alabama allows one buck per day for 56 days, whereas Pennsylvania allows one buck per year. My own state of New Jersey allows the possibility of 22 deer per year per hunter.

I can't tell you whether your own state of Indiana can allow more than two deer per year. And I can't tell if any of the other states can allow more or less, because I don't have all the figures I need.

You can find out your own state's estimated deer population from your game department. Figure 30 percent of that for your annual take. Add up the state's estimated fawn mortality, estimated predation, actual roadkill by vehicles (adding at least 25 percent to that figure), estimated poaching, and actual hunters' kill, and see how close it comes to equaling that 30 percent allowance. If the total is less than 30 percent of the herd size, you can legitimately request your game department to liberalize the seasons. If you are at 30 percent or higher, the game department is doing its job. And we have to remember that they are on the scene, while we are looking on.

Getting back to what I know is at the heart of your question: Can Indiana allow three deer instead of two? Definitely not.

Q: I took a doe on New Jersey's doe day that had a lot of fat just under her skin as well as in her body cavity. We had a lot of acorns this past fall (1993) and our local farmers' corn crop was also exceptional. I have always heard that, when you have a heavy nut crop, it usually foretells a hard winter. I know that our deer are in good shape right now, but will they continue to be all winter? Can you tell if we are going to have a hard winter by the size of the nut crop? H. L., Somerset, New Jersey

A: I have not found any definite correlation between the size of nut crops and the severity of the winter.

I do know that in the fall of 1993, New Jersey and most of the northeastern states had fantastic acorn crops. Red and black oaks outdid themselves in the acorn production, despite midsummer drought.

Here in New Jersey, we had a wet spring, which allowed all of the vegetation to get a good start on the growing season. By June, the drought had begun. Some of the rolling fields of clover and alfalfa just came to a standstill on growth, although the level fields, with deeper soils, produced good crops.

Any deer with this much fat inside its body cavity can go up to 65 days without eating, and survive.

Ponds, lakes, and the Delaware River were exceptionally low, and many folks lost the water in their wells. Still, this did not seem to affect the deer.

However, not all of the oaks produced acorns. Most of the white oaks, the deer's favorite, did not produce acorns; a few individual trees did, and those that did produced abundantly. There were lots of pignut hickory nuts, but none on the shagbark hickories. I saw no beechnuts, but the beechnut is a very sporadic producer of mast, having about one good year out of five. Walnuts were plentiful. The corn crop was very good; the plants had gotten their roots down far enough to withstand the dry periods between the hard showers of July and August. All told, deer food was abundant.

I dressed out and butchered several deer that fall, and they were in better shape than any I have ever seen. As you mentioned, their entire bodies, just under the skin, were sheathed in fat, a much harder, suet-type fat than is usual. The fat of the back up over the hams and around the tailbone was at least 1 inch thick. Inside the body cavity, just in front of the pelvic girdle, the fat hung like bunches of cherry tomatoes. The fat was so loosely fastened to the back area that I could simply pull these little balls of fat loose. Just behind the junction of the front leg and scapula, and just in front of the back hams, were large triangles of fat. There was even a heavy lacing of fat inside the muscles of the hams, surrounding the blood vessels.

Tests done years ago by the Pennsylvania Game Commission showed that deer this fat would be able to go for as long as 65 days without eating a mouthful of food, and survive.

Q: I have been reading about the different subspecies of deer throughout North America. I was intrigued reading about Key deer. Are they really that much smaller than the deer we have here in North Carolina? Have you seen them? I hope to get to Florida next winter and wondered where the best place would be to see them. I will not be able to get down there before February. Will all of the bucks have shed their antlers by that time? Are they on the same annual cycle as our own deer? I would appreciate any information you can give me.　　　　　　　　　　　H. K., Greensboro, North Carolina

A: There are 17 subspecies, or different types, of white-tailed deer found in North America, north of the Mexican border. Some of the subspecies found on the islands off the coast of South Carolina and Georgia are subspecies only because of the fact that they are isolated on those particular islands. If you had one deer of each of these four subspecies in a pen, you could not tell them apart, and neither could the experts. When you look at a Key deer, though, you don't need to be an expert to know that you are looking at a different deer. Key deer are the smallest subspecies, but they are not really that much smaller than the little Carmen Mountain whitetails found in the

A Florida Key deer buck, our smallest subspecies.

Chisos Mountains of Big Bend, Texas. The Coues deer of Arizona is slightly larger also, but can be distinguished from the Key deer by its larger ears.

The subspecies found in your area of North Carolina is *Odocoileus virginianus virginianus*. An average buck in his prime will stand about 34 to 36 inches high at the shoulder. A really big buck will go 38 inches, but seldom more than that. An average Key deer buck will be 26 to 28 inches high at the shoulder. I know the buck in the photo on this page was a bit bigger than that. I would like to say that he was 30 to 32 inches high at the shoulder, but I can't be sure because I couldn't put my tape measure on him. Tape measures have the habit of shrinking everything; just ask a fisherman. Adult bucks average about 80 pounds in live weight. Coues deer adult bucks stand 31 inches high at the shoulder and weigh about 98 pounds.

Key deer are found only on the Florida Keys. The best place to find them is in the National Key Deer Refuge on Big Pine, Little Pine, Sugarloaf, and No-Name Keys. They are an endangered species with an estimated population of about 300. As an endangered species, no hunting is allowed.

An Odocoileus virginianus *borealis buck, our largest subspecies.*

By 1950 the population had declined to about 50 animals. Given their own refuge and under the protection of the Endangered Species Act, the population rebounded to around 400. Since that time, the deer have been in a steady decline due to land development and increased vehicular traffic. Some years the deer deaths due to auto collisions are around 65 animals, or almost equal to the annual replacement of deer in the herd. Free-roaming dogs also take a toll. The speed limit on the above-named keys is 35 miles per hour and strongly enforced, and still the killing goes on.

No, the Key deer are not on the same annual cycle as most other North American deer. They are a true tropical subspecies; fawns are born in every month of the year. I have been down there in February, and most of the bucks had their polished antlers. I saw no bucks that had cast their antlers, but I did see a couple of bucks that were still in velvet. The best 8-point buck that I saw had a swollen neck, indicating that he was still in the peak of the rut. Because the breeding cycle can continue all year, antler development can be seen in various stages year-round, but from my observations, I would say its peak is in January and February.

Q: I was doing some preseason scouting for deer on a farm that I bowhunt. I was sitting on the edge of an alfalfa field, just sitting, waiting, and watching. I knew that deer fed regularly in this field, and I wanted to see how many bucks there were. There are numerous deer trails leading into the field, which is bordered on two sides by woodland, and I wanted to check out which trails would be the best prospects. I have found that the same deer seem to use the same trails, even when there are numerous other trails they could be using.

I got to the field about 4:30 P.M. and sat with the wind blowing in my face. Fortunately, the woods are on the northern and western sides of the field, so the wind is usually in my favor. I was dressed in camo and sat with my back against a small tree growing in the fencerow.

While I waited, I was amazed at the large number of groundhogs that I saw all over the field. There must have been 8 or 10 of them. I have hunted this area for a number of years, but don't recall seeing that many ground-hogs before. This was in September 1994 and, as I watched the groundhogs through my binoculars, I was fascinated at how constantly they ate. They were real eating machines. My question to you is: Would a high population of woodchucks be detrimental to the deer population, particularly since they both were eating the alfalfa?   B. G., Reading, Pennsylvania

Woodchucks eat a lot of the same foods that deer do.

A: Your question came at a most apropos time. I have just finished doing a very crude survey on the effects of a high groundhog population on the feed available to deer.

I planted a 3-acre field on my neighbor's land with Pilgrim Ladino clover so that I could get good photos of deer feeding in the field. This is the third year since the field was planted and I've never had to mow and take any clover from it. The deer and groundhogs eat it all. I didn't realize how much of the crop the groundhogs got.

I sat out in that field in mid-September and, from where I sat, I could see 13 groundhogs at one time. I have never seen that many groundhogs at once on a 3-acre lot, and it made me wonder just how that could be. The answer was simple when I thought about it: It was the web of life.

The theory behind the web of life is that all things, no matter how insignificant they seem, are attached to and affect all other creatures. We talk about the balance of nature, but nature is seldom, if ever, in balance; it is usually like a pendulum swinging back and forth between the lows and the highs. Things may be in balance at the precise bottom of the arc, but that is only momentary; most of the time is spent between the highs and lows.

Our red fox population is very low right now because it is recovering from an epidemic of rabies. Red foxes are a major predator of groundhogs, effectively keeping their population in check, or balance if you will. With the red fox population low, the groundhog population is high, because the curtailing restraints are gone.

I'm sure that this is what happened in your area as well, because your area had the rabies epidemic one year before we had it in New Jersey.

There are 43,560 square feet to the acre; on 3 acres, that comes to 130,680 square feet. I checked out the area eaten by the groundhogs and discovered that about 50 feet from each major groundhog den, the clover was eaten almost to the dirt. There were 11 major dens in the field and 6 on its border, and I will count all 17 dens because the groundhogs on the border fed farther into the field, away from their dens, than did the groundhogs that had their dens in the field. Each groundhog had decimated about 100 square feet, or 17,000 square feet for all 17 burrows. The groundhogs had consumed at least 7.68 percent of the entire crop, and probably more.

To reduce this loss of top-notch deer food, I shot 9 woodchucks from one spot in 1½ hours, and a friend shot 10 more.

To take it a bit farther, I weighed the stomach contents of some of the biggest 'chucks; they contained between ½ and ¾ pound of green vegetation. This was the afternoon feeding, and I know these same 'chucks had been feeding in the morning. I believe it is safe to assume that the biggest 'chucks, up to 12 pounds in weight, were eating 1 pound of clover per day.

They are always heavy feeders, but in late summer, they respond to mandatory lipogenesis; they must layer fat upon their bodies in order to survive the winter.

A white-tailed deer in the spring and summer eats about 8 pounds of green vegetation per day for each 100 pounds of body weight. Those 19 groundhogs were eating as much food as a doe and her two fawns.

Would a high number of woodchucks limit the number of deer in an area? I doubt it, but they definitely are depriving deer of some highly nutritious food.

I sat out in the same spot in mid-October and saw five more groundhogs from the same spot. I know there are more I haven't seen.

Q: I'm not sure if you will be able to help me on this question. Two years ago I planted about 1½ acres of Ladino clover. This past year I noticed a lot of native grasses, weeds, and thistles taking over. Is there a spray that will kill the weeds and grasses and not harm the clover? I am also concerned about any type of spraying because of the animals, especially deer, ingesting it.   P. S., Gladstone, Michigan

A: I had the same experience. I planted about 2½ acres of Ladino clover and it was an almost pure stand for two years. The third year thistles came in, along with other weeds such as narrowleaf milkweed. The fourth year I had as much weed as clover, and the clover was dying out. This year, the fifth year, I had it plowed and planted with bird's-foot trefoil. I have been told that this will grow heavily enough to keep a lot of the weeds out, and that it will reseed itself. The trefoil I planted has taken a good hold on another field, despite a parching drought last year.

Ask your county agent about the spray. I'm antispray myself and know nothing about them except that I don't ever want to use them.

Q: I have a cabin in the town of Denning, which is in the Catskill Park in New York State.

Before last May (1996), turkey sightings began to decline. We went from having to wait for birds to cross a road to no sightings at all.

Deer sightings were a carbon copy of turkeys. We had seen deer on many occasions, and in several instances, locals were involved in deer-car accidents. Since last May, deer sightings have been few and car accidents involving deer have declined.

The area I had scouted for the upcoming deer season had several rubs and disturbed ground where deer had fed, but no scrapes. On opening day I hunted this area but saw no deer. Whereas in past years gunshots could be heard all day, I only heard three shots this year. During the remainder of the season, I hunted several different areas that I had scouted but, again, saw nothing.

After questioning other hunters, I found that their luck was as bad as mine. Some say they saw bears but not deer. It was obvious that some deer were in the woods, but what happened when the sun came up? With all these hunters in the woods, shouldn't the deer have been moving around?

Rangers said the coyotes were keeping the deer down. Could this be true?   B. R., Brockhaven, New York

A: You have to realize that my answer is based on general assumptions, since I have not been in the Catskill area in a long time. Even if I were there on the grounds, I might not be able to ascertain all the reasons for the decline in the populations of both deer and turkeys.

For starters, let's talk about last winter. I live perhaps 60 to 70 miles, or even less, from the Catskill region. In my home area, we had a total of 93 inches of snow. I did not hear of many deer or turkeys being found dead of starvation. I do know that, although I am seeing as many deer this year as in other years, I am not seeing nearly as many turkeys, nor are they in as many areas. Perhaps the hard winter reduced your deer population, if not directly through starvation then through greatly curtailed fawn production. I realize that most people would not be shooting six- to seven-month-old fawns, but at least you would be seeing them. And you didn't.

Black bears will eat every white-tailed fawn they can find.

Some hunters did see bears, but I have no idea whether it was more or less bears than usual. We are seeing many more bears in my home area, and this has to have an impact on the deer population. Black bears are notorious hunters of white-tailed fawns, just as grizzly bears in Alaska are hunters of moose calves. While the deer population seems stable in my immediate area, I know for a fact that there are not as many deer in the mountains behind my home, which is the main bailiwick of bears.

You say that the park rangers are blaming coyotes for the great reduction in the deer population, and I believe them.

In your scouting, you saw several rubs but no scrapes. The rubs could have been made by bucks moving through the area. I am afraid that the deer population in your area is extremely low; otherwise the hunters would have pushed them out.

Q: My family and I have been hunting a certain farmland woods in northern Indiana for 10 years now. Over the years we have killed a couple of large 10-pointers, many yearling 8- and 6-pointers, mature does, fawn does, and button bucks. When we first obtained permission to hunt the property, it was littered with scrapes, but scraping activity has seemed to gradually taper off; it is now virtually nonexistent. What might this be attributed to?

C. R., Hammond, Indiana

The constant cutting of the brush beneath power lines allows for the regeneration of excellent deer browse.

A: You did not say if you are seeing as many deer now as you formerly did. If you are not seeing as many deer, the cause may be overhunting. You are shooting every age class of deer. You may be putting too much hunting pressure on that particular herd and are slowly, but surely, wiping them out.

Or perhaps the woodland itself has matured and no longer produces the food and shelter that it formerly did. If brush is being cut in some areas, the deer may be migrating there instead.

Perhaps the food crops in the area have been changed so that the entire area is no longer attractive to deer.

If you are seeing as many deer as before but fewer scrapes and rubs, the herd composition has probably changed in favor of does. Where the ratio of adult bucks to does is 1:7 or more, the bucks will not spend as much time advertising their presence. They don't have to.

Q: We have a large coyote population here in Maine, and hunters and trappers are taking about 1,500 animals a year. I believe the coyote is a big-time killer of deer; as the coyote population grows, the deer population will go down. I also think that the coyote not only eats a lot of deer but has changed the deer's habits a great deal. I have noticed that when the deer are disturbed now, they run much farther than they used to. Ordinarily, when a deer runs off after being disturbed or even shot at, it runs as hard as it can until it reaches protective cover, then it slows down. Although I'm not seeing the actual deer, I have seen from tracks that the deer enter heavy cover and keep running. Have you noticed that this is happening?

C. P., Bangor, Maine

A: No, I have not personally observed this, but you are the third person who has mentioned it to me. We have coyotes up on the mountain behind my home, but not too many come down here to the farmland area. I can understand deer running farther when disturbed by coyotes, because coyotes definitely prey upon them; a deer would be anxious to put as much space between the coyote and itself as possible. I also figure that a deer knows, most of the time, if it has been disturbed by a coyote or a man. Reacting the same way to both predators would simply make no sense. Deer have always responded to man by bounding into cover and then slowing down or stopping so they can make full use of their senses, which they can't do when running.

Q: How can the state of New York believe that killing off the entire deer population will help the deer herd? This is what happened in Yates County, New York (Dundee area), and they destroyed a wonderful natural resource.

A: I have heard this same complaint from many hunters in many sections of the country: "Why is the game commission killing off all the deer?"

There are two answers, and at first they may seem to be contradictory, but they're not.

First, no game commission is ever going to try to kill all the deer, because its own survival depends upon the existence of those deer. Most game commissions are not funded from their state's general treasuries, but depend upon the money taken in from the sale of hunting (and fishing) licenses. Many people hunt small game and upland game birds but to them, *hunting* means hunting deer.

Just recently a game warden under whom I served as a deputy 40 years ago told me that the deer we had worked so hard to protect were now being "decimated" by New Jersey's liberal hunting seasons. But things have changed. The deer herds we protected are now too big. And even 40 years ago, we had far too many deer, and we finally got laws passed that did away with the bucks-only law.

As hunters, we would all love to have big deer herds. We would all love to see more deer, more of the time. Most deer hunters do not live on the land they hunt, but come from the city or urban areas to hunt.

All hunters love to see white-tailed bucks like this.

Hunters all over have to realize that, with an estimated 25 million deer in the United States and Canada, we now have more deer than we have ever had on our continent. We are not going to have this high a number in the future. Deer populations across the country are going to have to be reduced, they will be reduced, and most of it will happen because of more liberal hunting seasons like New Jersey's.

When deer herds were small and building, we were only concerned with the land's carrying capacity. The deer have exceeded that, in most cases, to their own detriment. Today, we also have to be concerned with the social carrying capacity—the wishes of the people who own the land that deer live on. Many people who don't want large numbers of deer. They may enjoy seeing a few deer, and they definitely don't want the species wiped out, but they don't want deer destroying their gardens and shrubs, or the constant fear of hitting one with a car. If the state game commissions do not take the initiative to reduce deer herds on their own terms, they will have the terms dictated to them by nonhunting voters. And there are more of them than there are of us.

Q: I would like to know what effect trace mineral blocks have on the growth of a deer's antlers. What time of the year is the best to have them out? Do deer tend these blocks from October to December?

G. E., Acme, Pennsylvania

A: Trace minerals are exceedingly important to all animals. Many areas never had a full complement of all the minerals needed for optimum growth, and many more areas have had their soils depleted of minerals by agriculture. Deer cannot maximize or reach their full body size, weight, and antler development without the proper minerals. As most of them can't get these minerals from the foods they ingest, they should be given supplements. It is equally important that all humans take a multivitamin each day because we, too, need a whole gamut of minerals that we don't get from the food we eat. Food, whether for humans or deer, cannot contain the minerals we need if the minerals are not in the soil on which the food is growing.

I put out a mineral supplement called Deer-Lix (see page 186), which I mix with Agway's granulated red mineral salt. The deer love it, and it is extremely beneficial to them. They eat huge holes in the ground to get the soil that is permeated with these minerals by the rain.

Deer will visit these mineral holes year-round, but they do so *least* often during the rutting season, from mid-October to mid-December. During these two months, bucks eat less and have other things on their minds than food. The heaviest usage is from mid-March through the summer, when the

A natural mineral lick that's been hit hard by deer.

bucks are producing antlers and the does are producing and providing for their fawns.

Q: Would you please settle a friendly argument? My hunting partner of many years claims that white-tailed deer eat grass, and I say they don't. When you see deer in a field, they are eating clover, not ordinary green grass. Who is right?   K. P., North Berwick, Maine

A: I'm glad you didn't bet any money on this argument, because you would definitely have to pay up. Yes, deer eat grass.

Deer are primarily browsing animals. I can't stress this point too highly. They prefer to eat the leaves off brush and trees over everything except acorns. They eat acorns because the nuts produce needed body fat, but leaves and new sprouts of twigs are their favored and, in most cases, their most nutritious foods.

In areas where deer numbers are high, most reachable leaves and twigs are already eaten, so the deer feed upon forbs and grasses. The deer prefer forbs, which are broad-leafed plants, to grasses; but when they don't have access to forbs, they feed readily upon narrow-bladed grasses. Deer feed

Deer feed heavily upon grasses, even pawing through the snow to get them.

upon farm crops because, in most cases, these crops are growing on land that once provided natural deer food. They still prefer browse to farm crops; when neither is available, they eat grasses.

Q: I am privileged to hunt on a friend's rural property near Waynesburg, Pennsylvania. It's an old sheep farm and consists of 120 acres. There are two flat fields that have not been cultivated for years.

We are considering planting crops to attract and hold deer and turkeys and to provide nutrition that will encourage bigger and better antler development. What would you plant? What do deer really like, seek out, in the way of crops that provide antler-producing nutrition? I have read a lot about deer clover. Does it work? Do deer really like it or is rye or corn better? J. L. H., Bethel Park, Pennsylvania

A: You have a golden opportunity to produce better deer through wildlife plantings.

First of all, contact the local farm agent in the county in which the land is located. Have him test the soils for lime and fertilizer requirements. Nothing will produce better antler development faster than a heavy application of lime, and most old fields need it.

The deer clovers that you see advertised are very good, but the seeds used were developed in Alabama and other southern states. These seeds may not do well in your area. Again, consult your county farm agent as to what would do best for you. Also, by buying the seeds locally, you can save a lot of money. I have been using a Pilgrim Ladino clover that does very well in northwestern New Jersey and should do well in your area. Bird's-foot trefoil is an even better option.

If the two fields lie adjacent to each other, I would plant one in trefoil for protein and one in corn for carbohydrates. By leaving the corn standing, you would provide good winter food. By using these two crops, you should be able to hold the deer on your land all year. The carbohydrates are needed to produce fat and warmth through the winter. Again, your county agent can tell you what mix of fertilizer to use with each crop and how much. Fertilizer is expensive, but it puts minerals into the ground that benefit the deer that feed upon the plants.

By all means keep these fields as fields. The deer would benefit briefly from the browse that would grow in the fields as they converted back into forest, but that source would be gone within 10 years. Research shows that fields produce as much as 100 times more forage for deer than does a woodland.

Turkeys will also feed upon the trefoil, and it will hold tons of the grasshoppers and crickets that they feed heavily upon. As the deer knock the corn down, much of that will also become available to the turkeys.

Q: My question is about feeding deer during winter months when snow is heavy and feed is limited.

This past year (1994) southeastern Pennsylvania, where I live, and parts of northeastern Pennsylvania, where friends and I hunt, were hit with several snowstorms. Some produced freezing rains that resulted in a ¼- to ½-inch ice crust on top of the snow along with subzero temperatures for days.

As an avid deer hunter and deer enthusiast, I was concerned that the deer were not going to be able to feed properly, and therefore might experience a deadly winter.

Well after all deer hunting was over, my friends and I took feed into these areas for the deer and turkeys, and planned on supplying more feed as long as the winter was bad. Because the deer hunting in previous years had always been good to us, we wanted to ensure that it would continue from year to year.

So people don't get the wrong idea, this feed wasn't for baiting, and all the feed was taken well into the woods away from roads so deer wouldn't end up prey for poachers. Our main concern was to help the deer herds through the winter.

Most of the feed we took into the woods was shelled corn (with some still on the cob), plus apples and sunflower seeds for the turkeys, but mostly corn because it was the least expensive.

Getting to my main question, are we really helping the deer, or could we possibly be doing them harm? The reason I ask is that a couple of different people told me they had heard that feeding deer corn during the winter was no good for them. No one seemed to know why other than it had something to do with their digestive system, which may not be able to digest the corn properly during this time of the year, or perhaps deer really didn't get any nutrients from it then. Is this true? If so, isn't corn better than nothing? Would you recommend feeding deer during the winter like we're doing or, if we continue, should we feed them something other than corn? Are we interfering with their natural cycle, and should we even feed them at all? J. A., Beaver Falls, Pennsylvania

A: The winter of 1993–94 was one of the hardest winters we have had in years, but the winter of 1994–95 was the mildest I have ever seen. We had only one snowstorm of about 8 to 10 inches, and only a few days below zero. And the deer came through both winters in good condition. Why? Both of the previous years saw record-breaking mast production, particularly among red and black oaks. (The white acorn crop was very poor and sporadic; we had none in my area.) Deer went into both winters hog fat.

You are right: There are two schools of thought about feeding deer in winter.

First, if deer are going into a winter in poor shape because of habitat destruction caused by overpopulation, then the objective should be to reduce the size of the herd by increasing the harvest. If the reduction is heavy, the habitat should improve over a period of about five years.

Second, if the deer herd is not destroying the habitat but a severe winter is causing undue hardship, and it is feared that losses from starvation may greatly reduce the herd, supplementary feeding may be advised.

There are a number of arguments against feeding, and they all have varying degrees of validity.

1. Deer that have yarded because of cold winds and deep snow will not leave the yard to go look for food. This means that you actually have to take the feed right out to the deer. In doing so you will disturb the deer,

A very thin white-tailed doe, feeding in overbrowsed habitat.

causing them to use up many more calories than they would if you had let them lead the sedentary life of a yard.

2. By making a trail into the deer yard to get the feed to the deer, you create an avenue directly to the deer that dogs, coyotes, and other predators can use to prey upon them.

3. In southeastern Pennsylvania, deer would be used to feeding upon corn and would readily eat it. In northeastern Pennsylvania, if the deer had not had access to corn, they probably would not eat it.

4. The big fear about feeding starving deer (which the deer in 1993 were not) is that the animals would gorge themselves on the supplied food and develop rumenitis, or bloat, which could prove fatal. This is a possibility, but I have not see it happen.

A starving doe, in an overbrowsed yarding area. Supplemental feeding at this point is probably pointless.

In the winter, the deer's basic metabolism slows down considerably so that they eat only about one-third of what they would eat under normal conditions. Even starving deer retain microflora and bacteria that reactivate when food is again ingested. The danger is that the deer may overeat. If a small amount of food is put out and scattered, there is little chance of this happening unless just one animal eats all of the available food. Their reduced metabolisms usually prevent deer from overeating.

If you had started putting out the food before the deer reached the starvation point, it is unlikely that they would overeat. You would not be able to put out any food for the deer before the closing of your last hunting season because, in Pennsylvania, that would be considered baiting and is strictly illegal.

Shelled corn is probably the best winter food you can offer provided the deer are used to corn. It is also the most inexpensive. Clover and alfalfa hay are also good, but both are basically protein foods, and what the deer need is carbohydrates to produce heat.

Whether you should feed deer or not goes back to the third and fourth paragraphs of this answer. I have in the past fed deer extensively during severe winters when I was chief gamekeeper for the Coventry Hunt Club. We fed the deer to ensure the survival of sufficient breeding stock.

I do have to stress that you can feed deer on the local level to help your particular herd. Do not expect the state game department to do it on a large scale; they can't afford to, and it probably runs contrary to their game management plans.

Q: I hunt 1,200 acres in northern Missouri. The land consists of cropland; some drainage ditches and creeks contain its only trees. My question is, do deer yard up in Missouri? It seems the deer are gone once the crops are taken out. I verify this by looking for tracks while rabbit hunting in the snow.

There is a huge band of woods 4 miles to the east that extends for a number of miles. Perhaps the deer winter there? Also, should this type of area draw in the same numbers of deer year after year?

M. B., St. Louis, Missouri

A: No, deer do not yard up in Missouri. They seldom yard up in my area either, except in a winter of severe weather and deep snow, and my home is at least 225 miles farther north than St. Louis.

Your deer's disappearance after the crops are harvested is the same situation you find in most of the prairie states.

The deer are undoubtedly using the timber band that you speak of as their wintering area. You could easily check this out by looking for tracks there. Even though the deer would concentrate in the timber, because it is the only cover available, that still does not fit the true definition of *yarding*.

In many parts of the country, deer only yard up when the winter is severe or the snow is exceptionally deep.

Yes, I would suppose that approximately the same numbers of deer winter in the timber each year; they have nowhere else to go.

Q: As a resident of New Jersey, I was wondering if you could help me get my hands on any information concerning the deer problem and solutions in Princeton and Princeton Township. I never hunted before the age of 30, but at 39 I am now an avid bowhunter who resides in Mendham Township. I don't know if you saw or read anything about a deer hunt in Lewis Morris Park in Morris County. I took part in this hunt in order to help thin out their deer. I had three does spoken for, but shot only two. Because of the bad press coverage, the new mayor of our town and neighboring Harding Township wants very much to stop hunting (discharging of firearms). This area, Zones 9 and 13, is overrun with deer. Most people I meet are very open to hunting, especially bowhunting. I try to inform everyone I meet and have no problem getting permission to hunt.

I have called the Great Swamp Refuge and have gotten some very helpful information. Also, I have spoken to the biologist from the park hunt. I plan on attending all township meetings concerning a ban on hunting, and I'm looking for as much information as I can find to defend at least bowhunting. I'm sending you just a sample of articles that have been misinforming people.

The past nine years have been a wonderful experience and education. I do not plan on sitting still and not standing up for what I believe. If there is any information you can get me, or anyone you could put me in touch with, I would greatly appreciate it. Thank you.

J. M., Brookside, New Jersey

A: I have read the various clippings that you sent me, and am familiar with the refrain that they all sing.

It is my viewpoint that the greatest problem confronting hunters from the antihunters or, worse, the animal rights people is that the two groups don't even speak the same language. As more and more people move off the land—and more than 90 percent of our population has—they not only lose touch with their past, they also lose touch with reality.

People who grew up on farms understand that you can pasture only so many animals on so many acres before the pasture is ruined and the animals starve. This basic premise is easy to extrapolate to game management. It seems that the premise would be easy for everyone to understand, especially today when we constantly see television newscasts showing humans starving to death because of overpopulation. A piece of land will support just so many individuals, be they animal or human. When an area becomes overpopulated by any species, that species is wiped out by disease, starvation, or stress.

I was brought up on a farm where we killed the animals we ate; the meat did not come prepackaged in cellophane, it came in hair or feathers. We learned to kill in as quick and humane a fashion as was possible. Although all life is sacred, ours was more sacred than the animals'. This is a biblical dictum.

The major difference of opinion stems from the semantics of "animal welfare" and "animal rights." The majority of people, including the farmers, ranchers, hunters, trappers, and fishermen, are all interested in animal welfare. The main thrust behind wildlife management is having the proper conditions for the natural propagation of wildlife without the destruction of their habitat. Animal rights proponents claim that all creatures have the same rights as humans. This is clearly a personal viewpoint with no biological validity. I'm not sure that anything we say, write, or explain to the animal rightists will ever change a single one of their minds. To them, facts only cloud the issue, and facts will never change personal belief or prejudices.

Thankfully, the animal rights folks are a definite minority. We do, however, have to recognize the rights and needs of the suburban population—the landowners on whose property many deer live. While most of those folks are not antihunters, they may be against hunting as the main means of game management. It is important that we hunters understand this distinction, and that we hear and respect their opinions. Coalitions must be formed, with all sides of the issue represented, all options must be studied, a consensus must be reached, and the final decision must be satisfactory to the majority of the representatives.

I understand what you are trying to do and commend you for it. I have spent a lifetime lecturing and writing, trying to do the same thing.

The best source of up-to-date information on this subject is the booklet *An Evaluation of Deer Management Options.* It can be ordered from the New Hampshire Fish and Game Department, Wildlife Division (2 Hazen Drive, Concord, NH 03301). Send $1 for shipping.

Also, the *Guide to Urban Bowhunting* is available from the National Bowhunter Education Foundation (267 East 29th Street, Box 250, Loveland, CO 80538).

These booklets present the hunter's side of the issue based upon scientific facts.

Q: I hunt in northeastern Michigan, and where I hunt, we have a lot of spikes and only a handful of 4-pointers or better. To increase the number of quality bucks in our area, I believe that we should let the 4-pointers and better go and concentrate on the spikes and does. All the small bucks that we have taken this year were about a year old and weighed about 140 pounds, but the antlers ranged from a 6-pointer down to a 1½-inch spike. Is this bad genetics? D. G., Utica, Michigan

A: Whitetail bucks should never have spikes. They really shouldn't have 4 points either. When bucks have either, it is usually the result of the deer not having enough nutritious food. Please note that I said "nutritious" food; they usually have sufficient food, but it may not necessarily be nutritious.

Genetics does play a very important role, and some spike bucks do have deficient genes, as was proven in an extensive experiment carried out in the Kerrville, Texas, Research Station a number of years ago. The study received tremendous coverage. It started a nationwide killing of spike bucks in the name of good deer management. What was overlooked was the fact that Texas, prior to that time, had a law on the books forbidding the harvesting of spike bucks. If any bucks had deficient genes—and some did—they were allowed to live and become old enough to become breeders. This situation could not occur, and did not occur, in any other states that I know of, because spike bucks in other states had always been legal and were taken before they became breeders. When the Texas law was changed, the problem was partially solved.

What the entire furor over the harvesting of spike bucks did was mask the investigation of the real problem. The Texas finding was hailed as the answer to the problem of spike bucks. As I have already said, it solved part of Texas's problem: It got the law changed. It did not solve the problem in any other state where the spike bucks were not protected.

We are always looking for the quick fix, and shooting the spikes was taken to be that fix. But the problem was, is, and always will be the availability of sufficient nutritious food.

If you were to do an extensive study of the food that a deer gets today in a particular area and check it against what it ate as preferred food 50 years ago, you would find that the lists would be extremely different. What a deer eats as preferred food today may not be preferred food at all, but simply the main food available. When the deer population was below the carrying capacity of the land, deer could pick and choose among the various foods and eat only the most nutritious. When the deer population exploded and the number of deer exceeded what an area could produce in food, most of the desirable, nutritious plants were entirely eliminated. According to Pennsylvania State Foresters, deer overpopulation has changed the whole complexion of the forest. Entirely different plants, shrubs, and trees are now growing. The only vegetation that could survive the onslaught of the deer was vegetation the deer really didn't care for. The deer have completely annihilated some plant species.

What is the answer? You said it yourself: Shoot more does. If you have to reduce the herd further, shoot the spikes. To produce quality deer, you have to give them an abundance of nutritious food, and you can't have that with an overabundance of deer.

One of the main reasons that trophy deer management fails, or is doomed to failure before it gets started, is that most hunters, and the general public, want to see lots of deer. Most hunters are willing to harvest any deer so long as they can get a deer—and there is nothing wrong with that. But while we have lots of deer eating lots of food, we will not be able to produce many trophy bucks.

The weight of 140 pounds for the 1½-year-old buck you shot is a respectable weight for his age bracket—not the best, but good. Because that buck also had 6 points, he would have been well on his way to becoming a trophy buck if he had lived longer.

A big buck in rut. If you have many deer in an area, eating lots of food, you won't get many trophies like this.

Chapter
6

Breeding

Although most hunters have never seen deer breeding, the breeding season—that is, the rut—is the most important time of the year for the buck and the most exciting time of the year for the hunter.

It is during the rut that the bucks are at their magnificent best. This is the culmination of all of their preparation for the past 11 months. It is what they were designed for.

The rut is when the hunter has his best chance of taking a trophy buck, because this is the only time that a buck will let down his guard, be it ever so slightly. Don't think that bucks throw all caution to the wind, because they don't. However, this is the one time of the year when, responding to his biological urge to pass on his genes, a buck is likely to make a mistake.

It is during the hunting season that a knowledgeable hunter will employ antler rattling, grunt tubes, scents, and so on, to help trick the buck into making that one mistake.

It is the breeding season that actually starts the deer's annual cycle.

Q: I have often seen bucks chasing after does during the rutting season. In all those years, I have never actually seen a buck catch a doe. I always thought that, because the bucks were bigger and stronger than the does, they would be faster and have no trouble catching them. Are the does actually faster than the bucks?
T. L., Trenton, New Jersey

A: When you watch the track and field events in the Olympics, you don't see men and women competing with each other. Although the fastest women runners can easily outrun most men, they cannot outrun the fastest men runners. It has to do with size and strength. It's the same with the deer.

Much of the chasing you see is more ritualized than flat-out running. It's part of the courtship procedure.

Even when a doe is ready to be bred, she will run from the buck. And every time the buck approaches the doe, he runs at her. She may have every intention of standing for him, but she will run 100 feet or so before letting him catch up and mount her. Although the buck breeds her about six or seven times in her 28-hour estrus period, he runs at her each time, she runs off each time, and then she stops and waits for him.

If a doe is pre-estrus and being constantly harassed by a buck or bucks, she will not only run off but employ different stratagems as well. She will crawl into impenetrable thickets where the buck, with his antlers, cannot follow. She will crawl under downed trees that are held up slightly from the ground by their branches. She will join an estrus doe, and the buck tending that doe will keep all other bucks away.

Sometimes a buck can't catch a doe that doesn't want to be caught, because she usually gets more rest than he does. As soon as a buck starts to run a doe, that stirs the interest of every buck in the area, and they get busy trying to run each other off. While this occurs, the doe gets a chance to rest. The bucks are really tired all the time during the rutting season.

Q: On March 1, 1993, in Colchester, Connecticut, my brother-in-law saw a buck breed a doe. He said that the buck did not have antlers. I think it was a button buck. I have seen button bucks try to mount does before, but never successfully. What do you think of this, as well as of the lateness in the year?
C. L., Wallingford, Connecticut

A: You will have to read my book *The Deer of North America* again. There I state that a buck is capable of breeding from the time he peels the velvet from his antlers in September until February or March. The enlargement of the testicles, spermatogenesis, and a flood of testosterone are what prompt the velvet to dry and be removed. The process prepares a buck for the breeding season.

Most bucks shed their antlers in December or January, after the rutting season is over. However, they are still capable of breeding. If they can find an unbred doe, they'll breed up until February, March, or later. Last April, I saw a buck without antlers breed a doe.

North of the 32nd Parallel, most does breed around November 10–12 or December 6–8, dropping their fawns in May or June. Every year I get many reports of hunters seeing fawns with spots in November, while these fawns should have lost their spotted coats in August or September. The fawns that are still in their spotted coats in November came from does that were bred in April. I have records of fawns that were born in January and February, which meant that the does were bred in June. These are most unusual occurrences, once-in-a-lifetime happenings.

Your brother-in-law gave the date as March 1, which would fall within this time frame, but it is exceptionally late. It was evidently the doe's fifth estrus cycle, and it seems most unusual for a doe to have been in heat on four prior occasions without some buck finding her and breeding.

Ordinarily, button bucks are not mature enough to breed. Still, in 1965 Helenette Silver, a biologist with the New Hampshire Game Division, recorded a button buck that was mature enough to breed. Ms. Silver had a large pen of fawns and, in the spring, several of the little does gave birth to

A five-month-old buck showing sexual aggression to his mother. He is not capable of breeding an adult doe because he is too small to reach her. Plus, an adult buck would not let him.

fawns. No adult bucks had ever gotten into the pen. She suspected the culprit was a little buck that had matured enough to have grown little antlers, ½ to 1 inch in length, that had pushed through the skin, hardened, and peeled by the time the buck was seven months old. Subsequent investigation by Silver and other biologists has since confirmed that, if a young buck is mature enough to form little antlers at seven months of age, he is mature enough to produce sperm and breed. Such precociousness is the result of a high-protein diet and genetics.

Q: I may have a partial answer to the question of white-tailed bucks holding their antlers into April.

I wish I could remember the names of the author and publication that I'm referring to, but the gist of the study is this: As long as there are does coming into estrus, the bucks will be stimulated to keep producing the full spectrum of hormones that keep them fit and ready to breed.

Here is Lenawee County, one of Michigan's Ohio-border counties, it is not uncommon to see very small fawns in October. Counting the months back for the gestation period, that puts the end of the rut into March. I once watched three large bucks with respectable head gear chasing a small doe in late March.

Hunting shed antlers has become popular around here, too. We use the rodent chew marks to guess when the antlers were shed. A friend of mine found a big set of sheds in a greening alfalfa field while woodchuck hunting in the last week of April. This set had no dirt on them and no chew marks, which made us believe they were recently dropped.

I don't have much scientific evidence to offer, but I believe what I have observed supports the study that I mentioned. Hopefully, someone else read the same article and can supply the specifics on this topic.

L. K., Sand Creek, Michigan.

A: You are the second person to mention the study in which the author found that bucks keep their antlers as long as does come into estrus. I am sorry that I have not read the article, but I do not dispute the author's findings.

To date, I have received more than 50 letters from readers who have witnessed bucks carrying their antlers until mid-April or longer. I have never had such an outpouring of mail in response to one of my questions. What it all proves is that this is not as rare a phenomenon as most of us had believed.

I am willing to bet that, if the occasional wild buck does carry his antlers longer than normal, it is a recent phenomenon caused by our moderating winters. I am also willing to bet that if we go back to extreme winters like the one we had here in the Northeast in 1995–96, you won't see bucks carrying their antlers late. If it is true that bucks keep their antlers as long as does are in estrus, hard winters will not allow late-born fawns to survive, and the cycle will be broken.

For thousands upon thousands of years, the bulk of the does in the northern states bred between November 5 and December 18, giving birth 203 to 205 days later. This birthing period allowed both the doe and her fawns to take advantage of warm weather and abundant food. Fawns that are born in August and September just cannot attain the body growth and fat needed to survive a severe winter. Because they are eliminated from the gene pool, they do not throw the regular breeding period out of synchronization with the seasons.

All the sighting of bucks carrying their antlers up to, and past, mid-April have been recent—over the past 15 to 20 years, the period corresponding with mainly mild winters. What we need to know is how many bucks carrying antlers late were seen 30 years ago, or earlier.

Most fawns in the northern three-quarters of the continent are born between May 21 and June 21.

Q: I have been told that a white-tailed doe is only in heat for about 28 hours. How many times in those 28 hours will the buck breed her? What does he do the rest of the time when he is not breeding her?

M. B., Springfield, Missouri

A: Bucks and does usually stay apart for most of the year, although they may concentrate in areas of food or shelter in the coldest winter months. Bucks become interested in the does in early October and really start to chase them with the beginning of the rut about the middle of October. The does will avoid the bucks whenever possible.

About 48 hours before the doe comes into her estrus period, she will, under the stimulation of her hormones, become very agitated and seek out the company of bucks. She will visit scrapes, she will urinate frequently, she will leave a trail that every buck in the area will home in on.

A number of bucks will be attracted to the pre-estrus doe, but the largest one will lay claim to her and attempt to drive all other bucks away. If he meets up with a rival buck that is his equal in size, one that he can't bluff off with a hard stare or a mock charge, a fight is practically inevitable.

During the 28 hours or so that the doe is in estrus and can actually accept the buck, he will breed her six to eight times.

A white-tailed buck chasing an estrus doe.

Credit: Len Rue Jr.

There is usually a time lapse of three to four hours between each copulation. Prior to copulation the buck will run at the doe with his neck outstretched and held low. The doe will usually run two to three times in a low, slinking fashion. When she stops, the buck may lick her vagina or may attempt to mount at once. Penetration does not take place with every mounting, because the orifice is small. Because both large and small does are bred, and because of the disparate sizes of bucks and does, the buck has to hunt for the opening with his penis. Upon penetration, the buck makes four to five small strokes and then, with a mighty thrust, he penetrates very deeply and ejaculates. With the deep thrust, the buck's head will rise way up; the doe will be driven forward a foot or more as the buck slides off her back. At times the thrust is made with such force that the buck's feet go out from under him and he comes crashing down.

The doe will immediately squat to urinate and sometimes to defecate. She will stay in that humpback position, straining, for as much as five minutes. Then she will lie down.

The buck usually remains about 50 to 100 feet from the bedded doe, standing guard to keep other bucks at a distance. Even if he lies down, he is constantly on guard, constantly alert. Any crow cawing gets his attention, any movement of a chipmunk or squirrel in the leaves gets his attention, any sound at all has his ears and head swiveling, swinging, trying to locate the cause.

Any big buck in the area will attempt to make a run at the doe now, if he can slip by the dominant, tending buck. However, it is the 1½- and 2½-year-old bucks that are the greatest nuisance. Like a bunch of horny teenagers, they constantly try to run the doe off. They don't dare face the dominant buck, but they can usually outrun him, so they keep up a series of hit-and-run attacks. The dominant buck can usually keep two or three other bucks at bay; more than that and he gets no chance to rest. So long as the other bucks remain at least 200 feet from the doe, the dominant buck ignores them.

While tending the bedded doe, the buck may feed upon acorns, fallen leaves, or whatever is available. Although he does not get as much to eat as he ordinarily would, he does get enough to spend considerable time chewing his cud while standing guard. While on guard, the buck prefers to stand uphill when possible. I have seen bucks get up on little mounds of earth to get enough elevation to see farther.

While either standing or bedded, the dominant buck may doze off, but a deep sleep is not possible because of the competition.

All told, a buck may spend three or, at the most, four days with the doe. He may be with her about 48 hours prior to her estrus period, 28 hours during her estrus, and 8 to 12 hours afterward. Then it's off to seek another re-

A yearling white-tailed buck breeding a doe.

ceptive doe. If there are many more does than bucks in a population, as is true in my home state of New Jersey, the buck may spend less time with each doe.

Although he is capable of breeding many more does, the buck probably breeds no more than three to four in the first estrus cycle, because most of them come into estrus about the same time. During the second cycle, he may breed three to four more, but I doubt very much if even the dominant buck ever gets to breed more than six to eight does per year.

Q: I would like to respond to the question, how long do white-tailed deer live?

Mr. C. W. Cain, living in Opelousas, Louisiana, had a doe live to the age of 25 years and 10 months. In that time she had 33 fawns. This can be confirmed by Mr. K. Sonnier of the Department of Wildlife and Fisheries in Opelousas, Louisiana.   W. J. G., Scott, Louisiana.

A: I certainly thank you for the information you have given me and the opportunity for confirmation. I know there are more records of size, weight, number of fawns, age, and so on that never get into the record books and

This 20-year-old doe gave birth to a single fawn when she was 19.

Credit: Irene Vandermolen

are thus never brought before the general public. This record age eclipses all former records by several years.

Q: This is concerning white-tailed fawns being born in October in the state of Georgia.

There have been two separate sightings of fawns still having their spots during the third week of October. Both sightings were from reliable people who are avid deer hunters.

One fawn was seen in the northeastern part of northern Georgia, and the other was in central Georgia.

My question is this: Is it possible for a white-tailed deer to breed late enough in the breeding season, or even after that fawns still have spots in the middle of October? What are the odds of this happening?

Also, in your opinion (which I value very much), what is the survival rate of fawns born late in the year? And will they be healthy deer if they do survive? W. S., Hoschton, Georgia

A: Yes, it is very possible to see fawns with spots in Georgia in mid-October. It occasionally happens in my home state of New Jersey, and we are much farther north. The deer in the Deep South—southern Alabama, Mississippi, Louisiana, and Texas—have their breeding season two or more months later than do more northern deer. In mid-December 1990, I was photographing deer just a few miles from Mobile, Alabama. I photographed a buck that still had strips of velvet hanging on his antlers that he hadn't rubbed off as yet. Ordinarily, bucks peel the velvet from their antlers 2 to 2½ months before the peak of the breeding season. Thus the buck I saw would reach the peak of the rut, the breeding season, in late February or early March. With the gestation period of the white-tailed deer being 200 to 205 days, it would be September before the fawns were born—and they would still have spots in late November or early December. You do not live very far north of Mobile, so the possibility of some of your does breeding much later than others should, or could, be strong.

Under normal conditions, over most of the whitetail's range in North America, fawns don't lose their spots until late August or early September, when they shed out their natal hair to grow their winter coats. So that would put your fawns about six weeks to two months off a normal sched-

A three-day-old white-tailed fawn.

ule. I don't know how much longer those fawns in Georgia would have their spots, so they could be as much as three months off schedule, but even that is not an improbable occurrence.

Adult does usually breed November 10–25, dropping their fawns in May or June. Doe fawns of the year that are mature enough to be bred usually breed in December, with their fawns being dropped in June. A lot of these later-born fawns will have their spots in September.

If a doe is not bred or does not conceive when bred—which can happen for any number of reasons—she will re-cycle and come back into estrus approximately 28 days later. She may actually miss two or three of her periods, which means she may breed in January or February and drop her fawns in August or September. Those fawns will retain their spots for about three months, or all the way into December.

In my area and farther north, where the weather does get quite cold and food becomes scarce, it is unlikely that these late-born fawns would survive. And it is better for the species if they don't. Being born so late, there is the possibility that they would carry genes for late breeding. Over millions of years the whitetail has evolved into a creature that drops its young in May and June when food, warmth, and survival chances are optimum.

In the South, where the weather is less harsh and finding food seldom a problem, late-born fawns have a good chance of surviving and developing into normal, healthy deer that may or may not breed in the normal period. It is not as important that they adhere to the November–May schedule, although I still think it's better for the species if they do.

Q: On February 17, 1992, while visiting our property in southeastern Allegheny County, New York, my wife and I observed a seemingly healthy white-tailed fawn that appeared to be about two weeks old.

What are its chances of surviving the cold with its summer coat?

How common is birth this early in the year? Am I right to assume that the mother would have been bred in July or August?

I would appreciate any information you can give me on this occurrence. F. H., Niagara Falls, New York

A: Yes, if the fawn was about two weeks old on February 7, the doe must have been bred in late July or early August. This is very uncommon, but not unheard of. I have reported on several births of fawns in January and February in the latest edition of my book, *The Deer of North America*.

In a warm winter, I'm sure this fawn would be able to survive. The fawns I discussed in my book were subject to much more severe weather and apparently survived, according to my correspondents.

It is very unusual.

Q: While fishing on a small inland lake in the western Upper Peninsula of Michigan this past summer, a friend and I observed something swimming across the lake approximately a mile from us. Although we had binoculars, we were unable to positively identify what it was. We decided to investigate. As we approached more closely, we saw that it was a white-tailed deer, and it looked to be a spike buck. However, as we got closer, it became clear that it was a doe with the top third of her right ear cut off. The same ear was also split longitudinally through the rest of its length, giving the initial impression of a short antler. This, in itself, seemed strange, and we decided to follow behind her at a distance during her ½-mile swim across the lake. Her tail was sticking up above the water and completely dry, which was also puzzling to us at the time. We both agreed, as we followed her, that it would take a powerful human to have kept up with her at the pace she was traveling.

As the deer neared the opposite shore, we shut the motor off and approached within 20 yards with an electric motor. When she got within 10 yards of the shore, we noticed a log lying parallel to the shore, at the surface of the water. We did not think that she would have any trouble going over or around the log, but as she got her front feet up over the log, it became clear that she was physically exhausted. We could hear heavy breathing and see her struggling to clear the log. As her hindquarters came out of the water over the log, we noticed something sticking out from her. When she finally walked out of the water, we were amazed to see the two front hoofs and head from a fawn sticking out of her. The fawn was dead, as evidenced by the tongue hanging out of its mouth, but we agreed that it probably had not died that long ago; it did not seem to be decayed to any extent. We also agreed that the fawn looked rather large and concluded that for some reason the doe was not able to birth it.

As she tried to jump another log on land, she toppled head over heels and lay exhausted for a few moments. We continued to follow her along the shore for approximately 10 minutes, using the binoculars. It was a fairly steep slope down to the lake, and she was obviously hesitant to ascend until she was rested. She finally made her way out of our sight and we sat in silence, trying to comprehend the bizarre event that we had just observed. Another bit of information that makes this story even more strange is the date on which it occurred—July 22.

We began asking ourselves several questions. One obvious one was, why did this doe enter the water? When deer are in labor, they normally find a secluded spot to have their young. I do not think this doe was in labor at that time, and perhaps she was feverish because of the dead fawn. Perhaps she entered the water in an attempt to cool herself. I estimated the doe's weight at 150 pounds, and so could not understand why she could not birth the fawn; it seemed to be coming out headfirst, as it should. We also thought that, if the doe were carrying twins, she surely would not survive. At the time we observed her, the doe must have been in fairly good shape, because she swam the ½-mile span of water in less than 10 minutes. Could you lend some insight as to why this doe could not birth her fawn, how frequently this situation occurs, and whether you have ever seen or heard of anything like what I have described? Unfortunately, we did not have a camera with us and so this will have to remain in our memories, which it will forever. J. C. and R. T., Escanaba, Michigan.

A: I can only surmise that the doe must have been pursued by dogs or some other predator. I cannot imagine a doe going into the water while giving birth unless she was forced to. You are right, they usually seek some safe, secluded area in which to give birth.

You didn't mention whether or not her split ear was a fresh split, although I imagine you would have noted it if the ear had been bloody. A bloody ear would provide good circumstantial evidence of a predator pursuing the doe, forcing her to escape by swimming the lake. Getting her ear caught on barbed wire could explain the longitudinal split, but I can think of nothing but predation that would cut the ear tip off.

We don't know whether the fawn was dead when she entered the water, but it would have drowned in a short time by having its head submerged. Because the umbilical cord was still fastened, the fawn could have perhaps gotten enough oxygen to survive if it could have kept its mouth and nostrils closed. It obviously didn't, as its tongue was protruding.

If the doe was approximately 150 pounds, she was mature and should have had twins. If the dead fawn was the firstborn, the second fawn would probably die in the womb. Because both the head and forefeet were protruding, there is a good possibility that the doe could abort and eject the fawn from her body. If the second fawn died internally, the doe probably would have died also.

I hope you realize that my entire answer is conjecture, as I try to piece together the puzzle you have presented. I did recently see and photograph a doe in water with a fawn protruding from her body. I believe she went to the water to cool off and drink, although she did feed there for just a few moments. After perhaps a moment or two she walked off and out of my sight, so I don't know the outcome.

I have seen pregnant does lie down in moist spots to cool their feverish bodies during the birthing period, but what you and I have witnessed is exceedingly rare.

Q: In early July, while driving across I-80 in Pennsylvania, I saw a number of deer killed on the highway. One doe was lying so that you could see she had a large milk bag. It was quite evident that the doe had fawns that she was nursing. What are the chances of her fawns surviving with the doe killed at that time? Will other does allow the orphaned fawns to nurse?

B. B., Youngstown, Ohio

A: Fawns orphaned at an age of four to five weeks have practically no chance of survival. Does bond themselves to their fawns right from the moment that they lick them clean of the amniotic fluids after birth. The does are imprinted on their fawns' odor and taste. From that moment on, the doe could find her own fawn among hundreds of others. The fawns are also imprinted onto their mother's odor but pay less attention to this than does do. This can be seen if you watch a large group of does and fawns feeding together in July and August. The fawns will often run up and attempt to nurse the nearest doe, particularly if she is also nursing one of her own offspring. The fawn is willing, but the doe is not. The doe usually sniffs the

A doe nursing her fawn. If orphaned at such a young age, the fawn would have little chance of survival.

fawn's anal gland or tarsal glands and knows instantly whether the fawn is hers or not. If the fawn is not hers, she will not allow it to nurse. At times she may be very aggressive to the strange fawn, even going so far as to strike at it with her forefeet.

I know of several captive does that would allow any and all of the fawns in the compound to nurse, so it could be that in the wild a strange doe would allow an orphan to nurse, but it's not likely.

Fawns start to eat vegetation within a day or so of birth. They will usually start to eat dirt, too, for its mineral content. However, such vegetation intake is minimal, and the fawns do not become ruminants until they are three to four weeks old. The fawns are dependent on their mother's rich milk until at least two months of age. Most fawns are weaned by four months of age.

Mortality for fawns under the best of conditions runs as high as 40 percent. The fawns of does killed in June and July are going to be part of that 40 percent. They just aren't going to make it.

Q: In southern Mississippi, where I hunt, the last 10 days of deer season (January 22–31) are bowhunting only. On January 25, I shot a nice healthy doe. After hanging the deer up to skin, I noticed that she had milk in her bag. From what I could see, there was no young inside her. Could she have been nursing a fawn at that time of year, or could she have had a fawn born late and not completely dried up? Is this unusual?

K. W., Tylertown, Mississippi

A: In northwestern New Jersey where I live, and in the northern three-quarters of the continent, most fawns are born in late May through June. Most of the fawns are weaned at about three to four months, which means that the doe's bag would dry up in September or October.

However, I have seen tolerant deer allow their fawns to nurse into November, long after they have lost their spots. As long as the doe continues to allow the fawns to nurse, her body will continue to produce milk.

The breeding season in southern Mississippi occurs about two months later than the rest of the country's. I photographed the peak of the rut in southern Louisiana the first week in January, which means the fawns would be born in July and August. On this schedule, the fawns would be weaned in November and December. Thus it would not be unusual to find a tolerant doe still nursing her young in late January and having milk in her bag.

It could also be that the doe did not breed during her first or second estrus. She may have bred even as late as March or April. Her fawn would

A tolerant white-tailed doe allowing her seven-month fawn to nurse.

then have been born in October or November, in which case weaning would not have been completed yet.

In the South, such late-born fawns could survive. In the North, particularly during a hard winter, late-born fawns usually die. There are records of fawns being born in every month of the year, although anything outside the regular two-month birthing period would have to be considered unusual.

A loyal reader from Prairie du Chien, Wisconsin, once sent me a copy of the *LaCrosse Tribune* in which Jerry Davis, the outdoor writer, documented a fawn that was born in mid-January. The fawn was spotted and estimated to be 2½ months old when photographed in late March 1988.

Now, all of this is very unusual. First of all, it is unusual for a doe to come into estrus this late. They have been known to re-cycle four times, and I personally know of a doe that re-cycled six times and then bred. Perhaps she didn't come into estrus in November at all because of a problem with her pineal gland, which triggers the onset of the estrus period.

It is unusual for a buck to be capable of breeding this late, because he is at a low point in his testosterone cycle. But it is possible.

And it is most unusual for the winter to be mild enough to allow the doe to get enough food to support both herself and her fawn.

Q: According to the television and the newspapers, this summer (1999) we are having the worst drought we have had since the Dust Bowl days of the early 1930s. There are no corn or soybean crops left in my area. The government has declared our region a disaster area. What I want to know is how this is going to affect our deer hunting. I have seen some good bucks, but I don't think their antlers are as big as they were last year. In your opinion, what will be both the short-term and long-term effects?

P. W., Wheeling, West Virginia

A: I was raised on a farm, so I am always looking at farm crops as well as what I see in the woods. The drought of 1999 was the worst I have ever seen in my section of northwestern New Jersey. Not just the lack of rain but also the searing heat wilted the crops. The temperature was over 100 degrees on a couple of days, and near that mark for about a month. The rising heat produced quite a bit of wind, which literally sucked the moisture out

A well-hidden 10-pointer. In years of drought, deer body weights in particular tend to fall off.

of the earth and all the vegetation. Our countryside was as sere and brown as you would see in the West. The only thing that prevented more forest fires was the total lack of storms producing lightning.

Drought conditions can affect antler sizes. Bucks need good nutritious vegetation in June and July to maximize antler growth. Without it, there will not be many outstanding racks.

A dought can also wipe out acorn crops. In fact, in 1999 the black and red oaks were already dropping their acorns by August, pitiful little unfilled nuts scarcely larger than peas. What came down were mostly the cups of the acorns. Deer fatten faster on acorns than on any other food. In a drought year there will be few, if any, acorns on which to fatten.

There may also be little or no corn crop, and corn is a very important source of the carbohydrates that our deer depend on in order to fatten for winter. Although soybeans are exceptionally high in protein, they too were devastated in 1999.

Vegetation is affected. Deer begin creating browse lines in summer, because there is no other food—leaving nothing at all for the winter, for either deer or bears. There can be tremendous bear problems in drought years, because there is almost nothing for the bears to fatten on in the mountains. The deer and the bears will be very competitive for food. Suburban households will see more damage to their shrubs a lot earlier than normal. Deer will not be in any condition to withstand a severe winter. Herds may be cut back by 25 percent or more due to starvation.

CHAPTER

7

Deer Facts

The detective Joe Friday, on television's old *Dragnet* series, wanted "just the facts, Ma'am."

As with everything else, there are old wives' tales, there is hearsay, there is just plain baloney. Based on a lifetime of experience with deer, I've tried to give you just the facts.

Q: I hunt deer in my home state of New Jersey and in Maine. I keep close tabs on Maine, and read each year that the state produces hundreds of deer weighing more than 200 pounds, and some even near 300 pounds. But in all my years of hunting there, the biggest deer I've shot weighed 187 pounds field-dressed. Still, I was mighty proud when I showed that buck to my friends at home.

Why are the Maine bucks so much larger than New Jersey bucks? Why are bucks in some areas so much larger than does? B. C., Belleville, NJ

A: Basically, New Jersey's deer and Maine's deer are of the same white-tailed deer subspecies—*Odocoileus virginianus borealis*—and should be similar in size. However, Bergman's Rule of Heat Conservation states that members of the same species will be larger the farther north, or south, they are found from the equator. Larger size and body weight creates less surface area per pound of weight, which helps prevent heat loss. New Jersey is at the southern fringe of the *O.V. borealis* range, while Maine is at its northern end. Maine has more severe winters than New Jersey, which promotes larger deer, even though they are of the same subspecies.

I would think your big Maine deer was 2½ to 3½ years old, and I would also guess the larger deer you read about are older than 3½ years. White-tailed bucks are not fully mature until after age four, when they are capable of producing their largest bodies and antlers. Before then, a lot of their food intake goes to building a larger body. When they mature, they no longer must divert nutrition to body growth. The nutrients can then be used for larger antler mass and body weight.

In New Jersey, 85 percent of our bucks are shot when they are 1½ years old. Therefore, most of the state's bucks never reach full maturity unless they find a haven in a wooded suburb.

Hunting pressure in Maine will never be as heavy as it is in New Jersey. Maine has vast wilderness areas with inaccessible swamps that provide great cover for whitetails. In New Jersey, roads crisscross almost every hunting area. These differences in access and hunting pressure allow Maine deer to grow older and larger than New Jersey deer.

To conserve body heat and energy, northern deer tend to have larger body weights and sizes than southern deer

Sexual dimorphism is not totally understood. Most male mammals are larger than the females, but in birds of prey the females are usually larger. In whitetails, this weight difference might favor males as much as 2:1, although it is usually less.

It is easy to postulate that male mammals are usually larger because the largest and strongest of them do most of the breeding. They need this weight and size when fighting rival males. This would be genetic selection. It is also readily seen that the animal with the largest antlers or horns is usually the dominant animal.

Another factor in size differences between bucks and does is that the female reaches full maturity in two years, while the male requires four. Those extra two years allow the buck to grow larger, a distinct advantage in social standing or dominance.

The advantage for the doe is that the nutrients that would have increased her body size after age two are instead diverted to nurturing her fetuses and fawns. Does' smaller size also increases their winter survival rates, because they can thrive on a smaller food supply than bucks can. This ensures that there will be does surviving until spring to perpetuate the species.

Q: On several occasions you have stated that the peak of the breeding season in southern Louisiana occurs after the first week of January. Based on my observations, I agree.

I have a friend in a hunting club on Davis Island in the Mississippi River between Louisiana and Mississippi. He said after the club instituted a management program and reduced the doe population for a better doe:buck ratio, the herd's peak breeding season moved up three weeks to about the third week of December. Why would reducing the herd's doe population move the breeding season forward?   L. P., Monroe, Louisiana

A: I can't tell you from personal observation why this would happen. I must rely on research by other individuals for possible answers. For example, Michigan deer biologists Louis Verme, John Ozoga, and J. Nellist found that when they penned white-tailed bucks and does in close proximity, the does came into estrus earlier than normal. They reasoned that the odor and attention of the males so stimulated the females that their bodies induced ovulation earlier.

As I have often said, a buck is capable of breeding anytime after his antler velvet peels. From the rut's onset, bucks in the wild are constantly testing the does' readiness to see if they are coming into estrus.

Still, the most likely reason for the earlier breeding cycle on Davis Island is the island's management program, which is directed by Professor

Harry Jacobson of Mississippi State University. Before Jacobson's plan began, the herd's adult sex ratio was out of line, with many more adult does than adult bucks. As a result, many does were not bred during their first estrus cycle. This caused the rut to be less intense and spread out over a much longer time frame.

Jacobson does not believe that the change in the rut's peak is a result of the social and/or phenomenal effects that Verme, Ozoga, and Nellist documented in penned whitetails. Rather, by shooting more does and allowing more bucks to reach maturity, the Davis Island herd now has a higher percentage of adult bucks, which means there are more bucks to do the breeding. A higher number of bucks helps synchronize the rut, and allows most does to be bred during their first estrus cycle. This shortens the rut considerably, because few does are re-cycling 28 days later. In addition, when a good number of older does are removed from the herd, the younger does typically breed earlier.

These same phenomena have been recorded in South Carolina on lands managed by Professor David Guynn.

Q: I recently read in an outdoor publication that the states of New Jersey and Maine have issued warnings on eating deer liver. Since my family and I always eat the livers from the deer my friends and I shoot, I am very concerned.

Could you explain these warnings? Also, if there is any danger from eating deer liver, does it exist in only certain areas or in all of North America? The health of almost every deer hunter in the country could be at stake.

H. W., Charlestown, Rhode Island

A: Upon receiving your letter, I contacted Dr. Doug Roscoe of the New Jersey Division of Fish and Game. Roscoe participated in the study that prompted the warning.

The study had to do primarily with the retention of the toxic metal cadmium in the deer's liver. The study was begun several years ago and is ongoing. It is conducted primarily on the outer coastal plains of New Jersey, which have very sandy soil with an acidic pH.

The bulk of the pollution was airborne, coming from automobile emissions and the burning of fossil fuels. Electrical plating is a major source of such pollution.

Since the ocean dumping of sewage sludge has been barred, there has been a greater use of such sludge as agricultural fertilizer. Prior to the study, there was little monitoring of the toxicity of any metals in the sludge. Now all sludge is tested and can be used on the land only if it meets the criteria for the acceptable amounts of these toxic metals.

A number of important developments have taken place since the study was begun.

The study was instigated when the EPA's "food basket" studies showed that traces of harmful metals were being found in most of the basic foods we eat. (The FPA periodically checks certain foods across the nation for environmental pollutants.) Cadmium was showing up in nonlethal but higher-than-expected amounts. In an effort not to exacerbate the cadmium levels in our diets, the New Jersey division studied deer livers—because the livers of all grazing and browsing animals are known reservoirs of toxic metals—and put out the warning that you read about. The warning was intended not to prevent people from eating deer liver, but to make them aware that the livers did have traces of the metal, and that they should not eat excessive amounts of deer liver.

Studies have proven that there is less cadmium in a younger deer's liver than in an older deer's. Younger animals just haven't consumed as much vegetation in their shorter life spans. The toxins are deposited from the air into the soil, then absorbed from the soil by the plants, which are in turn

Most of New Jersey's bucks are taken at 1½ years of age.

ingested by the deer. The toxins are concentrated in the liver as it filters the deer's blood of impurities. The majority of the deer taken in New Jersey are young, which greatly minimizes our exposure to cadmium.

The latest food-basket study results showed that the levels of toxins in our foods have dropped significantly. This, in turn, means that any toxins ingested from deer liver would have less of a cumulative effect, because we are now exposed to fewer toxins overall.

Again, let me stress that the state was not trying to scare anybody. It just proves that the New Jersey State Division of Fish and Game is doing an excellent job of staying on top of what could have been a potential hazard.

Q: I have just read the latest edition of *The Deer of North America.* Your chapter on automobile accidents struck me because of my recent experiences in this area. I thought you might be interested.

I have belonged to a volunteer ambulance corps for more than 30 years and have made over 2,000 calls. Prior to October 1989 I had never been to a car-deer accident. In early October we had a very heavy snowstorm, downing many trees and wires; we were without power for a week.

Since that date I have been to 11 car-deer accidents, and the ambulance has responded to others when I was not on call. There were many more car-deer accidents with no injuries.

All this occurred within a 5-mile radius of Nassau. Any explanation?

After the ambulance hit two deer on different occasions, we put alert whistles on it. Two times I have seen that they work.

C. A., Nassau, New York

A: I have no explanation as to why you had no previous deer-car accidents before October 1989. There certainly must have been a goodly number of deer in your area prior to that time.

The reason that the deer kill started in mid-October was that this is about the time the bucks begin to respond to the rutting season. During the rutting season they become much more active and increase the area they travel in five- or sixfold, up to 10 to 12 square miles. They are also more apt to travel during the daylight hours during the rut, something they usually do not do the rest of the year.

I am pleased to hear that deer alert whistles worked for you. I had the misfortune of hitting 12 deer in the years before I put whistles on all my vehicles.

Q: My brother was hunting the southern tier of New York the weekend following Thanksgiving. There was fresh snow on the ground and my brother was stillhunting when he put up three deer from their beds. He began tracking them and noticed that one of the deer stopped and urinated five times in the first few hundred yards of its bedding site. What got my brother's attention was that each spot of urine was as blue as windshield washer fluid.

What could cause a deer to urinate *blue?*

D. G., Whitesboro, New York

A: This is going to be a very short answer, because I have to say I just don't know. I have never seen this myself, nor have I heard or read about it. Yellow urine is normal; a deeper orange to almost red is sometimes seen in late winter; but I've no idea what would cause the urine to be blue. It is also unusual for a deer to urinate so many times in such a short distance, especially when it knew someone was right behind it. The frequency of urination leads me to believe that the deer was injured internally. Perhaps an injury to some organ caused the blue coloration.

Q: Unless I miss my guess, the deer that your reader from Whitesboro, New York, saw passing blue urine on the snow had been feeding on eastern red cedar *(Juniperus virginiana)*. November is a little early in the year to see this, but it is common in deer wintering in areas where eastern red cedar is a predominant plant species.

My first observation of this took place during the winter of 1968 when I and other members of the bureau of wildlife were carrying out our annual deer wintering area checks in the region. We were in a wintering area in southeastern Dutchess County in which red cedar was the predominant overstory species. The snow was deep and the deer were confined to trails, so they were eating practically nothing but red cedar. The only urine stains we observed were blue.

Incidentally, this wintering area was subdivided and developed in the mid-1970s. Deer no longer concentrate there during the winter.

I hope this provides an answer to the reader's question.

G. C., Regional Wildlife Manger,
New York State Department of Environmental Conservation

A: I know you didn't miss your guess; you have had too much experience in the field.

Red cedar is a dominant plant in our part of northwestern New Jersey as well. In fact, it is one of the pioneer trees in our abandoned fields. From my window I can see an old field covered with hundreds of red cedars about 12 feet tall. And this year has been a fantastic one for berry production. Some of the cedars were so heavily loaded with berries that I just had to photograph them. Songbirds—particularly robins, mockingbirds, catbirds, and waxwings—were gorging themselves. And the deer eat a lot of them, too, yet I have never seen the blue urine you mention.

I'm not doubting for one minute that the blue urine you saw was caused by the berries, but I picked up one more thing from your letter. You said, "The snow was deep and the deer were confined to trails, so they were eating practically nothing but red cedar. The only urine stains we observed were blue."

I think that perhaps the reason the urine you saw was blue was that the deer were starving, while the deer I have observed were not. It is well known that in times of midwinter food shortages, deer are cannibalizing their own fat reserves and even muscle tissue, which turns their urine to an orange color instead of yellow. Deer that are eating nothing but red cedar berries may have blue urine not only from the berries but also from their metabolisms. Because the deer in my area were eating a much more varied diet, perhaps the blue color in the berries was not concentrated enough to color their urine.

I looked up Whitesboro on the map and saw that it was located in the Adirondack foothills, where winter food is usually in short supply. Undoubtedly the deer my reader was reporting on were also feeding almost exclusively on the berries.

By the way, wild turkeys are tremendous competitors for these berries. In the snow, turkey tracks can be seen going to and from every cedar tree. Of course, the dense cedar branches hold most of the snow up so that the ground beneath the cedars is snow-free. The fallen berries are easily picked up.

Q: I read the question that was sent in about blue deer urine in the snow. Here in Illinois I see this quite often. In this area it is caused by deer eating berries from buckthorn trees or shrubs. As trees, they are relatively short in height. The tree has berries about the size of small blueberries or the thickness of a standard pencil. It holds its fruit through most of the winter and sometimes into spring, with the berries falling randomly throughout that time. In times of need, deer seem to rely on them quite heavily, digging in the snow for the berries. I find the snow all trampled up under the buckthorn trees. I believe the berries must have some nutritional value for the deer, which search them out in times of snow-covered ground and cold to nasty weather. The berries seem to get them through the hard times when all other food is scarce. In some areas there are groves of buckthorn, and the area will look like a deer yard. All around, in these groves, you can see bluish green to blue urine stains in the snow. I believe the color difference of bluish green to blue is determined by how many berries a deer consumes. At times I'll find branches broken down. I'm assuming the larger deer, probably bucks, break them down to get at the berries that won't fall off. Sometimes I'll follow a big buck trail, and I have noticed that they more often leave darker blue stains in the snow.

Conservation groups in and around the area consider this tree or shrub a nuisance and therefore try to eliminate it. There is a volunteer group that calls itself Friends of the Prairie. I have to wonder. They chop, cut, and/or burn out the buckthorn in an attempt to restore the natural prairie grasses. Apparently the tree is one of the first plants to leaf out in the spring. By doing so, it destroys plant life in the understory by blocking out the sun's rays. In times of need, when I'm around these trees and they are holding berries, I will give them a good shaking to knock some berries to the ground for the deer. If you should do such a thing, be careful not to get the berries down your neck and in your clothes; they will stain if smashed. I have also noticed that some early-arriving migrating songbirds and others also rely on these berries when the weather catches them off guard. Let your readers know so they can help out our wondrous whitetails whenever, if ever, they see these trees with little black berries on them. Knock some berries down even if the weather is not cold and nasty and there is no snow. That way, if things do get rough, the deer can at least dig them up.

C. G., Worth, Illinois

A: I thank you for your information and I'm sure my readers are gaining valuable knowledge from it, just as I am. After reading the previous letter from New York State, it is evident that when deer feed primarily on blue berries, it will change the color of their urine. Your letter also points out that this condition exists in times of deep snow, when berries are the major food.

I can understand what the prairie group is doing and why. In Florida they are trying to eliminate the imported Brazilian pepper tree. However, in both cases, the shrubs are extremely beneficial to the wildlife, including deer, that feeds so heavily on their berries. I feel, as you do, that it would be wise to let these food trees continue to grow.

Q: I have a question about buck behavior. I watched three dogs running along a deer trail on the opening day of muzzleloader season. Shortly after the dogs went past my stand, a buck came down the same trail with his nose to the trail, following the dogs. Is it normal for a buck to be checking the whereabouts of dogs so closely? This was less than two minutes after the dogs went through.

Even though there is a dog quarantine during deer season here in northern New York State, some homeowners will not adhere to it. We had to contact the DEC about this, which did nothing until deer season was over and the dogs chased a doe into the path of a truck; they finished it off after it landed in a roadside ditch, then proceeded to chase the yearling doe accompanying it. A hunter witnessed the dogs chasing the doe prior to the accident. He reported this to the DEC, and they came after the doe was killed. They disposed of the leader of these dogs. It is illegal to shoot dogs running deer here.   R. S., Dexter, New York

A: The action of that buck following the dogs' trail is most unusual. Ordinarily, a buck would try to put as much distance as possible between the dogs and himself.

I can only hazard a guess that the buck was following the track of the doe that the dogs were following. You did not give me a date when you saw this occur but, if it did occur during the breeding season, there is a chance that the doe was in estrus. If this was the case, the buck was evidently more interested in the doe than he was afraid of the dogs.

In the northern states, dogs are one of the greatest hazards that deer have to face.

In the southern states, deer seldom get weakened by starvation conditions, nor do they experience snow crusting. Food is generally in good supply, and a well-nourished deer can usually escape from dogs.

In the North, in winter, domestic dogs are a major predator of deer.

Credit: Lou Stout

In the North everything is in the dog's favor, particularly if he is a well-fed household pet. It behooves all hunters, particularly deer hunters, to promote the passage of township leash laws so that dogs cannot run free. If your area has such laws, make sure that they are enforced. Report every loose dog you see to the proper authority. In the past, we have had feral dogs in my area that wreaked havoc on both deer and livestock. However, it was only when some livestock was lost that something was done. All too often the dogs belong to people who have just moved to a rural area after having lived in the city. When they get to more open areas, they just let their dogs run free. As deer hunters and lovers of wildlife, we have to see that this doesn't happen.

Q: I live on a farm in southern Oklahoma. On June 1, 1995, I observed peculiar behavior involving a coyote and a white-tailed doe.

At daybreak, I was peering out my front door when I noticed a big coyote leisurely trotting across my south pasture. Suddenly a white-tailed doe exploded from the woodline and sprinted directly at the coyote. The coyote quickly altered its course and hightailed it away from the unneighborly doe. The doe continued to chase the coyote for about 1/4 mile, until the coyote disappeared into the creek bottom. The doe then returned to the woodline where she had had first appeared, but remained on the alert and focused on the direction into which the coyote had disappeared. She made two other dashes in this direction, but returned each time to the woodline. The coyote never reappeared, so I assume she was successful in running him out of the area.

Is it safe to assume she had a fawn in this area? Also, is it common for a doe to be so aggressive in protecting her area?

R. O., Ardmore, Oklahoma

A: Yes, you can bet that this doe had a fawn hidden somewhere nearby.

I have never seen a white-tailed doe chase a coyote, but I was once fortunate enough to videotape a pronghorn doe run a coyote right out of sight. The coyote, thinking it would escape, ran to a barbed-wire fence and ducked under it. The doe never hesitated; she jumped right through it and kept the pressure on the coyote. She had made several short chases prior to this but, evidently, her patience had worn so thin that on the last chase she pushed the coyote out of the county. At no time was the coyote as close as 300 feet to the fawn. The doe didn't wait until it got close; she took after the coyote as soon as she saw it.

I have seen does chase off dogs, and I have seen them decoy a dog by running close to, and in front of, him.

I really have no idea what percentage of does would make an aggressive charge at a predator. I have to believe that it would be a very small

Fawns are practically odorless for their first week of life.

number. A larger percentage might try to decoy the predator. The largest percentage of does would probably take off, leaving the fawn's own protective devices to save it.

For their first five to seven days, fawns are practically odorless. Their protective coloration makes them extremely hard to see. The fawns themselves hide under vegetation. When startled, they go into a state of suspended animation for several minutes in which they stop breathing and their heart rate is greatly reduced. That all of these ploys are highly successful can be seen by our increasing deer populations throughout the nation.

Q: I thought that you might be interested in an observation I made on one of our ranches in Wyoming.

In September 1992, one of our bowhunters saw an eagle hit a yearling doe that was trotting across a meadow. The deer was not knocked down, although the hunter heard a very loud thump upon impact. Have you ever seen anything like this?　　　　　　　D. W., Block Island, Rhode Island

A: I have seen a golden eagle try to take an adult red fox on three different occasions. I saw a great horned owl that had attacked a white-tailed fawn and been beaten off by the doe. I have read numerous reports of golden eagles attempting to take mountain sheep lambs and being foiled by the ewe's defense. I have not seen or even heard of an eagle attempting to take prey as large as a yearling doe.

Q: I read with great interest your advice on butchering deer.

Could you give me more information on the prescapular and popliteal glands? I have never heard of them before. When I was younger we used to remove the hock gland on the hind legs, but then everyone started to say that this was not necessary. I will do anything to keep that wild taste you sometimes get in game meat out. G. L., Dumont, New Jersey

A: I butcher all of my deer with just a knife, because I bone them all out. I don't cut through any bones, because I remove each of the four basic hind leg muscles, muscle by muscle. When people use a band- or handsaw and cut through the leg bones to get a larger steak, they are wasting their time, because the muscles will separate themselves when the meat is cooked. I also don't want to spread any of the fatty marrow over the meat. If the meat is to be frozen, it is the fat that will go rancid in about 60 days.

When I butcher, I bone all of the meat and remove every smidgen of fat, fascia, and tissue that I can. By doing this, I automatically remove both the prescapular and popliteal glands.

The prescapular gland is a grayish, oily gland about the size of a jelly bean. It is located in the fat directly under the scapular, or shoulder, blade. The popliteal gland is slightly larger and located in the triangular chunk of fat found on the forepart of the deer's ham or haunch. If both of these glands are not removed, they will give the meat an unpleasant odor and taste. If you remove all the fat, these glands are automatically removed.

I have never had the "wild" taste that so many complain about with any of the deer I have butchered. The key is to remove *all* fat.

The hock glands do not have to be removed. However, because I always hang my deer by the head, I saw the leg bones off just above the hock, or tarsal, glands before I skin the deer prior to butchering. This completely eliminates the chance of my accidentally touching those glands and transferring any of the scent to the meat.

Bon appétit!

Q: On two or more occasions, after carefully butchering the deer, we placed the meat in the refrigerator. The next day or two, upon checking the meat, some of it had turned a blue-purple and smelled really bad. Wherever it touched another piece, that part also turned purple. Could you please tell me what went wrong? G. C., Sayreville, New Jersey

A: I honestly can't tell you just what might have gone wrong, because all you say is that you butchered very carefully. Let me tell you what I do, step by step, and perhaps from that you can see what you did wrong. Many readers may also gain some additional knowledge.

I gut my deer just as soon as I absolutely can—the minute it stops kicking—because that is just how fast the bacteria in the stomach start to cause bloating.

I have worn a sheath knife on my left hip since I was 9 years old and since I was 20, many years ago, I have been wearing a 6-inch Randall number 3 hunter. I realize that you can work up a deer with a smaller knife, but I feel naked without my Randall; it's an extension of my hand.

With my deer lying on its side, I take my knife and cut a circle around its anus. Then I roll the deer onto its back and straddle the carcass with the deer's two front legs between my legs as I face the animal's rear.

I pull the deer's skin up just behind the rib cage as far as it will go. Then I carefully insert the knife through the skin and make a shallow cut all the way up the deer's pelvic area, being careful not to cut the paunch or intestines. (On a buck, I cut around the scrotum and sever the penis.) If you get your deer at once, the paunch and intestines should lie down within the body cavity, as the gas has not built up as yet. Then I take my knife and, cutting to the left of the sternum, sever all of the ribs up to the base of the neck. Do not cut the skin this high if you are going to have your deer mounted.

With the rib cage wide open, I reach in and cut the deer's windpipe and esophagus loose as close to the neck as possible. I cut the flaps of the diaphragm loose from the rib cage to the backbone. I then lay the deer on its side and pull out the heart, lungs, and diaphragm. You will need to carefully cut the kidneys loose with your knife. Be careful not to break the bladder, and carefully pull the rectum through. Roll all the entrails out on the ground, roll the deer up with its back up, and spread the hind legs so all the blood drains out of the chest and body cavity. I then hang the deer up by its neck and spread the ribs open with a stick so the body heat leaves the carcass as soon as possible.

Aging meat can only be done properly at a temperature of between 34 and 38 degrees. Any colder and the meat freezes; any warmer and bacteria multiply too fast, spoiling the meat. So I do not let the carcass hang any longer than overnight, just until the body heat is gone and the meat has firmed up.

I then skin the deer from the neck down. Again, do not do this if the buck is to be mounted. After the hide is off, I use a small propane torch to singe off any hairs that may adhere to the carcass. This is the fastest way to clean the carcass.

I always bone my deer, so I lay the cleaned carcass on a table and sever the legs. I cut the loins loose from the backbone. I then remove the tenderloins from inside the body cavity and remove as much meat as I can from the ribs and around the neck bones. I remove all the fat and tissue that I can.

Great care should be taken to remove the prescapular glands buried in the fat beneath the shoulder blades and the popliteal gland buried in the fat on the forepart of the ham. These glands are ¾ to 1 inch in length and gray in color; if left on the meat and cooked, they will give it a bad taste and odor. Removing as much fat and tissue as possible will allow you to keep your venison for a year or more if it is properly wrapped and frozen. The fat will go rancid in about six months, even if it's frozen.

My wife wraps the meat as soon as I cut it up with plastic wrap and butcher paper and seals it all with tape. We freeze the meat to be used for stews and burger in large chunks and cut or grind it as we need it. This prevents air from getting between the cubes or ground meat and lessens the possibility of freezer burn.

When finished, be sure to scrub your cutting area with an antibacterial cleanser.

Q: I was just reading about the old doe that C. W. Cain had here in Louisiana that lived almost 26 years. I thought you might be interested in a doe my sister had for a few years. The doe was only a few days old when she was captured and given to my sister. She was kept in a pen until she was about a year old and became very tame. It got to where the gate on the pen could be left open and the deer would stay inside. Wild deer were often seen close by, and the tame doe started going off in the woods with them, but she would always come back. My sister did not know it wasn't legal to keep a deer and, after the first year, she was never kept penned up anyway. About the third or fourth year the game warden came by and told her she couldn't legally have the doe and two fawns she had by then. My sister tore down the pen, but the deer stayed around anyhow. The old doe was around for about seven or eight years and gave birth every year, usually to twins. Once she was gone all summer and showed up in the fall with a very crooked front leg that had been broken but healed up. Once some dogs ran her into the plate-glass front of our school auditorium. She made a big crash but wasn't harmed. None of this is unusual, but there was one thing I thought might interest you. For two years in a row, the doe gave birth on September 5 and always returned to where the old pen had been to do so. Have you come across deer giving birth at this time of year before? Thank you for listening. J. G., Goldonna, Louisiana

A: I had to get out a map to see just where Goldonna is in Louisiana. I located it and, just so my readers will know, it is a little north of Natchitoches or just about on the 32nd parallel north. I mention that because the time of deer breeding and birthing changes south of the 33rd parallel.

North of this parallel, most white-tailed deer breed November 10–25, with the peak coming November 10–12. Does that for some reason don't become pregnant will re-cycle 28 days later, December 5–20. Usually, any female fawns that have matured enough at seven months to breed will do so in this so-called second rut.

The gestation period for the white-tailed deer is generally 203 to 205 days, but it may be off 5 days of so in either direction, depending on the quality and quantity of the food available to the pregnant doe. Does bred around November 10 will give birth in the last part of May or the first part of June. Deer bred in the second rut will give birth in late June. Occasionally a doe may miss being bred in her second period and will then give birth in late July.

I have done a lot of deer photography in Louisiana and seen that the peak of the breeding season below the 33rd parallel is about two months later than north of it, or around January 5. That would make the birthing period the last part of July. If a doe missed her first period, her birthing period from the second rut would be the end of August. So, for your location, a doe giving birth on September 5 would not be unusual at all.

You bring up another very interesting point. You say that the doe gave birth on September 5 two years in a row. I am willing to bet that all of her other birthing dates were right around that time, too. Except in very unusual circumstances, most deer give birth about the same time each year; bucks, too, start their antler growth and drop their antlers at about the same time every year. Most creatures respond to a built-in time clock over which they have very little control.

We all respond to cycles that we may not be aware of.

The following pages show a doe giving birth—from labor to birth to newborn. The fawn is able to stand in 20 minutes.

The Deer Hunter's Encyclopedia

The Deer Hunter's Encyclopedia

Q: A member of my hunting group has the good fortune of owning 160-plus acres in Salem County, New Jersey, along the Delaware River and its extensive marshes. He has tried to limit the deer kill with respect to bucks, to help produce larger racks. There have been numerous 18-plus-inch spreads seen and taken on the farm. He does not shoot does.

The parcel is a combination of open woodland and farm fields. The adjoining parcel has several hundred acres of corn and soybeans. Due to the high deer density, the farmer on the adjacent parcel applied for and received a permit to shoot excess deer. To my knowledge, there is no limit on his kill amount. Rumor has it that he has taken more than 100 deer. Fawns, does, and bucks were piled up to spoil. I can't fault the farmer for trying to save his crops. What books on deer management do you recommend that I could purchase for my friend that emphasize the taking of does to balance a herd? My friend is still not convinced he should shoot does.

M. B., Mullica Hill, New Jersey

A: While 160 acres is a nice piece of ground, it would be virtually impossible to hold deer on such a small area.

Yes, I can't fault the farmer either. When I was chief gamekeeper for Coventry Hunt Club in Pahaquarra Township, we had a farmer who rented the river bottom lands for corn. The deer did eat his corn and, by special permit, he shot them by the hundreds. He also won an award for the highest yield of corn per acre in our county year after year. Although I always felt that he shot too many deer, perhaps he had that high yield per acre because of this. I always wanted him to shoot just the does, but he shot bucks, does, and fawns.

It is common knowledge that if you want to produce trophy bucks, you have to reduce your overall deer population below the carrying capacity of the land.

My own book *The Deer of North America* gives the basics of deer management, spelling out why does must be shot. The definitive book on the subject is *Producing and Harvesting White-Tailed Deer* by Dr. James C. Kroll (School of Forestry, Stephen F. Austin University, Nacogdoches, Texas 75962).

Q: My son discovered a big buck's hot area this season. He saw him twice and knows that he hung around there plenty. Deer sign was everywhere, especially on two high hills off a logging road. The area was sheltered by hemlocks; it had a brook on one side, a rock wall on another, and a heavily used deer trail below, running between his lookout areas and a large beaver swamp. We located three scrapes in this spot just before the season ended. The trees around were smashed with rubs. There were also deer droppings of all sizes and colors. The ones that my husband puzzled over, which covered these two hills, were cylindrical and

Clockwise from upper left: deer pellets when browsing, rabbit pellets, porcupine pellets, deer pellets when feeding on grasses and soft foods.

lightish golden in color, although under the pine needles they seemed harder and browner. They are soft and shiny when fresh. Anyway, they are not deposited in little piles like regular deer pellets, but just scattered all over. There is a cornfield nearby. Could that affect the way a deer defecates? We've never seen anything like it. When you sit, you just see more and more of them.

They are in the two bed areas we found and on the trails between the two hills. Can you tell if something else is making these droppings? We know there are foxes and coyotes in this area.

M. S., Rochester, New Hampshire

A: My guess would be that the droppings are those of a porcupine. The drawings you made are ¼ inch in diameter by 1½ inches in length. The 1½-inch length is right for porcupine, but a diameter of ½ inch instead of ¼ inch would be more normal. I have never seen porcupine droppings squared off as you show in the second drawing. All of the porcupine scat I have seen has been well rounded.

Another reason for my guess is that you are in good porcupine country; most of New England is, and you said that the area is sheltered by hemlocks. Hemlocks are a favored food of porcupines. The next time you are in the area, check out the uppermost branches of the hemlocks to see if you can see the white wood showing where the porcupines have eaten the inner bark.

Deer also favor hemlock areas because they, too, eat a lot of hemlock. Deer will feed under the same trees that porcupines are eating, because feeding porcupines often drop the outermost tender tiny tips. They don't do this purposely; they're just clumsy feeders. It isn't likely you will find many of the dropped tips, because the deer eat them as fast as they fall. The amount of food dropped by porcupines is not going to provide a meal for deer, but during the winter starvation months, every little bit helps.

Q: I have penned white-tailed deer, and I have a lot of questions. What food do they like best? How much protein should they have? What minerals should they have? Should bucks have more protein than does? What worming program works best? Does it help to feed calcium and phosphorus to the bucks for antler growth? Is there a book on raising penned whitetail deer? I have your *Deer of North America*.　　　　　O. B., Bremen, Indiana

A: Deer prefer white oak acorns, apples, and soybean sprouts about in that order, but I assume you are talking about foods that are commercially available.

I have found that the Agway pelletized dairy Crunchy 16 is an excellent food that deer love and thrive on. As its name implies, it has 16 percent protein. The many studies done on deer nutrition generally agree that deer need a 16 to 18 percent protein diet in order to maximize their body and antler growth.

There are commercial deer foods that have a higher protein content—one is reported to have 30 percent, probably due to having more soybeans in it. I have never used any of these feeds, so I can't tell you if they are worth the extra money that they cost. Nor can I tell you if the deer can utilize the extra protein. It may be similar to taking more vitamins than your body needs. With the exception of vitamins A and D, the body simply excretes any surplus vitamins that it cannot use. No deer study recommends more than 18 percent protein, so anything above that may be superfluous.

The protein feeds are best for deer from March through to the first of November. Then the deer prefer corn. Deer go through a period called mandatory lipogenesis, starting about the third week in September, which coincides with, or may be prompted by, the dropping of the acorns. If there are acorns available, the deer will feed upon them almost exclusively because of their rich carbohydrates. The deer instinctively know that they have to build up their body fat in order to survive the winter. After the acorns are gone, deer will travel several miles to feed upon corn if there are any farms in the area. So I feed corn from November through to March.

The best hays to feed are trefoil, clover, and alfalfa, in that order. Do not feed the horse hays of timothy and orchard grass.

Commercial feeds are all fortified with vitamins and minerals, so deer need little in the way of supplemental minerals. However, I use Deer-Lix mineral supplement (see page 186) mixed in with red mineral salt for both penned and wild deer. You can't feed them too much, but I want to make sure that they have all the minerals possible available to them at all times.

I cannot recommend a worming program because I have had no experience with them.

Both does and bucks should be fed the same high-protein mineralized foods, because equal demands are being made on their bodies. While calcium and phosphorus are being drawn from the buck's body to produce antlers, the same minerals are being drawn from the doe's body to produce her fawns. And I want to stress again that the doe's bloodline and genes are as important in producing good bucks as are the buck's, and maybe more so.

Q: This may sound a little weird, but I was wondering if you could help me find a way to get a fetus ruler in order to find out when our does are

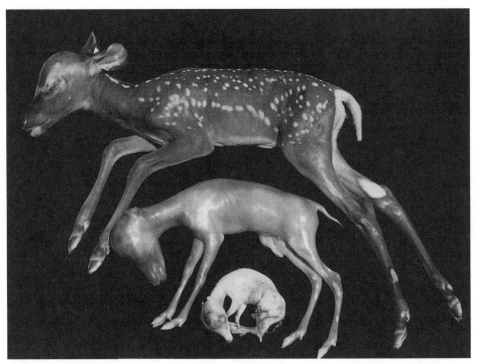

White-tailed fetuses, from bottom to top: 90 days, 130 days, and 185 days.

The Deer Hunter's Encyclopedia

being bred. I cannot seem to find one anywhere, but I know they are out there.

I live in Susquehanna County, Pennsylvania, and would be interested in hearing you speak. Is there any way we could set up something? I am 20 years old, am very involved with white-tailed deer, and study them constantly here at college in Bloomsburg. I would love to become a photographer and write on the whitetail someday.

B. L. R., Bloomsburg, Pennsylvania.

A: I do not know of a "fetus" ruler. In the research that I have read, an ordinary ruler is used.

A fetus is not measured from the tip of the nose to the end of the tail, as is done for most other mammalian measurements. Because a fetus is usually found in a head-down position, the measurements are taken from the top of the forehead, or the front of the crown, to the base of the tail. On page 236 of my book *The Deer of North America*, I have given the facts that a 90-day fetus usually measures 6½ inches, a 120-day fetus measures 10½ inches, and a 150-day fawn measures 18 inches. Reading the full paragraphs should give you a reasonably accurate guesstimate of the date of conception, eliminating the need for a fetus ruler. Unless you kill the doe, I don't know how you would use the ruler.

I also don't see the need for one. You live in Pennsylvania, at the same latitude as I do in New Jersey, and I can tell you, based on a lifetime of deer study, that the peak of your rut is going to be between November 9 and November 12, with most of your does being bred November 7–15. Any variation of a day or two from this norm is caused by the weather; a dark September or October will push the peak up a day or two.

Any doe not bred in this period will cycle 28 days later, the so-called second rut. Doe fawns that have achieved a body weight of about 80 pounds will also breed during the first week in December.

Yes, I am still doing my white-tailed deer seminars and you can get all of the information on times and fees by calling my office at (908-362-6616).

Q: I have heard it said that a deer gets up like a cow rather than like a horse. What do you say? I have seen a lot of horses, but I've never seen one lying down or getting up so I don't know what they do. What is the difference in how a horse and a cow get up? B. T., Matawan, New Jersey

The following pages show how a deer gets up. It first raises up on its front "wrists." It then raises its hindquarters completely, then its forequarters. Cows get up in a similar fashion.

The Deer Hunter's Encyclopedia

A: I was raised on a farm and, in the late 1930s, we did all of our farm work with horses. We had a dairy farm, so I have had lots of experience with both animals.

A deer gets up like a cow. It raises itself up on what would be the wrists of its forelegs. Then it raises its hindquarters completely, and then extends its forelegs to raise the front part of its body. The entire process is well documented in the accompanying series of photos.

A horse heaves itself up on its front feet completely, then raises its hindquarters. And no, horses don't lie down as often as cows; even when they are very young or very old, horses seldom if ever lie down.

The Deer Hunter's Encyclopedia

A healthy white-tailed buck, well fed and in his prime. If chased by well-fed, healthy dogs on crusty snow, the buck's chances of getting away are not good.

Q: While deer hunting this past gun season in the western Maryland mountains, I observed two big black dogs running several deer. There was no snow on the ground and the deer were about 200 yards ahead of the dogs. Hunting with dogs is not allowed in Maryland, so evidently these were wild dogs trying for a meal or tame dogs just out for a good time. I have several questions. Do you think the dogs can actually catch the deer? How much of a threat are dogs to our deer herd? And how far will the dogs chase the deer, and will the deer come back to the area?   P. T., Lewes, Delaware

A: There is no doubt that large, well-fed dogs can actually catch large, well-fed deer. In winter, when deer are not well fed, the job is easier for the dogs as the deer are weakened. On a crusty snow, it's a cinch for dogs to catch deer, because the deer's hooves will break through the same crust that supports the dog's weight.

If you were to read the research literature, you would get conflicting reports. The most extensive, documented studies have been done in the southern states. The conclusions are that, in most cases, dogs are unable to catch deer. However, it must be remembered that because of the milder winters, lack of snowfall, and more available food, southern deer are not as winter-starved as northern deer. Being in much better physical shape, they have an easier job outrunning the dogs. Also, most southern lakes, rivers, and bayous are ice-free, so many southern deer escape by taking to the water. That's not an option that northern deer have. By taking to water, the deer can outrun the dogs or, as usually happens, the dogs lose the deer's scent trail.

In the North, free-ranging dogs are perhaps the deer's greatest enemy, not counting actual starvation. From personal experience, I know the devastation that feral dogs can inflict on deer. Well-fed house dogs are an even greater threat, because they are in prime condition. Thankfully, in many areas pet dogs are not allowed to run loose these days. This should be made mandatory in all northern states.

When well-fed dogs chase deer, they often don't catch or kill the deer outright. They do, however, contribute to many deaths by causing the deer to burn up calories in running, calories that can't be replaced in the absence of food. Exertion also makes deer vulnerable to death by pneumonia-type diseases.

When deer are chased by anything, they usually run in a large circle so that they remain in their own home range, where they know the terrain intimately. Their best chance of survival is to stay on that range. If a deer is driven from its home range by dogs, hunters, snowmobiles, or the like, it usually returns within a 24-hour period. It's as true for deer as it is for me: "There's no place like home."

Q: After 50 years of deer hunting and buying both buck and doe urine scents in bottles, I still do not know how they collect "fresh" urine from deer. What is the process from deer to bottle?

J. G. M. Kitty Hawk, North Carolina

A: Urine is collected from "farms" that raise a large number of deer. The deer are usually kept on slanted concrete floors so that the urine drains into a trough and can be collected. Some of the does are stimulated, hormonally, to re-cycle into estrus every few days instead of every 28 days, as is normal.

Is the estrus urine from hormone-stimulated deer as good as it would be from a doe naturally in estrus? I don't know. It is possible that the hormonal shot in the stimulated doe's urine might be detectable by wild deer.

How do they get tractor-trailer loads of estrus urine from even a herd of does? I can't answer that either.

I do know that urine taken from the bladder of a deer that has just been shot is an attractant to other deer, because I have used it. However, such urine—even from a doe in estrus—is not as good as urine that has been voided naturally by the doe, because it has not passed through her vaginal area and has thus not picked up any of her estrus secretions.

Q: A coworker of mine, who thinks he is a part-time biologist, informed me that after yearling bucks are born, they stay with their mother for one year, then move about 1½ miles away after that year. If this is true, what happens to them if the woods they are born in is no bigger than a 2-mile radius? He also said that deer ticks live only on the edge of a woodline— approximately 30 yards into the woods. Could you enlighten me on these two theories? Thank you.   K. W. W., Yardville, New Jersey

A: A doe's fawns stay with her until they are almost one year old (yearlings). Prior to giving birth to her next set of fawns, the doe drives off her yearlings from her birthing territory. She also drives off other deer that might trespass on this territory. The yearlings of all does wander, bed, and feed in the corridors and on the edges of all the does' birthing territories. Being driven from their familiar home range is why so many yearling deer

A doe with a five-minute-old fawn. Her efforts to drive away her spike yearling before giving birth apparently failed in this instance.

are killed by automobiles in late May and early June. About 50 percent of the yearling bucks disperse for good at this time, and telemetry records show that most of them move about 5½ miles.

When fawns are about two weeks old, their mother no longer defends the birthing territory, and the matriarchal groups reform. Now the yearling does, and the 50 percent of the yearling bucks that did not permanently relocate, rejoin their mothers. Those young bucks that do rejoin their mothers are usually driven off by their mothers and the other adult does in their group just prior to the breeding season in fall. These young bucks also move about 5½ miles, which greatly cuts down on the chances of inbreeding.

There are many different types of ticks: Dog, wood, deer, and (in the South) Lone Star ticks can be found anyplace throughout the deer's range. Northern ticks don't observe any neat 30 yard limit. However, your friend is correct in one sense, because ticks are found much more often in high-grass fields than they are in the woods.

Play it safe and spray your pants and socks with Permanone before entering the woods.

The L. L. Rue Catalog Available

Our catalog features a selection of the finest photographic and outdoor equipment, accessories, books, and videos available. Of special interest are the Rue Ultimate Blind, which can be completely set up and ready to use in 30 seconds; the Groofwin Pod, which allows you to photograph from your vehicle window with tripod stability; and the Rue professional photo vest. Other items include camera packs, tripods, tripod heads, protective wraps, lens cases, photographers' gloves, camera mounts, shoulder stocks, and many other useful and unique accessories. Our carefully selected line of nature, outdoor, and photographic books includes many written by Dr. Rue: *How I Photograph Wildlife and Nature, The Deer of North America, Way of the Whitetail, Whitetails, How to Photograph Animals in the Wild, Cottontail Rabbit,* among others. Videos by Dr. Rue include *Basics of Bird Photography, Advanced Birth Photography, Rutting Whitetails,* and *An Eye on Nature.*

For a free catalog, please contact: Leonard Rue Enterprises, 138 Millbrook Road, Blairstown, NJ 07825; phone (908) 362-6616; fax (908) 362-5808.

Websites. For purchase and information about Rue videos, go to www.ruevideo.com. For purchase and information about Rue books and catalog items, please go to www.rue.com..

INDEX

squatting, 97–99, 140
squirrels, 29–31
stands, 2, 7
stare downs, 99–101
stomach, 163–64, 172–73, 178
subspecies, 204–6
supplements, 186, 195, 214, 267, 268
swallowing, 166–67

tails, 173–74
Tanck, Jack, 170
Taylor, Joe, 187, 188
"territorialism," 92, 118, 151
testosterone, 38, 64–65, 81, 83–85, 157–58
ticks, 275, 276
toxins, 248–50
tracks, characteristics of, 161–63
trophy deer, 27–29
turkeys, 4, 96, 129–30, 141–42, 252

understory, 192–93
urination, mule deer, 36, 107
urine
    as bait, 20, 37, 119, 274–75
    blue, 250–53
    during breeding period, 36, 102
    in butchering process, 181
    licking, 113–14
    during rutting, 38
UV blockers, 8–9

velvet, 47, 54–57, 76–77, 80–85, 86, 206, 236
Verme, Louis, 247, 248

walking, 123
Warbach, Oscar, 10
warning signals, wildlife, 29–31
water
    and birthing, 238–39
    as defense, 108–9
    requirements, 138–39, 147
Watson, Wyndle, 59–60
weather's effect
    antlers, 81, 86, 230–31, 244
    drought, 243–44
    fawns, 237
    feeding habits, 104
    on food supply, 92–93, 243–44
    rutting season, 143
    scent, 115
    wind, 104, 135–36, 144, 194–95, 196
    winter, 153–54, 210, 217–21
whiskers, 171–72
whistles, alert, 250
wind, 104, 135–36, 144, 194–95, 196
woodchucks, 207–9

yarding, 143–44, 221
yearlings, 157, 275–76